INDUSTRIAL LIGHT & MAGIC

The Art of Special Effects

INDUSTRIAL LIGHT & MAGIC

The Art of Special Effects

THOMAS G. SMITH

Introduction by George Lucas

A Del Rey Book

BALLANTINE BOOKS • NEW YORK

Library of Congress Cataloging-in-Publication Data

Smith, Thomas G. (Thomas Graham). 1938–
  Industrial Light and Magic.

  "A Del Rey Book."

  1. Cinematography—Special effects. 1. Title.
TR858.S65 1986   791.43′024   86-3298
ISBN 0-345-32263-0

Manufactured in Japan

First Edition: November 1986

10 9 8 7 6 5 4 3

*T*o the men and women of
Industrial Light and Magic, whose enthusiasm and
craftsmanship have brought pleasure to millions of
filmgoers around the world. And to the great filmmakers
George Lucas and Steven Spielberg, whose film genius
inspired them.

CONTENTS

ACKNOWLEDGMENTS

In August 1985, Industrial Light and Magic quietly celebrated an anniversary. It had been ten years since its beginning in Van Nuys, California; many who had been there had left and now I, too, was going. But as the general manager of ILM for more than four of those ten years, I felt a record of that decade should be somehow memorialized. Therefore, I proposed this book to Anita Gross, Director of Publishing for Lucasfilm. With her encouragement and the support of the staff at Ballantine/Del Rey, the project was undertaken.

I have received the help of scores of individuals: some former ILMers, some current ILM employees, and others who assisted in a variety of ways in compiling the massive amount of verbal and visual information necessary to tell the story. Among the former ILMers, I was greatly aided by Rose Duignan, Joe Johnston, John Dykstra, Ralph McQuarrie, Jon Berg, Phil Tippett, Harrison Ellenshaw, and Richard Edlund.

Still at ILM and, by their contribution, vital to the success of this book, were Warren Franklin, Chrissie England, Bruce Nicholson, Kenneth Smith, John Ellis, Kerry Nordquist, Mike MacKenzie, Roberto McGrath, Lorne Peterson, Steve Gawley, Dennis Muren, Ken Ralston, Michael Pangrazio, Chris Evans, and Craig Barron.

At the Lucasfilm archives, Debbie Fine, Barbara Lakin, and Kathy Wippert provided photos and records from the past ten years.

Ed Catmull, leader of Lucasfilm's Computer Division and perhaps the most knowledgeable person in the world on the subject of digital effects, provided necessary technical guidance in this exciting new field.

Outside the Lucasfilm family, I would like to thank Steven Spielberg and Kathy Kennedy of Amblin' Entertainment for their assistance in providing material from *E.T.: The Extra-Terrestrial* and *Poltergeist*. At Paramount Pictures, Harve Bennett helped provide visuals from the *Star Trek* films. Early historical photos were furnished by the Museum of Modern Art in New York City.

Kent Smith, a man with immense energy, a complete knowledge of film, and a fine command of language, helped in the assembly of the manuscript, along with extensive editorial assistance. And Mari Mine-Rutka, writer of Ewokese and English, also made an important contribution to this book.

I would like to acknowledge Annie Berardini, whose good humor, organizational skills, and lightning typing ability kept everyone on track.

Then, a special thanks to my wife, Elaine, whose patience and good taste helped guide me through the intense days and nights of labor, thus enabling me to complete a task that turned out to be far greater than I ever suspected it would be when I first proposed this project.

Finally, my deepest gratitude to the quiet power behind the success of Industrial Light and Magic, George Lucas, who has been an enormous influence in my own life and whose inspiration to hundreds of people both inside and outside Lucasfilm has written an important chapter in the history of motion pictures.

INTRODUCTION

In 1986, Industrial Light and Magic celebrated ten years of motion picture special effects work. This is an achievement unrivaled in the history of visual effects.

It all started in 1975 in the corner of a California warehouse. We had assembled a small group of enthusiastic and dedicated men and women, to create effects for a film I was directing called *Star Wars*.

Despite their independence from Hollywood, ILM has gathered acclaim from both the public and artists within the industry. They have won Academy Awards for their work on *Star Wars, The Empire Strikes Back, Raiders of the Lost Ark, E.T.: The Extra-Terrestrial, Return of the Jedi, Indiana Jones and the Temple of Doom,* and *Cocoon.* Their first television work *The Ewok Adventure* was awarded an Emmy for visual effects. In the first decade, the only time that ILM did not win an Academy Award for special effects was when it was matched against another ILM nominee that *did* win.

Of the top ten most successful films of all time, ILM has contributed to half.

As ILM grew, it attracted and trained new talent. It now handles several major film projects simultaneously while maintaining the quality of craftsmanship that has earned it its reputation. Like a successful film star, ILM is sought out by every major studio when effects work is called for. They are now pioneering in the use of digital images, painted directly on the film by computer controlled lasers.

To me, however, ILM is more than machines and technical processes. ILM's success springs from the creative spirit of the men and women who work there. Since the days of the first *Star Wars* movie, that enthusiastic and wild spirit has been viewed by some film industry executives with suspicion. Yet were the ILMers to be tamed into corporate soldiers, the creative army would quickly lose its unique spark.

In 1979, I hired Tom Smith to manage Industrial Light and Magic. He came on in early 1980 while we were finishing work for *The Empire Strikes Back* and departed four and a half years and ten films later. This book is the product of his experience plus hundreds of personal interviews and historical research. We hope that it will help to chronicle that amazing decade of visual effects achievement . . . the first ten years of ILM.

George Lucas

CHAPTER 1

HOW IT STARTED

Before irrigation, the San Fernando Valley north of Los Angeles was a desert. Even now, when the summer sun beats down on the clay soil, temperatures rise above 110 degrees. But running water and freeways transformed this barren expanse into a patchwork of Los Angeles suburbs, one indistinguishable from another. In 1975, a new enterprise moved into a recently constructed industrial building in the valley across the street from the Van Nuys Airport. The outfit was headed by John Dykstra, a six-foot-four-inch long-haired, bearded young man. Film director George Lucas had commissioned Dykstra to create the visual effects for a film Lucas had in production called *Star Wars*.

Lucas's ideas for the film were embodied in the *Star Wars* script and in the form of a dozen or so production paintings by illustrator Ralph McQuarrie. Out of this small portfolio, an entire universe awaited creation and filming. The new special effects enterprise that would bring this universe to life was named by George Lucas Industrial Light and Magic.

Dykstra recruited a small team, who began customizing the empty building, turning it into a combination film studio, optical house, model shop, and design facility. Technicians were hired to build

George Lucas lines up a special effects shot for *The Empire Strikes Back*.

new film equipment, while young electronic and computer geniuses devised revolutionary ways to use computers to control and coordinate the movements of model ships and camera cranes running along their smooth rails. Artists designed spacecraft and model builders constructed ships that would be used in the film.

Fifteen minutes by freeway to the south lay Hollywood. There had been a time when all the major studios supported their own special effects shops, staffed with masters of the art. But effects shops had been phased out along with other specialized facilities, as the studios went from self-contained production centers to mere sound stages controlled by landlords and suites of executive deal makers. By the time George Lucas was making *Star Wars*, no studio had a special effects facility; he had to create his own mini-studio to do the work.

However, Industrial Light and Magic in no way resembled the typical Hollywood studio. Outside, it looked like all the other industrial-style buildings in the valley. Inside, it was staffed with very young technicians, some barely out of college, few over thirty, some even under twenty years old. Film animator Peter Kuran was still in school when he offered to work for free on a trial basis; after two weeks he was on the ILM payroll full time. The doors at ILM were open twenty-four hours a day; technicians and artists worked without regard to time clocks or job classifications. They were children of the sixties, and many rebelled against authority figures and traditional work rules. There were no dress codes and no specified work hours; designers built models, and modelmakers ran cameras. But there was a strong esprit de corps and feeling of purpose in the building, the kind of enthusiasm that you get with a race car team building a winner for the Indianapolis 500. The involvement was with the cause rather than with the money: somehow the group felt they were a part of something really important.

To an outsider, the atmosphere at ILM was sometimes quite relaxed. Joe Johnton, fresh out of art school when he started work at ILM as a sketch artist and designer, recalls that every conceivable holiday was celebrated not with a day off but with an in-house party, often during normal working hours. One Halloween he dressed as a fish with a large fish mask over his head; he could only see out of the fish's mouth. While he was wearing the outfit and pouring himself a drink at the coffee machine, a 20th Century–Fox executive unexpectedly showed up through a side door to check out this nonconformist facility Fox was paying for. Joe greeted him with a "hello" from inside the fish head and nonchalantly returned to his drawing board.

Occasionally other unannounced visitors representing the studio's interests came to witness firsthand what was going on. On one sweltering summer day, everyone deserted their jobs inside the non–air conditioned building to take turns on a water slide that had been set up outside. Even Jim Nelson, the head administrator and stern father figure of ILM, was persuaded to take off his shirt and give the slide a try. He hit the water—just as a carload of executives from Fox were pulling in for a spot inspection.

John Dykstra was moving a refrigerator with the forklift one day as George Lucas and producer Gary Kurtz pulled into the parking lot with some studio executives. John lost control of the load and dumped it on the pavement. As the refrigerator smashed on the ground, the horrified ILMers suddenly realized that a limousine was in the parking lot. They looked up. Their eyes met the shocked faces of George Lucas, Gary Kurtz, and men wearing business suits and ties. . . .

In a period of a year and a half, however, this irregular band of individuals remodeled a building, hired a full staff, built a technical facility complete with custom-made cameras, and created the special effects for a film that stunned audiences all over the world. It was a great once-in-a-lifetime experience for all.

When the *Star Wars* effects were completed, the exhausted ILM crew scattered all over the world to rest. Some went to Hawaii; others to Mexico and Europe. Nothing was crated up; things were left pretty much the way they were on the last day of work. The lights were turned off, the door was locked, and

Snapshot taken during an outing of the ILM crew in late 1976.

everyone said good-bye. Though they all felt it would be a good film, they had no idea of the unprecedented success that it would have. There were no other projects for the staff to return to. It seemed that ILM would disappear, just as most temporary motion picture units disband after a film is completed.

However, with the unexpected success of *Star Wars*, and the complete saga still to be told, George Lucas decided to embark on the next episode: *The Empire Strikes Back*. This time, however, ILM would move to Northern California, near Lucas's home and film editing facilities. George had carried a dream ever since he was an assistant to Francis Ford Coppola: to build a film production center in Northern California. Now he had the money to begin realizing this dream, and from now on Northern California would be ILM's home. So it was that in 1978, certain key people were invited to move to San Rafael, California, and become a part of the new ILM. Many of the old ILM artists were called north: designer Ralph McQuarrie, artist Joe Johnston, visual effects supervisors Richard Edlund and Dennis Muren, and scores of others. John Dykstra, however, did not join ILM. He stayed in Southern California to form his own special effects facility, Apogee.

Special effects are not only a way of filming spaceships and laser blasts; there are many applications of this branch of film technology. Special effects are used in motion pictures when scenes are desired that would be impractical, expensive, dangerous, or even impossible to film in a normal manner. In the last few decades, the audiences' appetite for spectacle has increased, while the cost of motion picture production has multiplied tenfold. This has led the more imaginative filmmakers to look to visual effects as a way to expand the scope of their films while still maintaining a practical budget.

Special effects are almost as old as the invention of movies. Around the turn of the century, when the French magician Georges Méliès saw his first film in Paris, he immediately grasped its potential for magic. His early films, *Indian Rubber Head* (1901), *Voyage to the Moon* (1902), and *The Conquest of the Pole* (1912), employed nearly every type of visual effect currently used at ILM. Méliès did not film in color (he did, however, employ scores of women to hand color each print) and, of course, he worked half a century before the invention of the computer. Nonetheless, his films were remarkably inventive.

In the early 1920s when the large motion picture studios consolidated and gathered in Southern California, they built complete production facilities, providing practically every service for themselves within studio walls. Not only did they maintain creative talent under contract, they also owned the physical plant to "manufacture" scenery, furniture, miniature models, and to design and machine special camera equipment and even process their own film. It was assumed that all films required services provided by the special effects department. Every studio budget form had a section devoted to "tricks" (as effects were then called), and most films used them. There was a strong economic reason for this: the special effects shop could help cut the budget on set construction, reduce the number of extras needed in a crowd scene, and eliminate the need to go to distant locations. Screen credit, however, was often denied to the special effects artist, for it was felt

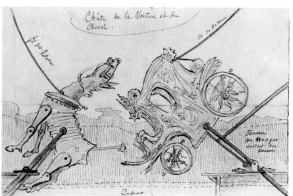

by the studios that the audience should not be told that tricks were used.

The studios not only controlled all aspects of film production, they also controlled the distribution of the product. They owned large chains of theaters and operated distribution organizations to supply these theaters with new films each week. In 1950, after twelve years of litigation, the Supreme Court of the United States ordered the large studios to separate the film production and film exhibition functions. The court regarded complete control over production and exhibition to be monopolistic, so MGM, Paramount Pictures, and others were forced to sell their theaters. At the same time, independent filmmakers began to make their films outside the studio system, without the big studio overhead to support. Audiences were also looking for more realism in film; they had gotten used to seeing real places in newsreels and were no longer content to have the idealized version portrayed by the studio artists. There was, therefore, less demand for the special effects technicians to simulate exotic locales behind the walls of a Southern California studio. Now it was the fashion to actually go on location. Almost overnight, the production giants closed the doors on

the scores of craft shops behind their walls, and the special effects departments were among the earliest victims. Craftsmen who had started in the early 1920's were now nearing retirement age, and newcomers were not sought to fill the ranks. Between 1960 and 1970, an entire generation of craftsmen were lost in the motion picture industry. So it was that when *Star Wars* was produced in 1977, George Lucas had to set up his own shop. Few of the new technicians he hired had

Above left: George Méliès' *The Man with the Rubber Head*, 1902. Here Méliès uses the same technique as for *The Dancing Midget* (page 7), only this time the second exposure enlarges the head size. Méliès appears to be using the same camera for both pictures. Even the shapes of the second exposed area are the same, suggesting that the same "matte" may have been used for both shots.

Above: George Méliès' *The Merry Frolics of Satan*, 1906. Satan drives a car on the right (in 1906, cars had a rather suspect reputation) and spooks a mechanical horse pulling the coach. This "stagey" look was common in a Méliès film.

Left: Mechanical layout for the stage effect used by Méliès in his film *The Merry Frolics of Satan*, 1906. This picture looks very much like current ILM drawings for trick set-ups.

had the opportunity to apprentice under the masters who had perfected their craft in the big studios of the earlier decades.

Though lacking in practical experience, this new generation of special effects technicians were energetic and young and they did have other experiences to bring to the job. They knew what they liked to see on the screen, and they set out to create it. But perhaps what separated this generation most from previous ones was that they knew the power of computer technology and how to use it.

Among the new members of the ILM staff, Richard Edlund and Dennis Muren had gained special effects experience working on TV commercials, and John Dykstra had worked for Doug Trumbull, who earlier had gained worldwide recognition with his special effects work on Stanley Kubrick's *2001: A Space Odyssey.*

Opposite page: This sequence of twenty photographs illustrates the highlights of Méliès' most celebrated film, *A Trip to the Moon,* 1902.

Left: George Méliès' *The Dancing Midget,* 1902. The image of the small ballet dancer was done using any one of several optical tricks. Most likely, her image was exposed in a second pass of the film through the camera.

Below: An art rendering probably painted by Méliès, an accomplished artist, of a scene for his film, *The Impossible Voyage,* 1904.

COPYRIGHTED
BY GEO. MÉLIÈS 1904
PARIS NEW-YORK

George Lucas, Dennis Muren, and Richard Edlund prepare a shot with the in-house-built VistaVision camera.

Dykstra had also freelanced in the effects field, but had little luck in landing a job on a film. His only feature film credit prior to *Star Wars* was Trumbull's *Silent Running*. But it was his work on a 16mm experimental project for the Institute of Urban and Regional Development that would, oddly enough, play a big role in revolutionizing special effects for *Star Wars*: it was there he learned to use a computer to control a movie camera, the birth of what is now known as motion control.

Motion control permitted the camera to move in a precise and repeatable manner. It also allowed the camera shutter to remain open during movement of the camera subject, creating a blurring of the image, something that occurs naturally in normal cinematography but was unknown prior to this in single-frame photography. This meant that in *Star Wars*, for the first time in a feature film, spaceships could race at unprecedented speeds across the screen without the stroboscopic jerkiness that would occur if they had been shot in the traditional manner. It also allowed many planes of action to be predictably planned and perfectly synchronized. Further, it permitted engine glows and running lights to be added to the spaceships with subsequent passes of the camera.

The computer had arrived on the scene. Special effects would never be the same again.

ROSE DUIGNAN

Rose Duignan was a twenty-three-year-old freelancer when she heard about a possible job in Van Nuys at ILM and went for an interview at the little industrial building across from the airport. She sat down and looked around the reception area. Obviously, decorations were not high priority in this production-oriented outfit. But she liked what she saw, and there was a certain spirit in the air. On a couch across the room sat a bearded young man in blue jeans. He didn't seem to have much to do and sat with his tennis-shoed feet up on the coffee table. Rose struck up a conversation with the receptionist. "How is it to work here? . . . Do you ever get to see George Lucas? . . . Is he nice? . . ."

When Rose was ushered into Dykstra's office, the kid on the couch got up and went into the office with her. "A bit cheeky," thought Rose. And even more cheeky when he plopped himself down on Dykstra's couch without a word and put his feet up on the boss's coffee table. Dykstra introduced himself to Rose and then introduced the "kid." It was George Lucas!

Rose worked at ILM for six months, through the last big push to get the effects for *Star Wars* done, then stayed with John Dykstra and worked on effects for the *Battlestar Galactica* TV show. She later rejoined ILM and became the production supervisor for *Star Trek II: The Wrath of Khan* and *Return of the Jedi*.

JOHN DYKSTRA

As a young man, John Dykstra earned his way through design school by taking still photos. Upon graduation, he worked on a number of projects: He signed up with Douglas Trumbull to work with him on *Silent Running*; he also had a job at Graphic Films while they were making *The Voyage to the Outer Planets*, a special film in the grand Omnimax format. However, his career was still in the fledgling stage when, in 1973, he took a job at the Institute of Urban and Regional Development (IURD) in Berkeley. This special group was associated with the University of California and was working on films designed to see if urban development miniatures could be made to look like full-scale construction. The test films were shot in 16mm using a snorkel lens to get in between the models and through the tiny streets; the project was strictly experimental and there was no thought of distribution, making the dry academic work seem an unlikely pursuit for someone who hoped to make it big someday in the feature film field of visual effects. Yet John applied himself to the job, as did his co-workers, Al Miller and Jerry Jeffress. The three saw the project as an opportunity to use computers to facilitate filming: Miller and Jeffress, electronic geniuses, hooked a PDP II computer to the camera shutter and a dolly mover to control the motions of the camera. The humble PDP barely had the power of a good pocket calculator today, but its use was still a remarkable innovation, heralding a new era of visual effects technology. At the time, however, Dykstra, Miller, and Jeffress were quite unaware of the significance of what they had done. They were just trying to do the job the best way they knew how.

By 1975, John was back in Los Angeles. The Berkeley project had run out of funding and it was time to find another job. He liked Douglas Trumbull and hung around his studio even when there was no work. There, he learned that George Lucas was looking for someone to do effects for a movie called *Star Wars*. Trumbull and Lucas had held some preliminary discussions, but it didn't seem the two would be working together. The determined young director had rather radical ideas about fast-moving spaceships performing acrobatics in the style of dogfighting World War II aircraft.

The experienced visual effects people didn't take George seriously. They told him such rapid movement would cause a

John Dykstra, the first ILM visual effects supervisor, poses with the Y-wing fighter.

Above: X-wing fighter built at ILM in Van Nuys.

Right: John Dykstra adjusts the first Death Star trench model filmed outdoors in the sun. Grant McCune is on the left.

Far right: Grant McCune makes an adjustment on a *Star Wars* model, "The Escape Pod." This was the very first shot that ILM completed.

Now their IURD experiments could be put to use. It was obvious that the only way they could achieve the sort of movement George wanted was by using a motion control system like the one they had developed in Berkeley. John used a new track and dolly to support a camera that was different from what was then conventionally being used. Normally, in special effects work, when a shot was to be duplicated and composited with other shots, it was filmed using 65mm film stock and camera equipment, which provided a very detailed, high-quality image that stood up well during compositing. But John faced a dilemma with this format: the equipment and the film stock were expensive and hard to find. However, John knew of a long dormant system that Paramount Pictures had used for Cecil B. De Mille's *The Ten Commandments*: it was called VistaVision.

The young *Star Wars* team adapted VistaVision for their special effects needs. They then went out and snatched up every-

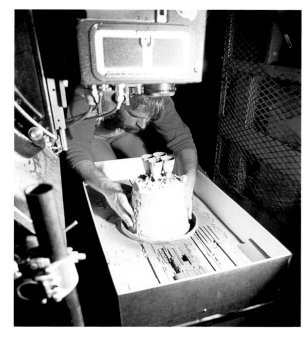

strobing effect on the screen, and they assumed George knew very little about special effects or science fiction. John, however, made no such assumption. He offered his services to George and to producer Gary Kurtz, and they signed him on immediately.

To begin with, the filmmakers had no studio, no camera equipment, and no models to film. Gary rented an empty warehouse in Van Nuys; John recruited many of his old friends for the project, and he also brought aboard several young students fresh out of art school, and camera operators and modelmakers brand new to filmmaking. Al Miller, his former partner from the IURD, came down to join the venture.

thing they needed at very low prices. Several years later, after the release of *Star Wars*, prices for used VistaVision equipment skyrocketed.

*T*he problem of choosing a good film and camera format was just the first of many challenges that John faced as ILM began to take shape. An accomplished aircraft pilot and a racing car and motorcycle driver, John had always been at home with machines. He had great faith in technology, though, and believed that imagination and engineering could solve any problem. ILM's high-tech environment suited him wonderfully. Under his guidance, many "wouldn't it be great if . . ." dreams became reality.

Part of John's success at ILM is attributable to his dynamic, charismatic personality. Six feet four inches, broad-shouldered, with a booming voice, he has a commanding presence. Yet John is also a sensitive individual who seems to know how to generate enthusiasm in his employees. During the making of *Star Wars*, he was constantly on the move through ILM's corridors, instruct-

Above: George Lucas points at the model of the T-16 spaceship from *Star Wars*.

Middle: Modelmaker Steve Gawley works on the first 3-foot-long Star Destroyer for *Star Wars*.

Below: The *Star Wars* landspeeder in the parking lot of the old ILM, driven by Bill Shourt (left) and Richard Alexander (right).

Below left: Steve Gawley's pickup truck in action, moving past the trench model with explosion.

John Dykstra stands next to Joe Johnston, dressed as Darth Vader holding a lightsaber.

ing, praising, laughing, and issuing orders. He'd quickly spot a person having a bad day, and, with his arm around the person's shoulder, they'd step outside for a frank and friendly discussion, and the person, cheered once more, would return to work. Those who worked for him were fiercely loyal.

When *Star Wars* was done, John went to Hawaii for a month to recover from the grueling one-and-a-half-year project. Though everyone had worked hard on it,

there was no premonition that this film would be anything very special, and no thought of continuing the operation after vacation. John planned to look for another job when he got back.

Of course, *Star Wars* changed a lot of lives unexpectedly, and John Dykstra's was one of them. He went on to form a company called Apogee, which he continues to operate out of the old ILM facility in Van Nuys.

Looking back now, he laughs as he recounts stories of the good times and points with pride to the picture of the assembled ILMers clowning it up in front of the camera back in 1977 when they were working on *Star Wars*. It is indeed a historic photo, freezing in time a moment when he led an enthusiastic yet relatively inexperienced team of rookies to win first place in the super bowl of visual effects.

RICHARD EDLUND

Most ILMers have an interesting story that explains how they got into the rather esoteric business of special effects. Richard's story is simple, yet perhaps one of the most colorful. He landed his first professional film job through the rather unlikely recommendation of an unemployment office. He had no connections in the film business but felt that he had special talents to offer, so he wrote a resumé and carried it to the California Office of Human Resources in Hollywood. Joe Westheimer, who ran a well-known and highly respected shop providing film titles and optical effects for television and feature films, read Richard's resumé and gave him his first break in the industry.

*I*n high school, Richard always had a camera with him. He took pictures for the school yearbook and even published some of his sports photos in the *Los Angeles Examiner*. He dreamed of someday becoming a photojournalist. After graduating from high school, he joined the navy, where he received further training in photography, including camera repair. Cameras fascinated him; he loved the concentration and precision required to strip a camera of all its watchlike parts and then reassemble it into a perfectly operating instrument.

The navy shipped young Edlund to Japan, where, unlike the typical GI, he studied Japanese language, culture, and literature in his off-duty hours. Years later, he would greet Japanese visitors at ILM and converse with the guests in their own language. While in Japan, he became interested in movies and decided that, when he returned home, he would study film. Although his high school academic record hardly recommended him, the University of Southern California admitted Richard into the film program. After two and a half years, with a close to straight A average, he decided to try his luck getting a job in Hollywood. Luck was indeed with him as Joe Westheimer came across Richard's resumé at the unemployment office.

At Westheimer's studio, Richard proved to be a jack-of-all-trades. He hand lettered movie title cards, repaired and built electronic devices, and photographed insert shots for films. He remained with Westheimer for four years and then, giving three months' notice, left to become a rock and roll photographer. It was the late 1960s and Richard claims to have become somewhat of a hippie. He moved to San Francisco and tried his hand at experimental film-making, supporting himself as a tour guide in the city, driving a cable-car-lookalike tour bus.

In 1974 he returned to movies, taking a job with Robert Abel, a special effects stu-

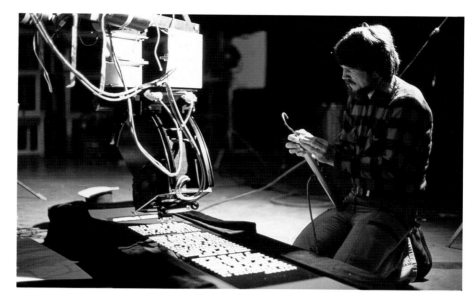

dio specializing in artful television commercials. While working for Abel, he got to know John Dykstra. Dykstra was discussing the *Star Wars* project with producer Gary Kurtz. Richard was electrified by the potential of the ambitious film project, and Dykstra agreed to hire him as Director of Photography if the project materialized.

Star Wars was a dream come true for Richard. It meant starting from the ground up, renovating an industrial building to make it into a studio, building the equipment to do the film work, and then learning to use that equipment like a virtuoso to do shots for the film. Richard recalls the first time he arrived for work at the new ILM. "It was a large, empty industrial building. All there was was a table in the middle of the floor with a telephone on it." The challenge was to develop the equipment needed to do the work. Richard, an admitted lover of hardware, was a key figure in equipping the new studio with the needed cameras. He helped scour the used equipment houses of Hollywood for the "trick units," as he calls them, needed to film the effects shots for *Star Wars*.

Above: Richard Edlund programs the opening title crawl for *Star Wars*.

Left: Richard Edlund operates a VistaVision camera, in the bed of a pickup truck driven by modelmaker Steve Gawley moving past the "trench," the grand finale in *Star Wars*. This high speed shot was done in the parking lot of old ILM.

Above: Modelmaker Grant McCune places a panel on the 3-foot Star Destroyer.

Right: The frame of the Star Destroyer on the left. Modelmaker Colin Campbell's prototype is on the right.

Far right: Parts for the X-wing fighter before being painted.

Then there were months of cinematography, including the spectacular pyrotechnical effects that provided part of the excitement of the *Star Wars* special effects. Richard loved filming these scenes. They required the use of a high-speed VistaVision camera; he located a forgotten one at Paramount Pictures that could run at 100 frames per second—no one since has been able to build a VistaVision format camera that could operate at that speed. It was one of those cases of superior craftsmanship from out of the past. He treasured this marvel of motion picture technology; but long after *Star Wars*, this one-of-a-kind instrument was destroyed by a careless operator who failed to lubricate the precision parts. Richard speaks of that camera today as one would of a lost friend who died needlessly.

For his work on *Star Wars*, Richard won an Academy Award, the first of four he would ultimately win while associated with ILM.

During the one-year hiatus of ILM, between *Star Wars* and *The Empire Strikes Back*, Richard shot effects for the TV show *Battlestar Galactica*. Then, in 1978, he was summoned to the new ILM in Northern California. Again a new facility with special equipment was needed, for a much more ambitious film project; Richard helped assemble the technicians needed to both build the facility and staff it for the big job ahead. One very striking aspect of Richard's personality is his powerful leadership ability. He oozes charisma. I have always felt that if Richard were shipwrecked with a boatload of world leaders on a deserted island, in a few years he would be elected emperor and the entire population would be happily at work doing special effects. For his key role on *The Empire Strikes Back*, he won his second Academy Award.

In 1980, George Lucas and Steven Spielberg were collaborating on a new venture unrelated to space, yet needing

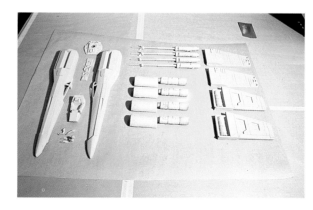

on his office wall as proof of his and ILM's respect for Ralph and of the company's indebtedness to Ralph's work on *Star Wars*).

Ralph was raised in a small town in Montana during the Depression. His grandfather had a little publication in town, and both he and Ralph's mother were active painters. At the age of ten, Ralph began art classes. His talent showed immediately, and upon graduation from high school in 1948, he began technical art classes. In 1950 he had landed a job at the Boeing Company in Seattle, where he was the youngest in a group of fifty or so artists. Later, the draft cut his tenure at Boeing short, and he was sent to Korea.

His experience in the army has had a profound effect on his life. Ralph carried his gun in the front lines and saw friend after friend killed in the sporadic assaults that continued despite the ongoing peace talks. Surrounded by bullets and shrapnel, he began to feel it was just a matter of time before it was his turn to die. With Chinese attackers on a hill less than fifteen yards away, he rose from his trench to hurl a grenade; before he could pull the pin, he felt a tremendous bang on the side of his head. Blood streamed from beneath his helmet and he crumpled to the ground. Miraculously, he was still alive. While bandaging his wound, his buddies examined his helmet, and found that the liner inside had stopped a bullet that would have otherwise torn into his skull and taken his life.

Ralph's survival in light of his friends' deaths haunted him. Never gregarious, when he returned home he found himself even less outgoing than before.

Ralph resumed his job at Boeing and later went freelance. He did a great num

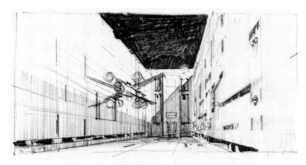

Above and left: The *Millennium Falcon* in Mos Eisley, and the X-wing flies through the Death Star trench. These were early conceptual sketches for *Star Wars* by Ralph McQuarrie.

Below: The Death Star trench model. This subjective angle was shot indoors with a painted backing to make it appear to go on indefinitely.

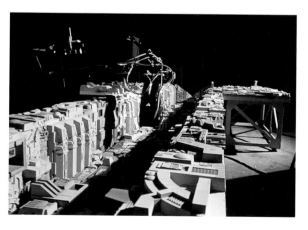

Following spread, four production paintings by Ralph McQuarrie:
1) Darth Vader fences with Luke Skywalker.

2) The *Millennium Falcon* docked in Mos Eisley.

3) Looking down the reactor chamber.

4) The *Millennium Falcon* flying into the Death Star hangar.

ber of technical paintings for NASA, an experience that would serve him in good stead later. He became expert in depicting spacecraft and hardware in realistic detail: just the sort of background ideal for someone who would bring the fantasy world of *Star Wars* to visual life.

While George was filming in England, Ralph took on several matte painting assignments for ILM, his first effort in this area. He went to the Disney Studios to see

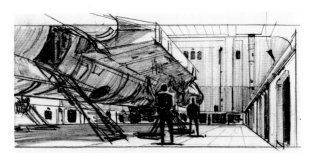

some of the matte paintings done there, and was astounded at how little detail there was in the work. He wondered how such paintings could be blown up to the full size of the theater screen and not look even worse! He sought out films with matte paintings in them to study their design, and made an interesting observation: though a screen is quite large, the apparent size of the screen was actually smaller than the size of the paintings, In a sense, the paintings were being not enlarged but reduced when seen in the theater. When he moved closer to the screen he found that the film grain became so coarse that the missing details were not noticeable.

Though he loved the concept for *Star Wars*, he never expected that it would be more than an average success. Science fiction films, after all, did not have a history of shattering box office records. So, after completing his work on the movie, he traveled to England to work on another assignment. He was out of the country when the film came out and missed the national excitement that accompanied the picture's release. Shortly after he returned to this country, he recalls exiting a subway station in New York City across the street from a theater where *Star Wars* was playing. There was a long line outside: it was the middle of a weekday yet people were lined up to get in. He crossed the street and quietly got in line himself. Inside the theater, the film did not surprise him as much as the audience's reaction to it. It was an incredible experience for him to see his designs and paintings hit such a responsive chord in the young audience.

When production for *The Empire Strikes Back* began, Ralph again joined in on the ILM project. This time he worked in the new Northern California facility as a

matte artist, contributing a great many paintings to the final film. But some of the fun had gone out of it for him; he felt that too much was expected, that he had to outdo his work on *Star Wars*. Ralph did not believe that art could come from such pressure. No enthusiasm is generated when no fun exists; for him the adventure was over

After *The Empire Strikes Back* was completed, Ralph left ILM to continue his freelance work. His next big challenge came when Steven Spielberg asked him to design the spaceship for *E.T.: The Extra-Terrestrial*. He submitted several concepts, and Spielberg picked the now-familiar cheerful little craft.

One of his most recent projects was as a production designer for the highly successful 1985 film *Cocoon*.

Today, Ralph is busy doing paintings for science fiction book covers and occasionally executing concepts and designs for films. He is one of the finest photorealist painters in motion pictures, and an expert at storyboard sketching and imaginative costume designs. He played an early and important role in the development of *Star Wars* and is highly respected by all who have had the privilege of working with him.

Left: Production sketches for *Star Wars* by Ralph McQuarrie.

Below, left: Production sketch by Ralph McQuarrie.

Below, right: Early sandcrawlers designed by Ralph McQuarrie. The originals of these McQuarrie sketches are quite small, some no larger than a postage stamp.

CHAPTER 2

VISUAL EFFECTS DESIGN

*I*n 1977, *Star Wars* burst upon the movie screen. Millions of filmgoers spontaneously cheered and applauded as a giant spaceship lumbered overhead. They sensed that this film would carry them into a new realm of film experience, and in the following two hours, they were not disappointed. It is interesting to me that most critics who reviewed *Star Wars* overlooked the powerful visual impact of this highly cinematic film.

The first ten minutes of *Raiders of the Lost Ark* also impart a powerful sense of visual design: the camera glides through a dark jungle, giving shadowy glimpses of the forbidding environment, and we move into an ancient tomb, scramble to dodge darts, and see our hero dangle over a deep pit. He is finally chased by a giant stone ball, only to dive free—into the midst of a threatening tribe of natives. This is followed by a classic chase on foot and an airplane getaway. Words cannot describe

Designer Joe Johnston (left) and special effects supervisor Dennis Muren discuss ideas for *Indiana Jones and the Temple of Doom.*

the pure excitement evoked by these images, developed under the direction of Steven Spielberg.

Scenes like these are no accident—all the special moments have been carefully planned. Spielberg does not just dream up amazing scenes on location. Like George Lucas, he is highly conscious of what he is doing cinematically. Communication with the audience is all-important, not just on the literary or acting level but on the cinematic level as well. Generally, reviewers will comment on acting (a dramatic art) or script (a literary art) or costumes and sets (a traditional design art) or even the music; yet rarely do they mention cinematic achievement, the powerful aspect of a well-designed film. In order to extract maximum impact from the cinematic element, both Spielberg and Lucas believe strongly in preplanning and storyboarding all their work, especially the special effects scenes. This is one of the tasks to which the ILM Art department is assigned.

The designers at ILM work in a small upstairs office next to the employees' coffee lounge. The walls are lined with burlap-covered bulletin boards with pictures pinned to them. These pictures range from work in progress to visual reference material such as old magazine photographs, classic paintings, and sketches the designers are considering either discarding or improving. This is the department where Yoda, the wise Jedi Master (from *The Empire Strikes Back*), the imposing mechanical snow walkers (also from *Empire*), the racing speeder bikes (from *Return of the Jedi*), and hundreds of other fascinating creatures and spaceships were born. The artists usually sketch in pencil and then finish the drawings off with ink and broad felt-tip pens in shades

When the storyboards are completed and the sequences are finally approved, they are duplicated and put in large three-ring binders. In the case of *The Empire Strikes Back*, there were almost 500 pages of storyboards. On *Return of the Jedi*, there were close to 1,000—a storyboard for nearly every special effects shot in the show. A complete set of these storyboards is also put on a bulletin board that runs down the main hallway in the center of ILM. If anyone is ever in doubt about what a shot looks like or where it goes in a sequence of shots, they refer to those storyboards. Some of the key personnel also have miniature versions of these pictures, to be carried around in their back pockets for quick reference when shooting scenes.

There are two major design responsibilities at ILM: one is for the creatures, spaceships, and sets; the other is to determine how the shots are to be composed.

of gray. (The storyboards will be photocopied, so color is not important.)

In the middle of a major production, such as *Return of the Jedi* or *The Empire Strikes Back*, all of the walls are covered with storyboards. For *Return of the Jedi*, on any one day there might have been five hundred storyboards neatly tacked to the wall. They were periodically rearranged or discarded as new ones replaced the old. This giant "comic book" view of the visual effects permitted rearrangement and redesigning before millions of dollars were spent chasing visual concepts that would not work.

THE STORYBOARD: BLUE-PRINT FOR EFFECTS

From the shooting script and verbal instructions from the director, a STORY-BOARD is created. It becomes the blueprint for the visual effects. Each drawing fits on a standard form which is designed with an area for a drawing of the scenes and below that, an area for a list of specifications, such as the number of photographic elements involved in the shot and the type of photography, whether animation, model photography, or miniature motion control photography.

*T*he method of design at ILM on a George Lucas film is one of close collaboration between George and the artist. George will propose an idea that he wants to execute, and artists in the Art Department will begin sketching an interpretation of George's verbal instructions regarding the spaceships or creatures he has in his mind. When a character or a spaceship is to be developed, an original sketch is followed by mock-up models. If it is to be a creature, such as Jabba the Hutt or a prototype Ewok, sculptors are put to work sculpting five- to seven-inch-tall versions of these creatures. The sculptures are painted, and a number of them are lined up on a table for George to inspect and comment upon. Usually, he will say something like this: "I like this one, this one, this one, and this one. Let's hold these others for

Gatefold: The further development of the storyboard painting as seen in *Star Trek III: The Search for Spock.*

A storyboard of a special effects shot for *Star Trek III* and the storyboard made into a painting.

later and deep six that one." The ones he likes may also be modified; maybe the ears of one should be substituted for the ears of another, one head might look better on another's body, and so forth.

When a spaceship is being designed, an artist will do a sketch of the ship and, if George likes the general look of the design on paper, a three-dimensional model will be built, usually out of paperboard. It is important at this point to hold it in hand,

rotate it, and see what it looks like from all angles, for it will, of course, be filmed from many sides and must look good from any point of view. Again, changes are usually made on these prototypes before work begins on the final model.

As the shooting progresses, the art director is often brought to the set to examine how things are coming together. Color combinations, the lines, and the general appearance of the scene are all checked. Most of the art directors at ILM are also first-rate model builders and sculptors who will often move into the model shop and work on the construction of prototypes for models or sculpt the little figure proposals for new characters and creatures in the films. An ILM art director rarely deals with matters that go beyond special effects, such as set design and costumes. The great exception to this is Ralph McQuarrie, whose concept paintings and sketches for *Star Wars* had a profound effect on all aspects of the film's design.

CINEMA WITH A CAPITAL *C*

When I first became involved with visual effects, one of its most fascinating aspects was the pure application of the cinematic art form as envisioned by the film aestheticians such as the innovative Rudolf Arnheim, Sergei Eisenstein, and the great MGM montage designer Slavko Vorkapich.

Most of the films we normally see are not good examples of what fundamentalist theoreticians would call pure cinema. Most films do, in fact, simply act as records of theater or literature. They are like postcards: not without function but not necessarily art, even though they may be a faithful representation of the object they depict. This is not so with most visual effects. Because they are designed in detail and carefully executed, it is possible to control nearly every aspect of their production. The special effects designer is not tied to lines of dialogue and the actions of

actors; imagination can be released to its fullest extent. With visual effects, the camera and its subjects are indeed free to move at will. Even the nature of the subjects photographed in most visual effects are entirely within the filmmaker's control.

What does this mean to the audience? Most people are not conscious of this esoteric aspect of cinema, and that is as it should be. Yet subconsciously they are very appreciative of directors who understand how to use this unique art form and who apply it in their films. Properly applied, Cinema with a capital *C* gives the

Far left: Early Luke Skywalker designs by Ralph McQuarrie.

Left: Early sketch of Chewbacca by Ralph McQuarrie.

Right: Layout of miniature prototype creatures for *Return of the Jedi*.

Below: ILM art director Joe Johnston works in his studio at ILM during *Return of the Jedi*.

an objective instrument, in theory dispassionately recording everything set before it, in practice the camera is always set in some relationship to the objects it is photographing. Determining that relationship is the role of the film designer. The designer may be an art director, a cinematographer, or a director. Should the scene be filmed from below, above, far away, or close? Should the camera move with an object or let it move away or toward us? The choices multiply the more one considers the variety of options available to the filmmaker.

Here's an example of how cinematic design can enhance a scene.

Imagine that a short two-line description in the script calls for a scene in which a spaceship is traveling toward a planet. The visual effects designer must figure out how to make this "live." There are several ways that this can be achieved.

The designer could, of course, have a fixed camera with the planet on the left and the spaceship moving toward it from the right: the camera doesn't move, the

viewer the feeling of three-dimensional flight. Rather than watching a flat, two-dimensional image surrounded by a black frame, viewing a well-designed film scene allows the surface of the screen to disappear and the frame around the image to be forgotten. The more cinematically the scene is conceived, the more the viewer feels carried into the space behind the surface of the screen, transcending the reality of sitting in a theater. Though the camera is

Gatefold: The asteroid chase sequence from *The Empire Strikes Back*, one of the finest examples of cinematic design for a special effects sequence.

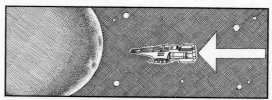

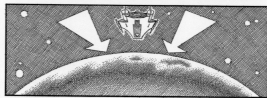

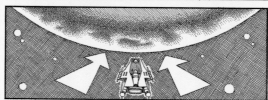

As you can well guess, there are endless possibilities that can result from combining these design elements. Some combinations will be more effective than others, but in all cases, it is the design of the shot that will either make it visually pleasing or not. The design is perhaps even more important than how the shot is finally executed. Therefore, the design is not only the first step in the creation of a visual effect at Industrial Light and Magic, but one of the most important ones.

Above: From *The Empire Strikes Back*—Princess Leia looks out her window in Cloud City. A shot that did not work too well because of perspective problems.

Left: Designer Joe Johnston stands before the hundreds of storyboards for *The Empire Strikes Back*.

DESIGN ALTERNATIVES
"A space ship approaching a planet," can be visualized in many ways. Here are four alternatives. The fourth one, shown here on the bottom, is the most dynamic of the four. The ship reveals more of itself as it roars over the camera and then turns toward the planet which hovers over it in the sky.

Right: McQuarrie thumbnail sketches for *Star Wars*.

Below: A Ralph McQuarrie sketch for a possible *Star Wars* poster.

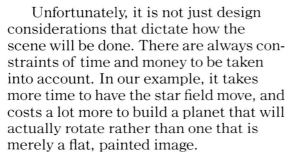

Unfortunately, it is not just design considerations that dictate how the scene will be done. There are always constraints of time and money to be taken into account. In our example, it takes more time to have the star field move, and costs a lot more to build a planet that will actually rotate rather than one that is merely a flat, painted image.

Some of the best examples of cinematic construction come from imaginative TV commercials, which are usually highly designed and preplanned. They can afford to strive for maximum cinematic impact, since their budget per second is often far greater than even the most expensive feature film.

But perhaps the most highly cinematic scenes ever done are those generated with a computer, since computer-generated images have total freedom of movement. The viewer can move from high over a (digital) city, swoop down to street level, roll along the sidewalk, and fly into a building and up the stairs. George Lucas's great interest in the possibilities of the digital

film medium springs from its enormous potential: the dream is for a day when the film designer will be able to sit at a computer console with total command of time and space. Meanwhile, those who appreciate this graphic side of film will find the best sampling of its pure art most commonly in visual effects.

Feature-film visual effects usually represent a very small percentage of the total film length and, therefore, are regarded more as seasoning than the main dish. Usually they deal with brief episodes with concentrated impact—moments such as the planet exploding in *Star Trek II: The Wrath of Khan*; the bicycles taking off and flying in *E.T.: The Extra-Terrestrial*; the *Millennium Falcon* going through an asteroid field in *The Empire Strikes Back*; or a giant Gorax attacking a small Ewok in *The Ewok Adventure*.

Since planning is a prerequisite for special effects, great care is taken, from the design of the objects within a shot to the design of the shot itself, to maximize their visual impact.

JOE JOHNSTON

In the summer of 1975, Joe Johnston went straight from college to working for a design company where he was earning $250 a week. The drive to work was a long hour and a half from his home in Long Beach, California, so when he was offered a job closer to home along with a fifty-dollar-a-week pay raise, he took it gladly. He had been out of school two weeks when he joined ILM in Van Nuys, where *Star Wars* was in production. John Dykstra told him the kind of shots director George Lucas wanted, and Joe got to work drawing. He had been working for several months, turning out sketches and storyboards, when he first met George in film editor Verna Fields's garage.

Asked about the atmosphere at the old ILM, Joe recalls: "We came from different backgrounds and that was what was kind of fun about it. We were just trying things that we intuitively thought would work. Sometimes they did, sometimes they didn't."

When the deadline for the effects was nearing, tension was building and some began to panic. Joe remembers one person who was big on computers and statistics who came in one morning with a long printout and announced to everyone that he had proven that there was no way they could finish on time. Since he did not intend to go down with a sinking ship, he quit. Years later, that same individual put out a flyer to get work in special effects. Heading his list of achievements was "Special Effects for *Star Wars*."

Joe says of design: "Design is intuitive. You have to give people something interesting to look at. It doesn't matter what it is, as long as it isn't boring. It might be a camera move or an interesting ship maneu-

ver. Perhaps a nice sweeping turn. Everyone notices if the shot is flat and dull. If the eye has nothing to focus on, it will wander all over the place. It is the designer's job to lead the eye into the frame and show it where to look.

"A good example of this is the opening scene from *Star Wars*. It blew people away because it was such a shock; they were forced to look at something. The lines of perspective were very strong on the Star Destroyer. It was all George's idea, and I'm sure that he had played it in his head a hundred times before he told me how he wanted it to look."

Joe attributes part of George Lucas's success in design to the fact that he is always looking for something unique, exciting, and "off-the-wall interesting." Most of George's ship designs are different. "Although everything has been done before," Joe says, "George somehow finds a way to do it better, differently."

After *Star Wars*, Joe worked on the television series *Battlestar Galactica*. Then, in 1978, he moved to Northern California to join the new ILM.

He feels that *The Empire Strikes Back* was his best work, partly because he was in on it right from the beginning and partly because he had the experience of *Star Wars* behind him. Two of his biggest contributions to *Empire* were the design of Yoda (which was sculpted by Stuart Freeborn) and the design of the snow walkers. In addition, Joe designed many of the visual effects shots in the film. "*Empire*," he says, "combined the spirit of experimentation with the big leap in technology."

After *Empire*, Joe played a key role in *Raiders of the Lost Ark*, for which he won an Academy Award in visual effects. On

Joe Johnston and Dennis Muren go over storyboards for *Indiana Jones and the Temple of Doom.*

Return of the Jedi, Joe began designing creatures and craft early on. His most noticeable achievements were the Ewoks and the speeder bikes. "I did hundreds of drawings of little furry guys in the woods. A lot of them were troll-like, gnomes. Some of them had cute little puppy-dog faces. George said, 'Make them cute.' So I did more drawings. Then I did one with a little bonnet with his ears poking out the top. George came in and said, 'That's it.' So that's how the Ewoks were designed."

The speeder bikes came more easily. George directed Joe to design something like a landspeeding motorcycle that had to be able to fly through trees. The speeder bike sequence in *The Return of the Jedi* is one of the most exciting effects sequences in the entire *Star Wars* trilogy.

In his personal life, Joe enjoys a bit of excitement reminiscent of scenes from the movies he works on. He is an ultralight pilot who flies his cloth and cable flying machine whenever his schedule and the Northern California weather will cooperate. The flying machine resembles a 1910 contraption and is powered by a motor barely powerful enough for a good-sized lawn mower. On one flight, his engine stopped unexpectedly while he was several hundred feet above the ground. Joe kept his cool as he reached up and grabbed the little handle attached to the nylon rope starter. He gave it a yank and it sputtered a few times, then stopped. The plane continued to drift silently downward. Joe tried it again and, like a cantankerous outboard motor, it finally sputtered to a start.

In his years with ILM, Joe worked on *Star Wars, Raiders of the Lost Ark, The Empire Strikes Back, Poltergeist, Return of the Jedi,* and, finally, *Indiana Jones and the Temple of Doom.* After *Indiana Jones,* Joe took a leave of absence in order to go back to college and study film. He enrolled at the University of Southern California film school, and there he practiced other aspects of cinema that he had never been involved with in his years with ILM. During the summer vacation from college, he returned to Northern California to act as production designer for *The Ewok Adventure.* He also did a little second-unit directing on this project. He likes directing and would someday like an opportunity to move into that aspect of filmmaking.

But if he never again works in film (rather unlikely) he still carries a lifetime of memories from being at the heart of one of the most wonderful film experiences of his time. He says, "I sometimes wish I could be hypnotized to forget how it was done and just enjoy each of the pictures I worked on as a film." Of all of them he still regards his first film, *Star Wars,* with the most fondness. "It's something that when I'm eighty-eight my great-grandchildren can tell their friends, 'See that old man? He worked on *Star Wars!*'"

NILO RODIS-JAMERO

ILM visual effects designer Nilo Rodis-Jamero was raised in Cebu City in the Philippines. His Catholic father felt that his son should become a priest and sent him to seminary, where Nilo spent four years of high school, but Nilo felt that to become a priest one should have a "calling," which he never experienced. He wanted to go to college in the U.S., where some of his close relatives were living. He passed the High School Equivalency test and was admitted to San Jose State near San Francisco, California. After graduating from college, he was hired by General Motors to work on car design for Chevrolet.

Meanwhile, Joe Johnston, art director for the newly reestablished ILM, was looking for someone to join him in the art department. He contacted San Jose State and asked for leads on new talent. They referred him to their star student who was now working for General Motors; by the time Joe caught up with him, Nilo was designing tanks.

Nilo had never thought of a career in film but was interested in what Joe was talking about. After a brief pause for reflection, he agreed to join the art department.

It was the summer of 1979, and the pace of the work at ILM was building up in preparation for the big push on effects for *The Empire Strikes Back*. Nilo was soon drawn into the excitement of planning the effects for the film, and though he had never had much interest in movies prior to his recruitment at ILM, he now became deeply involved in the *Star Wars* environment. He was in fact now in the very center of new ideas for the film.

He felt privileged to be associated with artists such as Ralph McQuarrie, Joe Johnston, and the man he calls the greatest designer of them all, George Lucas. "Lucas," says Nilo, "can design in any medium." Though George himself rarely puts pencil to the drawing pad, he knows how things must look and gives the artist the room needed to be creative. "With George's guidance, the designers are kept on track and constantly improving themselves because of his feedback."

For *The Empire Strikes Back*, Nilo put his talent to use not only in the design studio but the Model Shop as well. He was responsible for the design of Boba Fett's ship and built an early prototype. Unfortunately, Boba's role was diminished during late pre-production and the ship was seen only in a few shots.

Between *The Empire Strikes Back* and *Return of the Jedi*, Nilo played an important role in the design department at ILM. One of his bigger projects was *Poltergeist*; he worked closely with effects supervisor Richard Edlund and the film's producer, Steven Spielberg. His biggest challenge, however, was just around the corner: *Return of the Jedi*.

More than a year before principal photography commenced on this third film in

Visual effects designer Nilo Rodis-Jamero inspects a model for *Explorers*.

the *Star Wars* series, Nilo began sketching designs for George Lucas. He was not limited to the work that ILM was to do on this film—now he was branching out to propose ideas for costumes for the characters in the film. As the time approached to construct the creatures and build the costumes for the actors, Nilo took a leave of absence from ILM and became a key figure in the wardrobe department. He continued in that department until filming was completed, and then returned to ILM to assist in the post-production special effects work.

In one of his most recent projects, *Explorers*, he was given a great deal of latitude by the film's director, Joe Dante. Nilo found *Explorers* to be a synthesis of all he had learned in his first six years with ILM, and made use of his skills in nearly all phases of motion picture design.

When asked by young would-be designers how to get into the business, he recommends a broad academic background. He feels that education develops an individual's character and it is character, he believes, that is ultimately expressed in the work of the artist.

CHAPTER 3

MODEL CONSTRUCTION

Every one of the "core" ILM model-makers is a unique and gifted craftsman. One story illustrates the kind of talent inherent in this department.

In 1977, Bill George was in his early teens when he went to see *Star Wars*. Being an avid builder of models, he was very impressed with those he saw in the film. He went out and began to build replicas of the models that were being sold as kits. But one of his favorites—the Y-wing—was not available in kit form. He was disappointed to find that this one was not for sale, so he built one of his own design from his memory of how it looked in the film. Meanwhile, after the great success of *Star Wars*, George Lucas gave Alan Ladd Jr. of 20th Century—Fox the only Y-wing built by ILM for the film; Ladd put it in a case and displayed it in his office. Six years later, when Bill George was working at ILM on *Return of the Jedi*, George Lucas asked that ILM use a Y-wing in the new film. Alan Ladd Jr. was out of the country and the model was needed desperately. There seemed to be no way that we could get it quickly, and we were tempted to build a quick one just to get moving while we waited for Ladd to return. Bill George heard about the crisis and offered to bring in his copy. He told us not to expect much since it was one of his early works, but when we saw it we were astonished. Not only was it an absolutely professional model in every sense, but Lorne Peterson, who had worked on the original one used in *Star Wars*, said it was better than the one given to Alan Ladd Jr!

Bill George's model was used in *Jedi* and then purchased from him by ILM at the end of the show. It now sits in the *Star Wars* archives along with all the other important models from the three historic *Star Wars* films.

Opposite page: George Lucas stands among models from his three *Star Wars* movies. The unfinished Death Star from *Return of the Jedi* hangs above him.

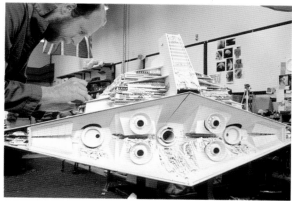

Above: Modelmaker Bill George works on a spaceship model.

Middle: Modelmaker Steve Gawley works on a Star Destroyer.

Below, from left: *Empire Strikes Back* Modelmakers Steve Gawley, Dave Carson, Paul Huston; back row: Lorne Peterson, Marc Thorpe, Michael Fulmer; middle row: Ease Owyeung, Wesley Seeds, Sam Zolltheis; foreground: Charlie Bailey.

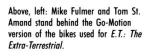

Above, left: Mike Fulmer and Tom St. Amand stand behind the Go-Motion version of the bikes used for *E.T.: The Extra-Terrestrial*.

Middle, left: The ILM *E.T.* crew, from left to right: Micheal McAlister, director Steven Spielberg, Pat Sweeney, Ken Smith, Michael Fulmer, producer Kathleen Kennedy, Warren Franklin and Dennis Muren.

Above, right: The stop motion puppets and bicycles prepared for use in *E.T.: The Extra-Terrestrial*.

Middle, right: Tom St. Amand adjusts the E.T. puppet on a bicycle.

Below, right: Modelmaker Charlie Bailey works on the interior of the Star Destroyer.

There is a core of less than ten model-makers at ILM, but this number is augmented when bigger projects require it. During *Return of the Jedi*, there were more than thirty people working on everything from spaceships to miniature redwood trees. Lorne Peterson shares the leadership of the department with Steve Gawley. The two are totally different kinds of personalities: Lorne is an organizer, a chart maker and planner, in addition to being a first-class modelmaker and designer, while Steve is a hands-on team leader, capable of inspiring fellow modelmakers to turn out incredible amounts of work when the push is on.

Mike Fulmer came to ILM as a journeyman welder, specializing in large oil drilling rigs and pipelines and structural steel frames. Nothing could be further from the kind of delicate work he now performs at ILM: he welded the tubular frames for the five-inch bikes used in *E.T.* and made the silver dollar–sized spoked wheels; he also built the miniature Ford Tri-Motor airplane for *Indiana Jones and the Temple of Doom.* In order to simulate the corrugated metal look of the fuselage, Fulmer constructed a mechanical device that converted heavy-duty aluminum foil into perfect corrugated sheets.

Charlie Bailey races cars on the weekends and headed up the team that built the Jules Verne–like *E.T.* spaceship and a set of miniature Imperial walkers for *The Empire Strikes Back.* He couldn't afford a special race car so he modified his own and between weekend races drove it to work with the racing number still on it. One weekend, he wrecked his car during a race—he miraculously escaped with his life, but the car did not fare so well.

When they moved to Northern California to do *The Empire Strikes Back,* everyone thought that it would be a matter of simply restoring the old models from *Star Wars* and perhaps adding a few new ones. But it didn't turn out that way. For *Star Wars,* less than fifty models were built. For *Empire,* they added slightly over one hundred. For *Return of the Jedi,* one hundred and sixty new models were built! In all, Lorne Peterson estimates that over the past decade, more than five hundred models have been built by ILM for the Lucasfilm projects, including the Indiana Jones series.

Above: Modelmaker Randy Ottenberg works on the rigging for the galleon ship in *Goonies.*

Left: Modelmakers Bill George (left) and Chuck Wiley (right) build the hull for the galleon ship in *Goonies.*

Right: Barbara Gallucci places a miniature tree in a miniature set for *Return of the Jedi*. Special effects for some of the battle between the Ewoks and the two-legged walkers took place on this set.

Below: Barbara Affonso paints a tree for a *Return of the Jedi* miniature set.

Life at ILM can be pretty intensive in the Model Shop when a deadline presses everyone to their limit. During the making of *The Empire Strikes Back*, people were putting in long hours seven days a week. In an out-of-the-way area of the ILM building, used cardboard boxes were stored until the janitor could throw them out. Periodically, one very conscientious modelmaker would withdraw to this spot with a 2 × 4 piece of lumber. There he would bash the boxes and scream. Brian Johnson, one of the effects supervisors on *The Empire Strikes Back*, was passing through the area around ten o'clock at night when he heard the racket and rushed to witness the ritual. After seeing what was going on, he immediately came to Lorne to express his

concern for the modelmaker's sanity. "Oh," said Lorne offhandedly, "that's okay. He does that about every two days."

Since then, though, things have gotten a bit more relaxed, and the primeval screams have subsided. There isn't as much overtime, because there are more employees to share the tasks and the size of the workshop has grown.

If there were one word to describe how ILM performs its tricks, the word would be "miniaturization." Small airplanes, bikes, houses, trees, mine cars, cliffs, and on and on. By filming things on a small scale, Indiana Jones can seem to ride a mine car past molten lava and then be chased by a wall of water; E.T. and Elliot can fly on a bike past the moon; Luke and Leia can chase stormtroopers through a redwood forest on a speeder bike going 100 miles per hour; and a family haunted by poltergeists will see their tract house implode into a black hole. Sometimes, there are other alternatives to special effects, but there are substantial cost savings with special effects miniatures. In *Starman*, there were several shots of a railroad train shot at ILM. An entire freight train, with the surrounding desert terrain, was built by the ILM model shop. This was one of those times where a special effects technique was used because it would have been more expensive to shoot a real train. Though this seems strange, it turns out to be very difficult to coordinate real trains with a camera crew. The ILM models provided a less expensive—and more manageable—alternative. As special effect shots they are absolutely undetectable even to experts. And in all cases, these models *must* look real, and must have character.

Left, above: A miniature set-up of the two-legged (chicken) walker about to have its head crushed by two logs.

Left, middle: The moment of impact as two logs crush the head of the chicken walker.

Left, below: The chicken walker falls to the ground and explodes in the miniature forest set.

Above: Dennis Muren (behind camera) lines up the shot. The netting will provide a dappled light effect.

Middle: Chris Evans paints the backdrop for the miniature forest set for *Return of the Jedi.*

Below: Modelmaker/painter Paul Huston paints a miniature backdrop.

Above, left: Modelmaker Ease Owyeung and technician Mike MacKenzie work on the wiring for the *Millennium Falcon.*

Above, right: Modelmaker Paul Huston sets up the miniature city set for *Explorers.*

Opposite page: Cityscape model for *Explorers.*

With *Star Wars*, for the first time space hardware was given character. The ships looked space-worn, with holes and dents like the scars on the face of a Western gunman. This is not accidental: the designers and modelmakers were creating models with character, much like an actor might devise a subscript scenario to build on a character in a film or play, thinking about skirmishes that are never shown on film. The models are like icebergs, with only a small part showing but giving the impression that there is a lot of history there that we cannot see in the short period of the film.

The funky *Millennium Falcon* is not just a piece of space hardware, it is the cosmic version of a hot rod. The Imperial TIE fighters are more than enemy spacecraft, they *look* nasty. One is reminded of the attack of vicious bumblebees when a swarm of TIEs swoops down on our heroes. There is not the slightest regret when we see one of these black interceptors take a laser hit and explode. The giant Death Star, under construction in *Return of the*

Jedi, is ominous and represents the kind of large architectural structure where huge industrial conglomerates or heartless governmental bureaucracies reside.

A lot of artwork and many of the sets that are used in special effects do not look as good on close inspection as they do in the films. This is not true with models. The models built at ILM are amazing in their detail. On very close inspection one tends to see more than is ever apparent on the screen; each is an important character in the film.

ENGINEERING OF A MODEL

A MODEL made for an ILM film has to be more than just a good-looking piece of work. First, there are the practical considerations: on a big film an important model will be used every day for months, subjected to hot lights, sometimes rough handling, and occasionally collisions with computer-controlled cameras. For these reasons, the models cannot be too delicate or they will never survive the daily stress and will become a constant source of trouble during shooting. They are, therefore, much more durably constructed than mod-

Above: A group of people review the models, from right to left: model shop supervisor Lorne Peterson, archivist Debbie Fine, George Lucas, producer Howard Kazanjian, modelmaker Charlie Bailey, and ILM general manager Tom Smith (author).

Right: A tiny *Millennium Falcon*, not much larger than a quarter.

Below: A tiny Y-wing model.

els made for museums or crafted by the typical amateur hobbyist. The strength begins inside: the interior is fortified with a metal frame that is engineered to maintain the integrity of the model's shape and provide support when attached to the mounting pylons. Exterior articulation for the outer skin of the model cannot be so delicate that it requires constant maintenance. Often the exterior begins as a collage of hundreds of small plastic fragments, which then serves as a master from which a mold is made; this is the basis for vacu-form rugged panels that are applied to the exterior of the final model.

During filming, a model must be supported on a specially built pylon. When shooting from the front, the support pylon is mounted on the rear; when we look at the model from the rear, the pylon is mounted on the front. When seen from above or below, the pylon is attached to the non-camera side of the model and held solidly during the filming. These multiple support locations require engineering considerations that the home hobbyist does not have to deal with. Panels on the

exterior skin of the spaceships snap off to reveal each mounting point, and there may be as many as four mounting spots on one model. The pylon upon which the model is mounted is also quite complex: the more sophisticated versions have special blue lighting that surrounds them so that they will blend with the blue screen that serves as a background and therefore become invisible after being optically composited into a final shot. The pylon also contains precision motors that interface with the camera's computer, allowing the spaceship to move on several preplanned axes while being photographed. Apparent model moves are accomplished by moving the camera back and forth on its long track. With the combined capability of the camera and the pylon movements, the operator

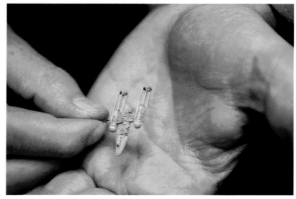

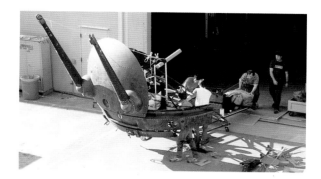

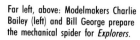

Far left, above: Modelmakers Charlie Bailey (left) and Bill George prepare the mechanical spider for *Explorers*.

Far left, middle: The model of the spider, used on *Explorers*, as it arrives for filming at the ILM stage.

Left: Cameraman Patrick Sweeney takes a meter reading for an *Explorers* miniature set.

Below: A composite shot showing the "clean-up" spider from *Explorers* as seen in the film.

is able to put the spaceship through an almost unlimited number of maneuvers.

Most models are filled with electronics. There are the lights in the engine pods on spaceships, lights that shine from the "windows" of the craft, and the concealed miniature motors that control wing flaps, puppet pilot head turns, and any other mechanical action that might be required of a model. The modelmakers at ILM have

had to be very innovative in the way lights are installed in these spaceships because there is very limited space in the average model to accommodate normal lighting. Though miniature incandescent bulbs are sometimes used, bundles of glass fiber optics (like a braid of hair) were used on the X-wing fighters, Y-wing fighters, and the TIE fighters. They were also used for the Star Destroyer, and Vader's Destroyer in *Star Wars* and *The Empire Strikes Back* because of the ship's limited space and the need for thousands of tiny window lights. Light emanates from one source at one end of the large bundle, and at the other

Right, above: Modelmaker Charlie Bailey and effects supervisor Dennis Muren examine the sophisticated engineering required in construction of the model *E.T.* spaceship.

Right below and far right, above: Detail of the *E.T.* ship's interior lighting, using quartz halogen sources.

Far right, middle: Visual effects supervisor Dennis Muren and technician Marty Brenneis, with the inner skeleton of the *E.T.* ship.

Far right, below: *E.T.* ship with engineers Marty Brenneis in the foreground and Gary Leo on the right.

Opposite page: The final composite shot showing the *E.T.* spaceship hovering above the town.

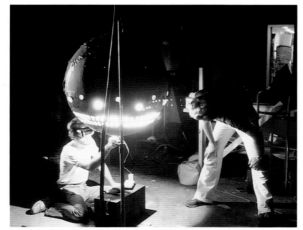

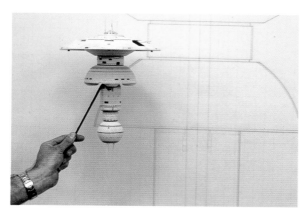

end each small strand is then brightly illuminated. The bundle was taken apart with the small hairlike fibers distributed to the interior of the small portholes of the ship, so when the fibers were illuminated, thousands of small lights shone like the lights of Manhattan on a clear night. Their great number and small size helped to communicate the idea of a large ship.

With all this mechanical and lighting gear crammed into these models, they have another unexpected need: air condi-

Far left, above: Blueprint and small prototype for the space station used in *Star Trek II: The Wrath of Khan.*

Far left, below: The aluminum outer skin of the *E.T.* ship.

Above: Ralph McQuarrie's design for the *E.T.* ship.

Middle: Modelmaker Charlie Bailey examines a small prototype of the *E.T.* ship.

Below: Steven Spielberg examines a model of the *E.T.* ship. Warren Franklin is on the left.

Gatefold: The *Millennium Falcon* races through a tunnel in the new Death Star in *Return of the Jedi.*

Above: The "esophagus" crew. Engineers, modelbuilders and stagehands were needed to operate the esophagus in *Poltergeist*.

Right: Interior of a model from *Star Trek III: The Search for Spock*, illuminated by neon lighting.

Above right: Modelmaker Barbara Gallucci and stage technician Ed Hirsh work on the esophagus for *Poltergeist*.

Below right: Head Stage technician Ed Hirsh inspects the esophagus for *Poltergeist*.

tioning! Almost every model is cooled with a compressed air heat-extraction system. Without this system, most models would melt from the internal heat of the electronic gear combined with the heat from the intense stage lighting that is focused on the model during photography.

When the Death Star was built for *Return of the Jedi,* large illuminated areas were made of brass plates that were etched to create holes where windows were to appear, and then backed with neon light tubes. This system was also used on many of the variety of spaceships created for the ILM *Star Trek* projects. Again this technique created the appearance of many light sources, but it also turned out to be less time-consuming than the fiber optical system, since there were no small fibers to be connected to the portholes.

Though some models weigh only a few

ounces and have no lights or mechanical parts, many models are complicated devices weighing hundreds of pounds and requiring a crew of stagehands to move them from place to place. When a model is delivered for shooting on the stage, it also comes with a substantial package of electronics to control the internal functions. These controls allow the model's miniature motors to interface with the computer that runs the camera. In addition, a power supply for the model's lighting is associated with each model.

Each model is a marvel of engineering and artistry. It is hoped by *Star Wars* fans the world over that someday these unique objects will be displayed in a museum for close inspection. When that day comes, viewers will be astounded that these models look even better in real life than they do on film.

The little boy in the *Poltergeist* bedroom about to be sucked into the esophagus.

Model of the space station used in *Star Trek II*.

Inset: The ILM crew works on the lighting for the space station used in *Star Trek II*.

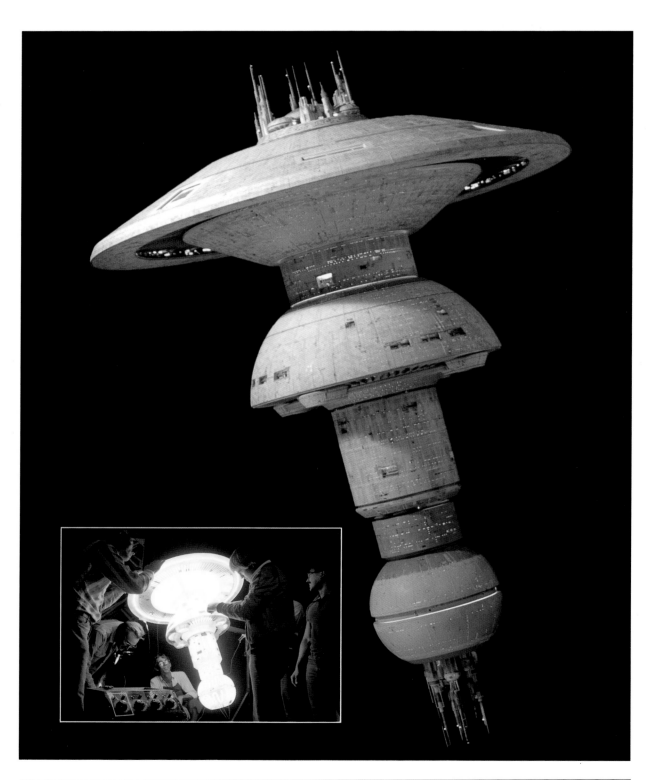

LORNE PETERSON

Ten years after ILM was established in Van Nuys, California, there were only seven of the original crew of seventy still working as ILMers. Model Shop Supervisor Lorne Peterson is one of the "magnificent seven." Lorne has seen a lot in his time at ILM, and almost as much before.

As a boy, Lorne was possessed by what he calls the "Old Michaelangelo Syndrome." He wanted to be an artist, and artists, he thought, should be able to do everything. The enterprising boy plunged enthusiastically into projects ranging from building his own bedroom furniture to entering local art contests and organizing backyard carnivals.

After high school, he attended Long Beach State. His college career lasted some five and a half years, including one semester of graduate work. First he thought he might go into architecture, then into teaching. Upon graduating, however, he found himself working in industrial design, building model prototypes.

A number of his classmates, like John Dykstra, found work with Douglas Trumbull on films such as *Silent Running*. Lorne and classmate Jon Erland had joined an industrial design company near Los Angeles. Because of the recession in the early 70s, business grew steadily worse and the two young men decided they might do better on their own. They formed a little company and were successful in a modest way, getting contracts to design sound speakers and furniture, trashcans, drinking fountains, and planters for shopping malls.

In the summer of 1975, Peterson and Erland decided to take a break from the hard work of running their firm. They went on vacation and hired someone to answer the phone while they were away.

Upon returning, they found they'd received a call from another Long Beach State grad, Bob Shepherd. The return phone number was wrong, and Lorne had to do a considerable amount of hunting around to locate Shepherd, but it proved to be worth it. Shepherd wanted to know if they'd be interested in working on a film project directed by the guy who did *American Graffiti*.

Lorne and Jon were hired specifically to build surface panels for the Death Star trench that Luke Skywalker would race past at the climax of the film. During their first few days at the new Industrial Light and Magic facility in Van Nuys, Lorne and Jon couldn't stop marveling at the amount of equipment and the number of artists that were assembled. There was energetic activity everywhere, and the two new recruits quickly plunged right in.

Soon after Lorne was hired to build models, he remembers seeing a slight, quiet, bearded man wandering through the model shop. Sometimes, this man would stop to see what Lorne was doing. Lorne would strike up a conversation with him and explain what he was up to. He knew some of the plot details of the science fiction film they were working on and so he told them to the bespectacled fellow. Lorne didn't know until later that he was speaking to George Lucas.

Because of his experience, Lorne found himself often called upon to give advice on which building materials to use and what procedures to follow, which led to additional duties as an administrator. He still, however, kept building models; he and Jon Erland concentrated on the Death Star trench, but also worked on the Tatooine Sandcrawler, the X-wing, and the

Imperial TIE fighters as well.

Once *Star Wars* was completed, Lorne remembers that there was a feeling among those who had worked for ILM that, since all that equipment and talent had already been put together, someday they might work again at the Van Nuys facility. Perhaps on another film like *Star Wars*.

Lorne was a bit disappointed when he was asked by Visual Effects Supervisor Richard Edlund to move to Northern California and start up a model shop for a new ILM; he thought it meant the familiar team from *Star Wars* would not be getting together again. But he decided to take the job anyway and, after finishing up his work on the television series *Battlestar Galactica*, he headed north.

In San Rafael, he found ILM reborn, with many familiar faces from Southern California all hard at work on the *Star Wars* sequel, *The Empire Strikes Back*. Lorne

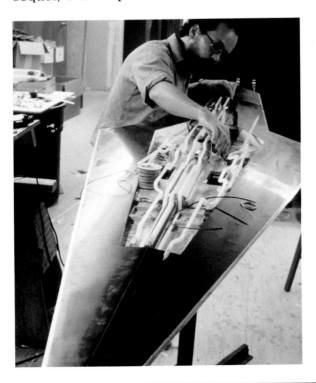

Modelmaker Charlie Bailey works on the interior neon lighting for Darth Vader's Star Destroyer.

now feels that this film was the most difficult project the ILM modelmakers have ever undertaken, because of the enormous volume of work they were given and the limited amount of time in which they had to accomplish it. Of all the models done for this movie, the construction of Darth Vader's Star Destroyer was the most grueling assignment. The ship, lit from within by neon lights shining outward through over 250,000 ports, had to be completed in only seven weeks. The resulting overtime costs put the final price tag of the vessel at over $100,000, making it the most expensive single model ILM has ever made. Lorne feels that the only project to compare with this was the ship for *E.T.: The Extra-Terrestrial*, which was far more complex, although cheaper to make because they had more time to do it.

Lorne describes George Lucas's reticent style of direction by saying, "It was never as if he walked in and lectured in the model shop. It was almost as if his direction glowed out of him—without his ever having to say more than one sentence here and two sentences there." He tells of saving up a series of questions to ask George about the progress of the model work. One evening he caught the boss wandering through the area, so he called him over and rattled off his list. George listened, paused, and then said slowly, "Well, I don't know, Lorne, do whatever you want to do. Building models is *your* job." Reflecting upon this, Lorne admits this was probably the right thing to say. It showed that George did not need to satisfy his ego by pontificating on every little matter and it also allowed those working for him room for creative decision making.

Lorne himself now has duties that are mostly administrative in nature. He realized, he says, that his model making was interfering with his management of the shop and that others were suffering for it, and so, reluctantly, he put aside many of his more enjoyable tasks. But he still can't resist getting at least one model in per movie. This was the reason, he says, he built the Boba Fett ship designed by Nilo Rodis-Jamero for *The Empire Strikes Back*.

The adventures of the old ILM and the endless weeks of *The Empire Strikes Back* are now behind him, yet he looks ahead to new challenges for those who have become the most renowned toy makers in the world.

STEVE GAWLEY

Steve Gawley had always enjoyed building models, and he was a good draughtsman. It wasn't surprising, therefore, when Joe Johnston, his friend and former classmate from Cal State–Long Beach, recommended him for a job as modelmaker on a project Joe had just started work on.

It was 1975 and the two buddies would drive together in Steve's new pickup truck to their place of employment, the ILM facility in Van Nuys. There, Joe designed models and Steve and the rest of the Model Shop built and painted them.

Steve remembers those times as the simple, good old days. "We bought parts for models at the surplus stores. You could go over and scavenge through old stuff . . . fans to cool the lights for the Rebel blockade runner," for instance. "The screening room," he says, "was furnished in early 'Goodwill' sofas—springs exposed—and your clothes would get caught. You'd get up and rip the seat out of your trousers. It was just a whole different thing. All the money was put into the show—not furniture."

His new pickup became the "ILM pickup." In the now famous Death Star trench run at the end of *Star Wars,* they had to get a high-speed shot of explosions going off in the truck as the camera simulated Luke's point of view. Richard Edlund mounted a VistaVision camera on the back of Steve's truck and had him drive through

the parking lot at thirty miles per hour only six inches away from the model trench, while explosions were set off and Edlund filmed the action. Steve was glad when they got a good take on that shot.

After *Star Wars,* Steve went on to become the Model Shop foreman and worked on *The Empire Strikes Back, Poltergeist, Star Trek II, Star Trek III, Return of the Jedi,* and *Raiders of the Lost Ark,* and *Back to the Future,* among others.

As Model Shop foreman, Steve primarily supervises special model building projects. He was in charge of the construction of the Death Star set for *Return of the Jedi* and responsible for all of the models used in *Star Trek II: The Wrath of Khan* and *Star Trek III: The Search for Spock.* He still, however, loves to dig in and become per-

Modelmaker Steve Gawley works on the detail underneath a small Star Destroyer.

sonally involved in model construction. He built a number of the models for *Raiders of the Lost Ark*; one of the more memorable ones was the miniature set for the climactic scene where the Nazis took the Ark to be opened in a remote canyon. As the wrath of God begins sweeping the evil soldiers skyward, a powerful fire storm sucks them upward. Steve built the small set upside down so that by reversing the shot, the flames would appear more natural.

One of his most interesting projects was the creation of the ghosts that also

Right: Modelmaker Steve Gawley and electronic technician Mike MacKenzie inspect the frame for the model car built by ILM for use on *Back to the Future*.

Below: Modelmaker Steve Gawley displays the *Back to the Future* DeLorean car.

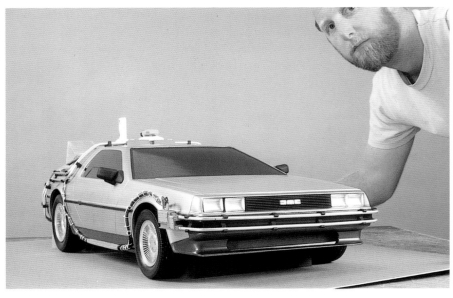

appear in the climax of *Raiders*. A number of complex ideas had been tried and had failed, then Steve thought of making a "ghost" of silk and swishing it through water. The silk was attached to the end of a wooden stick and looked like a mop. When it was swished through a large water tank with glass sides, the underwater effect looked quite spooky; it was filmed and then inserted optically into the live-action scene for the climax of *Raiders of the Lost Ark*. The overall effect was remarkable. In retrospect, he's not sure this was such a wonderful idea. He says, "I got stuck on top of this water tank for three weeks, moving the ghost back and forth!"

In *Back to the Future*, Steve Gawley led a team that built a model of the professor's DeLorean car. The model was then shot with the motion control camera just as a spaceship might be shot for *Star Wars*. Though it was only used for one shot at the end of the film, it was extremely important and effective.

At ILM, Steve's ability to inspire others and keep up morale even during the toughest assignment is universally recognized. On *Star Trek II*, with a sixty-hour, six-day-a-week schedule, he came up with an idea to cheer his beleaguered co-workers: "I used to make everybody come to work Monday morning with a joke. It started out as a diversion and then it started to become regular, and I guess for a few guys it became embarrassing. 'Hey, man, I need a joke for my boss on Monday. Weird guy, wants me to tell a joke.' But it was a good way to start the week. There's a lot to be said for humor," he adds, "and occasional breaks don't hurt either.

"There's a certain amount of craziness that has to be present in what we do," he says, "because it's really a taxing job. You have to go out and do some crazy things.

We used to launch rockets out in the ILM parking lot. We'd build these model kits— B-29 bombers—and shove skyrockets in them and launch them. They'd go up a couple of hundred feet and over about a block. Depending on where they landed, we would keep running; if they landed in the wrong spot, we would leave."

As fond as his co-workers are of him, Steve is equally fond of them. When asked how he feels about his time at ILM and the people he's worked with there, Steve says, "I'm really lucky. I'm proud to have worked with a bunch of guys that have done all of this. I know it sounds corny," he admits, "but I feel that way."

CHAPTER 4

CREATURES AT ILM

Lucasfilm has been in the creature business since George Lucas commissioned Ralph McQuarrie to sketch ideas for R2-D2, and a creature assignment brought Phil Tippett and Jon Berg to ILM. Since then, there have been creatures for every film in the Star Wars series and puppet stand-ins for real actors in each ILM film project. Some of the daring and spectacular stunts done in films are in fact performed by puppets that are either animated in stop-motion or manipulated by radio-controlled devices.

Dragonslayer had a creature as its star. The dragon had such a big part in the film that a special machine, the Go-Motion device, was built just to make its moves look more realistic. In *Raiders of the Lost Ark*, ILM puppets were used when the Nazi staff car drove off the cliff. The Nazis swept upward by God's wrath at the film's end were soldiers only seven inches tall. The shrinking, melting, and exploding

heads of our villains were also the product of creature builders at ILM.

No film has ever demanded the kind of mass production creature operation that *Return of the Jedi* did. More than a year

Above: Detail of cantina creatures from *Star Wars*.

Below: The ILM creature crew poses with cantina creatures from *Star Wars* (1977).

before the filming, George was proposing ideas for designers to work on. On one occasion, he sent over a print of a 16mm film showing a queen termite in her nest, tended by scores of smaller workers—she was a yellow quivering sack of slime. "This," George said, "is what Jabba the Hutt should look like in *Jedi*." With this for inspiration, several designers took a crack at what George was looking for, and small prototypes were sculpted and presented to George. The final result was a blend of ideas. When the final concept was chosen, it was kept top secret. No one outside of the small design group or those that had a "need to know" were permitted so much as a peek.

How do they make a stop-motion puppet like the tauntaun for *The Empire Strikes Back* or a creature like the full-sized Admiral Ackbar from *Return of the Jedi*? Though the specifics change from film to film, there is a general sequence of events.

Perhaps even before the final draft of the script is written, George will know that he wants a certain kind of character. The idea is then given to someone like Phil

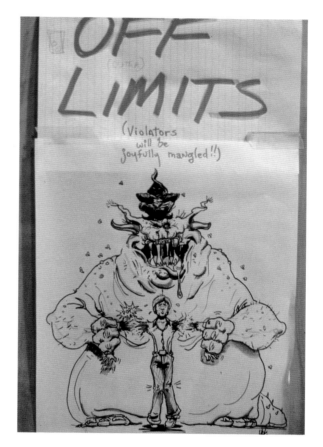

Far left: A bulletin board showing progress charts for the creatures in the *Return of the Jedi* creature shop at ILM.

Left: "Off Limits" sign from the creature shop at ILM in 1983.

Below: Salacious Crumb from *Return of the Jedi*.

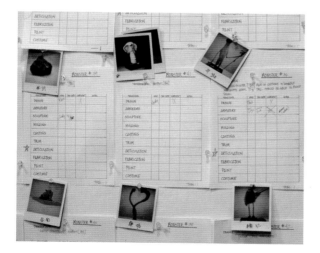

Tippett, who begins with some rough drawings or perhaps noting ideas as they occur to him. When he feels he has a design that shows some promise, Phil will sculpt a small prototype out of fast-drying clay; it may be given a coat of paint and some clothes. Then it is presented to George. After the miniature prototype is approved (usually with a few changes from George), a full-scale version is sculpted around a wire support. If a creature is to play in scenes with actors, its size must be of the correct proportions. Perhaps a human being can fit inside the creature to manipulate the body parts—the more human its shape, the more likely it will fit around a person.

Above: A background creature from *Return of the Jedi* made in the creature shop at ILM.

Right: The staff of the ILM creature shop poses with some of their creations for *Return of the Jedi*.

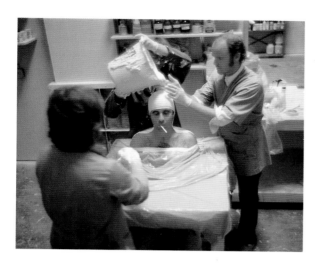

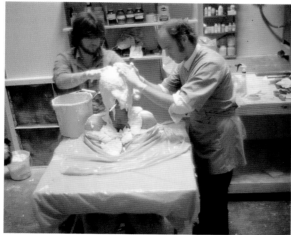

On the other hand, if it is a creature many times larger than a human being, it most likely will become a STOP-MOTION PUPPET. It will then be filmed as a miniature in a miniature setting and when humans must interact with it directly, optical trickery such as the traveling matte or rear screen projection processes will be used to make it appear as if both human and creature are in the same setting at the same time.

If it is to be a stop-motion puppet, a machinist such as ILM's Tom St. Amand is put to work on a steel armature that will ultimately become the skeleton for the creature. If it is a mask that must fit tightly over an actor's face, a cast is taken of the person's face and the sculpted piece is built right on top of that plaster visage.

Far left, top to bottom: An example of how a death mask was made for a creature in *Return of the Jedi*. With Phil Tippett directing, Stuart Ziff has clay poured on his head. The clay is molded around Ziff's head. Close-up of Stuart Ziff's head completely covered. This is a dangerous process and should not be tried by amateurs without expert guidance.

Left: A pig guard from *Return of the Jedi* showing the interior padding.

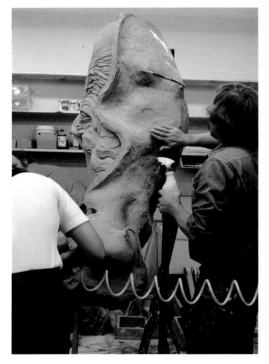

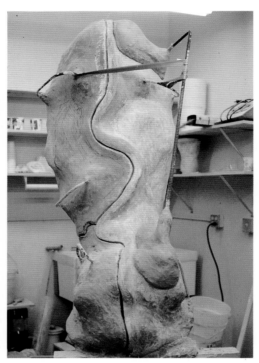

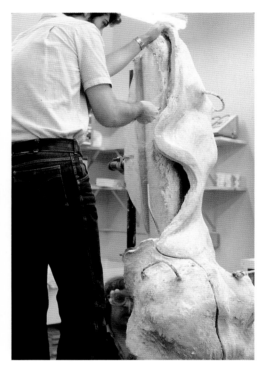

Making a mold of the giant head for the Ephant Mon creature in *Return of the Jedi.*

Far right: Tim Rose with completed Ephant Mon. Salacious Crumb is sitting on his head.

Opposite page: Ephant Mon and friend, Salacious Crumb, from *Return of the Jedi.*

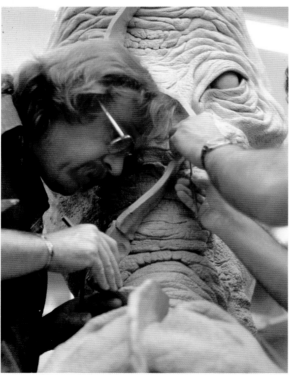

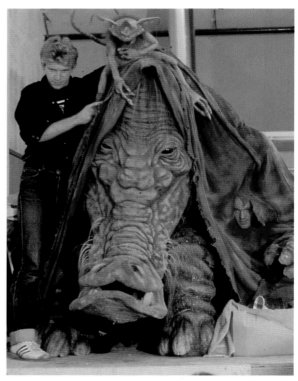

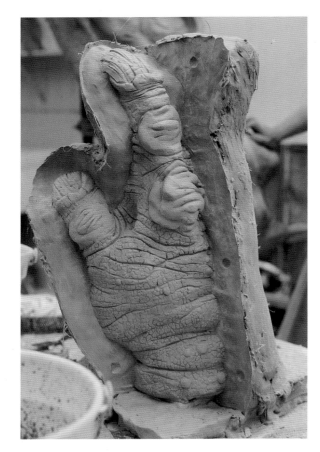

Right: Casting the Ephant Mon hand.

Below: Completed Elom head (left) and unpainted Tooth Face head (right).

Far right: Ken Ralston painting a dragonet (baby dragon) for *Dragonslayer* (1980).

The full-sized clay version is now surrounded by casting material and set to dry. When the cast is hardened, it is split open and the clay interior is removed, leaving a negative cast of the creature. With a stop-motion puppet such as the tauntaun, the armature is now fitted into the empty mold, and rubber is poured around it. After the rubber has cured, the cast is opened, and the beginnings of a stop-motion creature emerge. After it is painted and dressed with fur or other exterior skins, it is now ready to be filmed.

In a film like *Dragonslayer*, there were many puppets built in many scales. If a close-up of the dragon's head was called for, a Muppet-like version of the dragon was used, with an operator's arm and hand working the beast's head. In long shots, smaller versions were used; one was built for walking while another model was used only for flying. A dragon head, claw, and tail were made full-sized for use of the set in England, where the rest of the filming was done by the principal photography crew under the direction of Matthew Robbins. It was the mix of these assorted sizes that made the creature work properly.

Full-sized models are unwieldy, and often produce disappointing results. For *The Empire Strikes Back*, a full-sized taun-

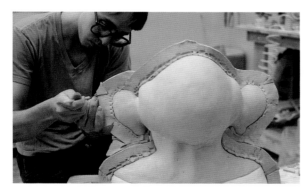

Far left, above: A mold of Nien Nunb, Han Solo's copilot in *Return of the Jedi*.

Middle: Kirk Thatcher and Wesley Seeds working on the mold of Nien Nunb.

Below: The finished version of Nien Nunb, painted and with his eyes in place.

Left: A loving hug from Dave Carson for Nien Nunb.

taun was built and shipped to Norway for use in the snow. Luke Skywalker was put on it and a futile attempt was made to make it look like he was riding a real beast. Not only did it look fake, on several occasions it simply fell over in the snow! The shots were never used in the final film. The same sort of disappointment occurred on *Dragonslayer* when a full-sized dragon was wheeled onto the set. Most of these shots also were canceled on the set or ended up on the cutting room floor. The history of film creatures is filled with attempts at full-scale versions and disappointing failures, yet film directors and producers seem to keep trying to make them work, for it is always more comforting to have the creature on the set with the actors, knowing when you have a good performance, rather than putting your faith in what the special effects crew might do with your scene later.

In one Hollywood film the central figure was a large apelike monster. Construction on the full-sized beast was slower than expected, and as the first day of filming drew near, it was clear that it would not be completed in time. The nervous producer tried to mobilize more craftsmen to speed up the work, but no more were available, so he located an Italian crew ready to take on a part of the work. Blueprints were

Far right: The *Poltergeist* creature which was originally modelled in clay.

Right: The molded rubber ghost from *Poltergeist,* shot in a tank of water to make its hair float.

Below: The final shot in the film—the *Poltergeist* ghost attacks the woman of the house.

quickly flown to Italy with instructions to build one of the monster's large hands. Now, with both crews working, they hoped to be ready on time. A few days before cameras were to roll, the Hollywood part of the beast was completed minus a right

hand, with the missing appendage on its way from Europe by air. It arrived and was hurriedly uncrated. Inside the box was a masterpiece of Italian craftsmanship, perfectly conforming to the blueprints they had been given. The problem was, it was the wrong hand. There were now two right hands and no left. When they recovered from the shock, one old-time stagehand remarked as he repacked the box, "Well, that's the trouble with these big Hollywood movies: the right hand never knows what the left is doing!"

However, there *are* many successful full-scale creatures in films. In *Return of the Jedi*, Jabba's palace was filled with vile creatures, most of whom were designed at ILM and many built in Northern California. They were large fellows and not easy to operate. Cables resembling bicycle hand brakes are attached to a movable body part and then threaded through the beast and out the back or down below and out of camera sight. A hand grip is then attached to the cable so that, with a simple squeeze of the operator's hand, the creature will wink an eye, wiggle an ear, or sneer. Large body parts, such as arms or a big jaw, are commonly operated with direct hand grips or guided by rods. For *Return of the Jedi*, sometimes there were as many as ten operators working Jabba the Hutt, with each person responsible for some articulated function. In *Star Trek III: The Search for Spock*, ILM's Ken Ralston (cameraman, sculptor, sketch artist, and visual effects supervisor) built and operated a villainous doglike pet. The beast was operated from below in a small space under the raised floor of the spaceship. These uncomfortable circumstances are not unusual for puppeteers in films.

The Muppet movies rely on hidden operators for nearly every scene. Lanky

From top to bottom: Creature technician Randy Dutra with the clay version of the Rancor Pit monster built for *Return of the Jedi*. Unpainted Rancor on the right with the Rancor prototype on the left. Phil Tippett spray-painting the Rancor Pit monster. Phil Tippett puts the finishing touches on the Rancor Pit monster.

Jim Henson, one of the Muppet creators, spent an entire day hidden in a fifty-gallon steel barrel submerged under water in order to operate Kermit the Frog sitting on a log in a pond. When they aren't hidden under or behind the set, film puppeteers are swallowed up inside the creature itself. While the filming takes place, the creatures require constant attention between takes to repair inevitable tears in the fragile rubber, which is chosen for how it looks rather than how it wears. Mechanical parts often require maintenance to function as they should. The operators inside are provided with water and cooled by portable fans—which, because of the noise they make, cannot be run during filming.

It would be wonderful if all creatures could have motors inside them that make them do exactly what is called for by the director. A sort of *Westworld* robot concept would be nice, but unfortunately, this rarely works; the motors are too large and the number of them to operate the scores of parts is too great. Sometimes, however, a

Below: Camera operator Kim Marks in the foreground and effects supervisor Dennis Muren on the right shoot the Rancor Pit monster. The piece of glass in front of the camera lens is used to soften the image.

Right: The completed Rancor Pit monster as seen by the camera.

Below, right: The entire Rancor Pit crew, counterclockwise from left: cameraman Dennis Muren, camera assistant Kim Marks, puppeteers Dave Sosalla in the dark distance, Phil Tippett and above him Tom St. Amand.

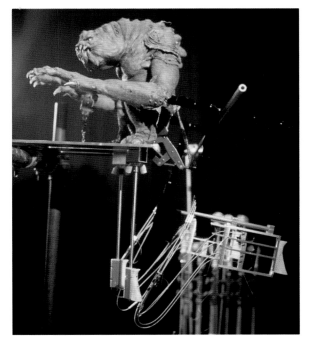

motor is hidden inside a puppet when its movements are simple. In *Indiana Jones and the Temple of Doom* a small remote-controlled and motorized puppet was used inside one of the victims to be lowered into the hotlava, and full-scale human dummies were powered by compressed air—driven motors and thrown off the suspension bridge during the climax of the film. Their lifelike movements were quite convincing.

The future of puppet control seems to lie somewhere in the computer technology and the miniaturization of motors that will become available in the next few years. The question is, will the computer make a puppet run in front of the camera, or will the computer eliminate the camera altogether and create the whole scene on a piece of film scanned by a laser?

I would like to think that people will still be able to use puppets and masks as they have for centuries, to enterain each other.

Far left, above: The Rancor Pit monster complete with cabling ready to be used on the set.

Middle and below: Puppeteers operate the Rancor Pit monster.

Above: The Rancor Pit monster as seen by the camera

Left: A Nazi officer in *Raiders of the Lost Ark* as his face shrinks.

Right: The wax version of Toht, the Nazi villain in *Raiders of the Lost Ark*, as his head melts.

Left: Teek from *Ewoks: The Battle for Endor*. Articulation of the face is accomplished by this behind-the-scenes crew of puppeteers.

Right: Teek, from *Ewoks: The Battle for Endor*.

JON BERG

Jon Berg's parents must have been perplexed by their son. His teachers told them that he wasn't performing to capacity at school; he seemed to spend all his time and energy tinkering in the garage. This in itself wasn't so unusual for a teenage boy—after all, Jon's brother loved to work on cars—but Jon was out there building a rubber monkey. A rubber monkey? *Why?*

It started in his early childhood. When Jon was only three or four years old, his big sister took him to see a movie called *Mighty Joe Young*, which featured a formidable gorilla created through special effects. It was so frightening to the little boy that he spent most of his time with his

hands over his eyes, and later on, he could recall only the film's title and a few dreamlike images. In fact, as he grew older, Jon couldn't decide if what he remembered *was* a dream or if there had actually been a movie that he once had seen. Meanwhile, his family had taken him to see many other movies, particularly Walt Disney cartoon features, and Jon had become very interested in animation. He started to make flip books, with drawings that changed slightly on successive pages. When the pages were rifled quickly, the fleeting image seemed to move. Jon made a nice little profit selling these creations to classmates.

Then, Jon found out that the *Mighty Joe Young* of his childhood was indeed a real movie. He was thrilled, and immediately wanted to know more about the special effects that had left such a strong impression on his young mind. He learned about stop-motion animation, and withdrew to the garage to build rubber puppets.

Jon did a stint at Santa Monica College, where he took courses in several fields, including photography and art. He was driving a cab in Beverly Hills when an acquaintance got him an interview with Cascade Studios, a company specializing in television commercial work. The company was doing a series of commercials on the Pillsbury Doughboy and Jon got involved in animating the chubby little character. At that point, he thought his position with the company would be temporary, but there was a lot of stop-motion work and Jon stayed on. The House of Chocolate Man, Kellogg's Little K Man, Speedy Alka-Seltzer, and scenes with dinosaurs were some of his

The Wampa snow creature from *The Empire Strikes Back*. Phil Tippett operates the Wampa.

assignments; he was also the hands and feet of the Jolly Green Giant for the vegetable commercials.

At Cascade, Jon became friends with Phil Tippett and Dennis Muren. In 1976, Dennis got involved in the special effects for *Star Wars*. When he learned that the film needed additional creatures for its alien cantina scene, and that the fellow who was supposed to be working on this was still tied up with another project, Dennis took some creature concepts Phil and Jon came up with to director George Lucas and producer Gary Kurtz. Phil and Jon were hired by the new ILM monster model shop.

After Jon and Phil designed monsters for the now famous cantina, George Lucas had another problem for them to solve: he had planned to have a chess game in *Star Wars* using miniature people as pieces, but a film had just been released with a similar idea in it and George had to rethink his plans. He decided to use miniature creatures instead, and called upon Jon and Phil to figure out how to do it. They came up with the kooky chessboard creatures used in the game between the Wookiee Chewbacca, and the 'droid R2-D2. After designing the figures, they got involved in the stop-motion animation of them as well—they were becoming utility scene-savers and never knew when they would be called upon next. One day, Jon received a call from the set saying they needed a monster for the trashmasher scene. Jon and Phil stuck an eyeball on a stalk and, lo, another creature was born! (Jon would rather forget this one. He does not regard it as one of their best works.)

Jon left ILM after *Star Wars* was completed, but returned when work on *The Empire Strikes Back* began in 1978. On this film, he was primarily a stop-motion animator: beginning with Joe Johnston's designs, Jon built the menacing Imperial snow walkers that appear in the Hoth snow battles. His modifications made the miniature models workable for animation purposes.

Again working on short order, he and Phil Tippett also produced the Wampa snow creature for this movie. Jon calls it "another one of our knock-together things," and describes their method of collaboration. "He'd say, 'We've got this thing to do. I'll get a block of wood and some hinges from the carpentry department and you get a crowbar.' And then we'd discuss how far we'd want the jaw to open up and I'd knock together something that we'd use as a puppet and then he would go and do his beautiful build-up work with all of the stuff—wax and fur and everything."

The Wampa is something "we all kind of fiddled around with," Jon says. Nonetheless, the sight of that giant snow monster rising up to attack Luke Skywalker is a terror not soon forgotten.

Jon finally left ILM in 1980, but returns from time to time to tackle various assignments, not all of them creature creation or stop-motion work. In 1984, he broke into acting when he played the monstrous Gorax in the Lucasfilm-ABC television film, *The Ewok Adventure*. He designed the creature, built the suit, and played the part. His interpretation of the terrifying Gorax played to over fifty million viewers on ABC one Sunday night in 1984; it also ran in theaters overseas. There have probably been millions of kids hiding their eyes, just as he did when his sister took him to see *Mighty Joe Young*.

CHAPTER 5

STOP AND GO MOTION

The Rebel Alliance is hiding out on a snow-covered planet in the Hoth System. Darth Vader, having discovered their headquarters, is landing his forces to destroy them and capture Luke Skywalker. Giant Imperial snow walkers spearhead the Dark Lord's attack. The Rebel troops wait anxiously as the fearsome, four-legged machines stalk closer.

This scene from *The Empire Strikes Back* contains some of the most imaginative uses of special effects in the *Star Wars* saga. The Rebel troops were added optically; the walkers were miniatures brought to life by a technique called stop-motion photography.

STOP-MOTION PHOTOGRAPHY takes advantage of the fact that movies are actually a succession of still images that, when projected quickly enough, allow us to perceive the images as one continuous motion. In stop motion, objects, usually miniatures or puppets, are photographed one frame at a time. In between frames, the objects are manipulated through portions of a movement such as walking, running, or flying. It is a painstaking, time-consuming process, but the end result is the same as with regular cinematography: when projected, the sum of the changes in position between frames is seen as continuous movement of the objects.

Snow walkers attack the Rebel forces—a composite shot from *The Empire Strikes Back*.

Stop motion is a technique with a long history in movies. One of the great masters of this method is Ray Harryhausen, who created the giant ape in *Mighty Joe Young* (1949), the beast in *The Beast From 20,000 Fathoms* (1953), and the many imaginative creatures in *Jason and the Argonauts* (1963) (perhaps the most ambitious stop-motion work in any feature film). Jim Danforth's work in *When Dinosaurs Ruled the Earth* (1970) is another masterpiece of stop motion. ILM has used stop motion many times and from it has derived a related technique called "Go-Motion." But when *The Empire Strikes Back* was being filmed in 1978 to 1980, Go-Motion was still a thing of the future.

Above: Doug Beswick animates the snow walker. Stop motion animator Jon Berg is in the center and Phil Tippett on the right.

Below: Designer Joe Johnston paints the snow walker

Left: Modelmakers Nilo Rodis-Jamero and Bill Beck put baking soda "snow" in front of the painted background for the minature walker set.

The snow scenes in *Empire* are full of stop-motion uses that presented us with a number of problems. In the Hoth snow battle, for example, there was a large snow field surrounding the miniature walkers. This meant that the animators (the people who move the miniatures between frames) had to assume all sorts of awkward posi-

Following spread: A photo composite shot of the snow walkers in action.

tions to manipulate the mechanical monsters without disturbing the snow. Some animators worked on their stomachs, stretched over the miniature set on supports that resembled diving boards; others worked from below the set, popping up to do their animation through a snow-camouflaged trapdoor.

During many of the snow battle shots, the camera was moving. Because of this, a motion control system was used to advance the camera during the exposure of individual frames. In one shot, the camera repre-

sented Luke Skywalker's point of view as he flew around and under the legs of one walker. This had to be executed between animated movements of the walker—which meant that if all went well, one such shot might be completed in a day. Many

Right: Jon Berg animates snow walkers for *The Empire Strikes Back*.

Below: Animator Jon Berg lines up a shot of the snowfield while the Dykstraflex moves in slowly, a frame at a time.

Far right, above: Close up of a miniature snow walker.

Far right: The machined precision parts needed for the animated snow walker.

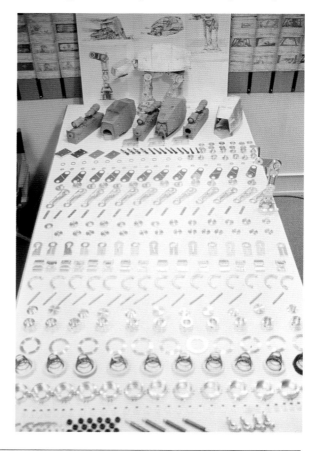

Phil Tippett animates the snow walkers for *The Empire Strikes Back*.

shots, however, required multiple takes.

One stop-motion shot from the Hoth scenes was remarkably well executed. When shooting in Norway with the actors, Mark Hamill (Luke) was supposed to ride a full-scale tauntaun. Rails were set up and mechanical devices arranged to simulate the movement of this strange beast. It turned out, however, that only the close-ups of Luke were usable because a full shot of the tauntaun did not work. Consequently, all the medium and long shots in this sequence had to be done with stop-motion animation. A puppet was made of the tauntaun, and one of Luke, dressed exactly as he was for the location shots. Phil Tippett animated the tauntaun.

A trapdoor would open from below the set, and Phil would surface with little steel pointers. The pointers would be placed around the tauntaun to indicate its starting position. Next he would manipulate the rubber creature with its rider, carefully moving the animated parts into a new position. After several minutes of adjustments, he would remove the pointers, smooth out any artificial snow that might have been disturbed, duck below the set, and close the trapdoor. An assistant near the camera would verify that the snow was not disturbed. One frame would be shot. The door would open, Phil would pop up with his pointers . . . And so forth. After twenty-four of these operations, *one second* of action would be on film.

And, of course, if a mistake were made, everything had to be started again from the beginning. A television camera with animation video recorder also monitored the process, so the small crew could occasion-

Above: A shot of the tauntaun on a snow bank from *The Empire Strikes Back*.

Inset: The steel ball and socket armature for the tauntaun puppet used in *The Empire Strikes Back*.

Right: Elephant used by the stop motion animators to study animal movements prior to *The Empire Strikes Back*.

ally play back the work as it progressed. Sometimes errors would be discovered on the spot and the crew could start again even before seeing the developed film.

In some shots, to add realism and introduce some naturalistic blurring to the movement, the tauntaun and the camera were moved with computer-controlled motors. But all changes in the physical movement of both the rider and the beast were done manually.

After all of this, the resulting shots were short, perhaps five to ten seconds in length. Of course, this whole process was the climax of months of preparation, which included the design and

building of the puppet and the machining of skeletal parts and exterior decorations, including the rider.

A stop-motion animator must be a special kind of artist. Along with the patience to sit for hours manipulating puppets, the animator must have an understanding and, indeed, an appreciation of animal movement. While preparing for the extensive stop motion in *The Empire Strikes Back*, Phil Tippett and Jon Berg studied the movement of an elephant. When birds in flight were to be emulated, they filmed and studied birds a frame at a time. It is perhaps no accident that many stop-motion animators are also good sculptors; a thorough knowledge of anatomy seems essential for success in this interesting field.

A DRAGON COMES TO ILM

When Industrial Light and Magic did *Dragonslayer*, new horizons opened in the field of stop-motion cinematography. The main focus of the *Dragonslayer* story was a giant dragon which terrified poor peasants, so the dragon *had* to look real. Matthew Robbins and Hal Barwood had written the story with the idea that the creative capacity of ILM's specialists could be used to do effects for historical events just as it had routinely done effects for the future. Drag-

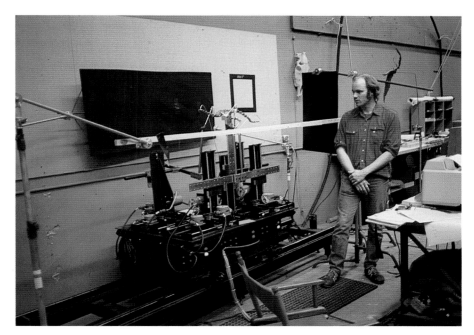

ons were not new to film, but the hope was that this dragon would look so real that the audience would forget the film cliché and respond with terror. This dragon, therefore, had to be better than anyone had ever seen before.

At first, Barwood and Robbins planned to use a full-scale dragon, to be built at Disney Studios. (The film was a Disney/Paramount co-production.) In fact, a dragon was built and sent from Southern California to Pinewood Studios in London, where the film was shot. It turned out, however, that the large mechanical creature built by the Disney staff couldn't act; it had about as much subtlety of character as a frontloading hydraulic-assisted tractor. This is not a criticism of Disney Studios; it is quite difficult, if not impossible, to build a large mechanical creature that will have the kind of articulation that is necessary. Real animals have a fluidity of motion that is not easily copied by even the most sophisticated machines. Even a fire-eating dragon has to show emotions, and this

Above: Phil Tippett ponders the armature of the dragon, which is connected to the Go-Motion device used in *Dragonslayer*.

Left: Ken Ralston animates the flying dragon in *Dragonslayer*.

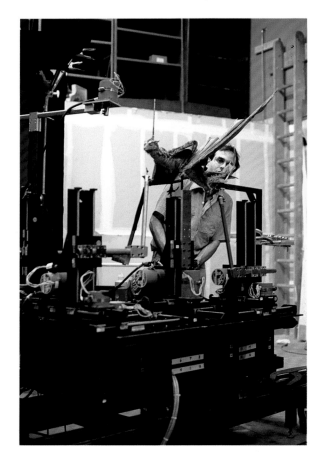

Right: Stuart Ziff works on the dragon mover.

Below: The dragon mover, also known as the "Go-Motion" device. Phil Tippett stands by as Stuart Ziff operates the device. The dragon is attached to rods you see on the left.

one for *Dragonslayer* flunked his screen test at Pinewood. There were a few scenes in the film where the big dragon was called upon to lower its head into the shot or reach in with a claw, but the role of the full-sized beast was seriously diminished. In the final cut of *Dragonslayer* there were only a dozen shots in which the whole mechanical monster was used. This left nearly a hundred shots where an understudy dragon (or parts thereof) was needed. As usual, the entire special effects project was storyboarded and laid out in comic-book form. The task looked immense: not only did the dragon have to look real, the show had to be done in record time. Dennis Muren was chosen to supervise the special effects and Phil Tippett was given the job of supervising the animation of the dragon. Ken Ralston would shoot and animate the flying dragon. The scenes where the giant mechanical dragon did not work were to be hand animated in stop motion.

In short, the challenge facing ILM was to do a major character for a film in stop motion and do it quickly. But there was a big problem. Stop motion has a major stylistic drawback, a generic flaw if you will: it does not look convincingly real. When done to perfection, the best that can be said about it is that it is good stop motion. It rarely looks real enough to fool a sophisticated audience into thinking that what they are seeing was actually filmed as it moved before the camera. The reason for this is simple: when you film a real animal in motion, each frame is exposed by the motion picture camera at a shutter speed of ¼₈th of a second, a rather slow speed for objects in motion, so there is blurring during the exposure of each frame. This blurring has the effect of smoothing out the movement. On the other hand, a stop

Phil Tippett works on the Go-Motion device used to animate the dragon for *Dragonslayer.*

motion frame is exposed while the puppet sits absolutely still. Thus, the image in each frame is very sharp and devoid of the blurring motion seen in live cinematography. As a result, this sharpness in stop-motion cinematography renders a somewhat stroboscopic, or jerky, image. When not directly comparing stop motion to live cinematography, one tends to overlook this peculiarity. However, when stop motion is intercut with real scenes, it does not look the same, no matter how well it is done. We wanted this dragon to look real, not just like good stop-motion work. There would be scenes in which the dragon would be composited into a shot done on location with real people, and the comparison might have presented huge problems for these shots in particular. The question was how to achieve a more realistic effect in stop-motion photography—or, how to get the "stop" out of stop motion.

GO-MOTION

We tried an experiment. Blue rods were attached to major body parts that would move when the dragon was in motion. (This part of the innovation was borrowed from Japanese rod puppetry.) These rods were then connected to "stepper" motors whose movement was controlled by a computer. As Phil Tippett animated the puppet, programmer Gary Leo at the computer recorded the exact position of the rods, creating "programmed" movements for the beast, based on the animator's design. The dragon's actions could then be replayed and filmed in a more traditional manner, only now the camera could expose the movement as it *occurred,* thereby filming the blur that had been missing in traditional stop-motion cinematography. A new name was chosen for the process: Go-Motion.

When I was called in to view the first test, even with the rods showing, I was astounded. The dragon did not look like the typical stop-motion puppet; its moves were completely smooth. It looked to me like someone had taken a lizard and attached it to a series of rods and filmed it as it walked.

We knew we had a good technique; the only question that remained was how to hide the rods. This problem was solved through rotoscope mattes created for each frame by the animation department, applied whenever the camera revealed the lower parts of the dragon. "Rotoscope matting" is an animation technique in which film is projected on the artist's easel. Each frame is then traced with great precision. Later this matte is used in the optical processes to eliminate unwanted areas of the original scene. In this case, the animated mattes were used to mask the rods when the Go-Motion dragon shots were optically composited into the shots with real people.

The Go-Motion system created a completely convincing dragon. When I'm asked which film I feel was our best effort at ILM, it is hard for me to select just one, but *Dragonslayer* ranks high on the list. Indeed, most special effects people hold this movie in high regard because of its use of the Go-Motion technique. However, in 1982, at the Academy Awards, *Dragonslayer* lost the award for Best Achievement in Visual Effects to another of my favorite ILM efforts, *Raiders of the Lost Ark*. Though Dennis Muren lost to *Raiders'* Richard Edlund that year, the *Dragonslayer* effects supervisor didn't let the loss keep him down. The following year,

Below: Steel armature used for the Rancor Pit monster in *Return of the Jedi*.

Right: Detail of the jaw armature for the Rancor Pit monster.

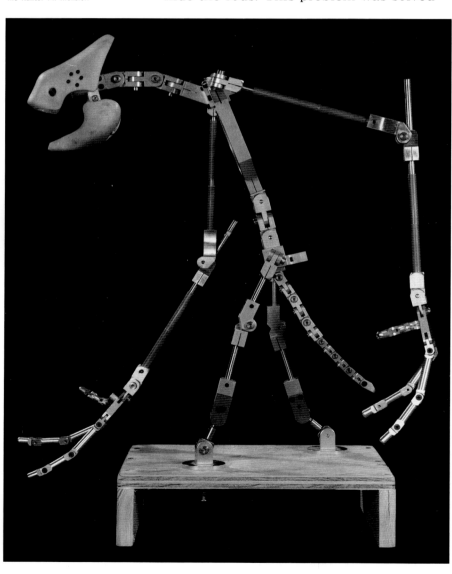

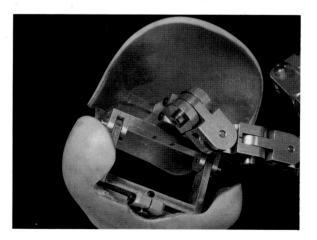

Edlund, nominated for his superb work at ILM on *Poltergeist*, sat in the Academy audience as Muren went up on stage to receive his Oscar for ILM's efforts on *E.T.: The Extra-Terrestrial*.

THE PROCESS: BUILDING THE PUPPET

As with larger creatures we've discussed in the previous chapter, a stop-motion character begins with artist's sketches. Once a design is picked, a small prototype sculpture is made; after this is approved, a full-scale clay model is sculpted. This becomes the master for a mold, which ultimately gives birth to the rubber puppet.

Before casting the rubber figure, a steel skeleton—the armature—is made, complete with machined ball joints whose tensions are adjustable. Machining these

mechanical joints is one of those very specialized skills held by only a handful of craftsmen throughout the world. Jiri Trnka, a Czechoslovakian filmmaker, has made scores of wonderful stop-motion films using hand-carved wooden joints. At ILM, machinist-animator Tom St. Amand painstakingly machines every joint of steel. He is without a doubt the best and most experienced person in the world at this rare skill.

Small parts, such as fingers, are sometimes given wire support. The rubber is then cast around the skeleton so when the creature emerges from the mold it is complete with all its "bones." All it needs is a coat of paint, a skin of fur, or perhaps a suit of clothes.

In nearly all the films done at ILM, stop-motion puppets double for actors in miniature scenes: the children on bikes in

Animators Phil Tippett and Tom St. Amand work on the puppets for *Indiana Jones and the Temple of Doom*.

Right and middle: Tom St. Amand uses stop motion animation for the mine car chase in *Indiana Jones and the Temple of Doom.*

Far right: The stop motion puppets used in *Indiana Jones and the Temple of Doom.*

Below: The lava pit victim in *Indiana Jones and the Temple of Doom.* This is a remote control puppet.

Opposite page, left: Cameraman Pat Sweeney inspects the baby spider from *Explorers.*

Right: Stop motion animator Tony Laudati animates the baby spider for *Explorers.* There was also a full-sized mechanical device about eight feet high, but the smaller stop motion version was used when the creature was needed for articulated action.

E.T.: The Extra-Terrestrial; the riders of the speeder bikes chasing through the woods in *Return of the Jedi*; the main characters in the mine car chase for *Indiana Jones and the Temple of Doom.* The reason is obvious: we are asking the puppets to do things that the actors would never be able to do.

In *E.T.*, the children on their bikes were partially automated with a variation of the Go-Motion technique. The front and back wheels of the bike were rotated by a computer-controlled motor and the rider's rider's legs, attached to the pedals, were also moved during the exposure. The resultant blurring and precison of movement contributed to an incredible realism in the flying bicycle scenes.

However, Go-Motion is rarely used in this type of short scene where human doubles appear, since the set-up for Go-Motion is too time-consuming to be worthwhile when the shot is brief. Stop motion will be used instead, as it is when production time and budget are short. This was the case on *The Ewok Adventure,* where Phil Tippett did an extensive stop-motion sequence involving Ewoks battling a monstrous creature called the Borra. Though Go-Motion would have been nice for this sequence, the realities of our schedule and the limits of our budget dictated the use of stop motion. Fortunately, Tippett's skill made stop motion an acceptable alternative.

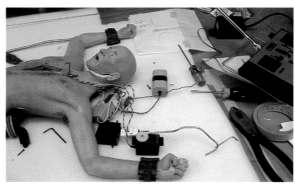

PHIL TIPPETT

Most objective reviews of feature film stop-motion animation rank *Dragonslayer* as one of the best if not *the* best example of the art form. All the special effects work for *Dragonslayer* was performed at ILM in 1980; the stop-motion animation was by Phil Tippett.

At ILM, stop motion is done as a substitute for real animals or moving objects and is integrated into films with live action. Consequently, it requires the highest technical proficiency in order to achieve maximum realism. Most of the time audiences have no notion (we hope) that the shots they're seeing use the stop-motion technique. Very few artists have mastered stop motion so completely that they can apply it in this realistic manner. Phil Tippett, however, is one who knows how to do it.

In 1958, when Phil was seven years old, his parents took him to see a movie at the Oaks Theater near his home in Berkeley, California. The film, *The Seventh Voyage of Sinbad,* was filled with spectacular special effects and Ray Harryhausen's stop-motion animation. Phil remembers the day vividly and asserts that the film changed his life. He fell in love with the spectacle, and was particularly fascinated with the stop-motion animation. By the time he was thirteen years old, he had spent the money he'd earned mowing lawns on an 8mm Keystone camera and was making things move in front of it. He filmed walking figures made of pipe cleaners and formed stop-motion action in clay, all shot one frame at a time. He found that when he worked it was so engrossing that he would lose all sense of time and place. His whole mind was focused on the scene he was filming.

By the time he was seventeen years old, he was being paid minimum wage ($1.50 an hour) to animate for TV commercials. The hard work and low pay was discouraging, so he put it aside temporarily to attend art school. After leaving art school, he did some animation for low-budget films and then returned to TV commercials; one of his jobs was to animate the famous Pillsbury Doughboy. While doing this work he began to develop working relationships with some of those who in five years would become important names in special effects: Jon Berg and Dennis Muren. Dennis had been working at ILM as a special effects cameraman, and at his recommendation Phil and Jon were hired to join the *Star Wars* production team and animate the miniature chess game.

When work began on *The Empire Strikes Back,* Phil began designing the tauntaun creature and animated all medium and long shots of Luke on the tauntaun. Phil also worked on the Imperial snow walkers, those giant machines that resemble iron horses, but he gives most of the credit to Jon Berg for animation of these beasts.

When *Dragonslayer* came along, Phil worked with Dennis Muren, Stuart Ziff, Gary Leo, and Tom St. Amand to develop to Go-Motion system. The results were incomparable to any previous stop-motion work.

During *Return of the Jedi* Phil ran the ILM creature shop, which provided more than half of the scores of creatures seen in the film. After principal photography was completed, he and Dennis Muren teamed up again with Tom St. Amand, Dave Carson, Randy Johnson, Jeff Mann, and Kim Marks to film the Rancor Pit monster. Phil also supervised the small two-legged walkers seen in *Jedi,* utilizing the Go-Motion system and linking it to the little walkers.

For his incredible contribution to *Return of the Jedi,* Phil was the recipient of an Academy Award.

CHAPTER 6

MINIATURE PHOTOGRAPHY

It all began with what producer Frank Marshall called "the $250,000 sentence," a four-word description in the script for Steven Spielberg's film *Poltergeist*: "And the house implodes." Marshall is referring to a scene in which the home of the Freeling family becomes so possessed by spirits of the dead that it is destroyed by implosion—it collapses upon itself and disappears into a black hole at its center. This was the effect that Spielberg wanted and what he asked ILM to do. Richard Edlund was the ILM visual effects supervisor for *Poltergeist*, and this was the kind of challenge he relished.

The concept for achieving the effect is a simple one to describe, but was difficult to achieve and fraught with danger. A miniature house, six feet wide and four feet high, was built, an exact copy of the one used in the film, which was in a new housing development near Los Angeles. The miniature was accurate not only in exterior detail but also in every interior feature. All furniture and window frames had concealed wires that, when pulled, would draw them toward a large black funnel. In fact, the entire house was destined to collapse and be "sucked" into this funnel, not only by the wires but through the use of a powerful vacuum, triggered by an electrically controlled valve. The event would happen rapidly, almost in the blinking of an eye, but it would be filmed by a high-speed 35mm movie camera running 360 frames per second so that when projected at a normal 24 frames per second, what occurred in one second of real time would be slowed down to fifteen seconds on the screen.

After several weeks of preparation, the beautifully constructed and fully furnished house was completed. It looked like a museum piece except for the bundle of

Below: Preparation of the *Poltergeist* house before it imploded, with modelmakers Marc Thorpe (left), and Larry Tan (right).

Right: Imploding house scene setup with the 35mm *Bruce Hill* high speed camera.

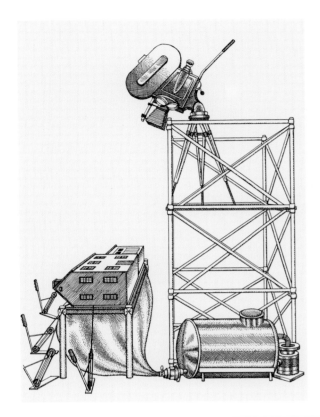

cables that extended ominously out the rear, away from the camera view—"booby trap" attachments that foretold the fate of this lovely model. It was then placed on its back over the black funnel. The high-speed camera was above on a high scaffold, looking down upon it. Because of the high frame rate and corresponding shutter speed (over 1/720th of a second per frame), a powerful bank of lights was focused on the house to light it. They would be turned on just seconds prior to activating the camera so that the heat from the lights would not literally melt the model.

It is usually very exciting to attend the filming of a shot like this, for unlike most special effects photography, which occurs very slowly, the high-speed shot happens rapidly and often the consequences are immediately obvious. This particular shot was especially dramatic because of all that was at stake: the model with its furnishings had been under construction

Left: The *Poltergiest* house collapsed inward when cables and a large vacuum device pulled all of its parts into a black funnel. A high speed camera looking down slowed the action and gave it the look of a full sized house.

Below: The collapsing suburban home built for *Poltergeist*, as seen in the final composited image.

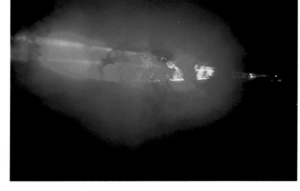

Above: The encased remains of the imploding house sent to Steven Spielberg.

Middle: Smoke and dry ice effects for *Poltergeist*, used as spirits who ward off human intruders.

Below: Cameraman Neil Krepela (behind the camera) shoots a tornado effect for *Poltergeist*. Stage technician Harold Cole works on the tornado.

for weeks, costing well over $25,000, and it would be destroyed in only a few seconds. A mistake at this time would be quite costly.

The exposure and lens focus was checked and the film threaded carefully in the camera and tested. A hush fell over the assembled spectators as Director of Photography Edlund yelled for silence. The cues had to be correct and clear so that we did not have a false start before the camera was ready or have the camera run too soon before the house was ready to collapse. At 300 frames per second, a normal camera load of 400 feet of 35mm film could run out before the action even began. It also takes several seconds for a high-speed camera to get up to speed, so several seconds are wasted at the start just waiting for it to reach the right velocity.

When all was ready, Edlund yelled, "Roll camera!" The camera began its rapid climb to speed, and the pitch of the motor's whirr grew higher and higher. (Some high-speed cameras have jammed at these speeds and literally exploded with film; everyone around the camera was aware of that possibility as the motor was approaching maximum speed). Then, above the roaring camera came the call of "Action!" and suddenly, all the wires were pulled, ripping the house apart and drawing its fragments toward the funnel. Now the vacuum valve was activated, and with a loud roar, small fragments were sucked toward the funnel.

Edlund and machinist Gene Whiteman, to guarantee that not one scrap of the house would survive, began blasting the remains with pump action shotguns. The roar of the vacuum, the blast of the guns, the ripping of the model as the cables pulled it apart, and the screech of the camera were almost deafening. In less than five second, it was all over. The house had disappeared into the funnel. "Cut!" And the camera coasted to a stop.

A cheer erupted from the onlookers. If something had gone wrong, it would have been silence followed by swearing. The final verdict, however, would not really be in until the film was returned from the lab and could be viewed the next morning at dailies. At ILM convention dictates that no one, no matter how important, project a shot alone before dailies—it is a group effort and we should all find out together if we succeeded or failed.

Sometimes what appears to be failure on the set is quite effective on film. Other times, what seems to be a complete success during the shooting does not look good at dailies and must be reshot. So it was a long wait that night for the scene to get back from the lab. Modelmaker Ease Owyeung must have had a particularly restless night: if the action was not good, he would have to start all over again and build another house, complete with furniture. The camera operator could not have rested easy, either. If he had made a mistake, it would be like dropping a game-winning touchdown pass in the Super Bowl.

The next morning, with the screening room filled to capacity, we ran the film. It was terrific. At least that is what *we* thought. Spielberg could not attend the screening because he was in Los Angeles directing *E.T.* at the time, so a print of the shot was sent to him. He would look at it during the noon break in shooting; we waited to hear his assessment.

When Steven ran the film in his screening room, he was as filled with anticipation as we had been. Still, he had to retain his objectivity and let us know if it did not satisfy him. The unprepared projectionist had no idea what he was running—per-

Above: An explosion in *The Empire Strikes Back*. This was shot in a large rented building with a ceiling higher than that of a normal sound stage.

Left: Cameraman Neil Krepela (left) and effects specialist Gary Platek (right) test laser effects for *Poltergeist*.

haps just more dailies from *E.T.*—so as the house slowly disintegrated and disappeared into itself, Steven could hear the astonished projectionist spontaneously shout out, "Holy shit, what was that!" It was indeed an amazing shot, and Steven loved it.

When ILM finishes effects for a film, a key model will often be mounted in a plastic case and presented to the director. All that was left of the *Poltergeist* house was a jumble of pulverized model fragments with

Opposite page: Final composite shot of Elliot and E.T. riding past the moon, from *E.T.: The Extra-Terrestrial.*

some cabling. This was cleaned out of the funnel and off the studio floor and encased in a plastic box, looking like something that had missed the trash pickup. It was sent to Steven, and he was delighted with his magnificent conversation piece. Later in his office, I saw it sitting prominently on his grand piano.

Why do some miniatures look phony the moment they come on the screen while others fool us completely? To begin with, the model work must be appropriately detailed. But even this will not look good if it is not well photographed. There are many elements that contribute to successful photography of a miniature; one that ranks very high is the apparent atmosphere in the picture. Even on a relatively clear day or night, there is a diffused quality to a normal atmosphere. A mountain several miles away will look hazy and desaturated; the mountain farther behind it will be even hazier. If a miniature of these mountains were built and filmed without this apparent atmosphere, it would look wrong from the instant it came on the screen, so diffusion is almost always used in some form when filming miniature objects. Smoke is one of the most common mediums for the creation of atmosphere: it

Far left: Visual effects supervisor Dennis Muren films an *E.T.* miniature.

Left: The *E.T.* ship comes in for a landing through smoke with the cameraman following the action.

Below: Modelmaker Scott Marshall works on a detail for a miniature in *E.T.*

Gatefold: The E.T. creature looks down into the valley of lights, created by the ILM matte painting department.

Far left, above: Visual effects supervisor Dennis Muren shoots a miniature set-up for *E.T.*

Far left, middle: A modelmaker adjusts the small model of E.T. in front of painted backing. Lights are created by holes drilled in board and backlit through colored gels.

Left: Dennis Muren sets up a shot of the E.T. puppet in valley setting.

Below: The valley of lights painting by matte artist Chris Evans.

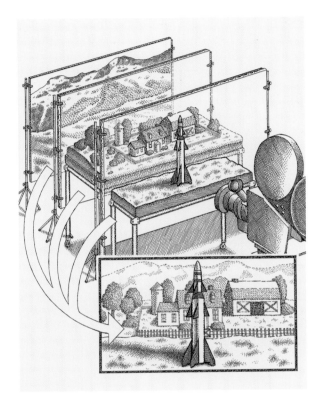

Right: **DEPTH ENHANCEMENT**
Placing layers of bridal veil between elements of a miniature set creates a look of atmospheric haze. This technique is commonly used at ILM when photographing miniatures. Too much sharpness in "distant" objects reveals the use of miniatures.

Below: Final composite shot of Elliot, E.T., and friends against the setting sun, from *E.T.: The Extra-Terrestrial.*

not only has the lovely quality of separating objects as they recede from the camera but, when properly lit, it also creates a wonderful mood.

Bridal veil material is another substance commonly used to add diffusion to miniature objects. When filming the Imperial snow walkers from *The Empire Strikes Back*, Dennis Muren separated the mechanical miniatures with bridal veiling; the closer ones had no diffusion, the second rank back had one layer, the third another layer. The effect was quite convincing.

Muren's photography of the Rancor Pit monster from *Return of the Jedi* was diffused with a combination of atmospheric smoke on the set and a sheet of glass placed at an angle to reflect a white card in front of the lens. It had the effect of "flashing" the whole picture. The effect was controllable by simply increasing or decreasing the amount of light on the card being reflected by the glass. Of course, there are diffusion glasses that are made by lens filter companies for the express purpose of being placed in front of the lens and thereby diffusing the image; they come in varying strengths and range from very subtle to heavy fog. The problem with them is that they diffuse all objects equally and therefore do not provide the separation necessary to replicate the way real atmosphere affects natural objects. Therefore, though diffusion filters can be used when filming miniatures, they are rarely used alone.

Fire, water, and billowing smoke are commonly called for in special effect miniature photography, but, unfortunately, all possess special problems when filmed in miniature. Neither smoke nor flames scale down well, and they do not look or act appropriately. Small flames do not look like very large ones, and when they are shot in slow motion, they take on an unnatural oily look. The movement of the smoke is also unreal looking.

AN IN-CAMERA MATTE SHOT

A miniature is often used to replace a full-sized set piece. Since the savings can be substantial. In the *Ewok II* film, there were several shots showing the large, dark Marauder castle, accomplished by using several techniques including matte paintings. But we also employed one of the oldest film tricks in the business: a matte box split. Here's how it was done.

ILM modelmaker Paul Huston constructed a miniature castle which was taken to the barren location. A camera mounted on a platform was pointed

Far left, above: Stage hand John Lister sets up the miniature castle for a "split screen effects" shot in *Ewoks: The Battle for Endor*.

Below: Modelmaker Paul Huston lines up the shot.

Left, top to bottom: Paul Huston cuts a matte to block off the lower half of the frame prior to shooting the first half of the "split" shot. Cameraman Rick Fichter covers the lens with bridal veiling material to diffuse the model castle (make it look as though more atmosphere is between camera and miniature). Paul Huston applies the matte to the top half of the matte box. Prior to action exposure on lower half, the bottom matte will be removed. Paul Huston applies a paper matte in front of the lens to block off half the picture.

toward a distant landscape. The model castle was placed before the camera at precisely the right level so it appeared to be sitting on the distant mountains. The lower half of the frame was then blocked off by taping black paper to the bottom of the camera matte box (sunshade). White bridal veil was placed over the camera's lens in order to provide an atmospheric "haze" for the castle.

The scene was then filmed by Cinematographer Rick Fichter. After blocking off the entire frame area, the exposed film was wound backwards in the camera, and black paper was positioned in the areas that had been clear for the first exposure, covering up the castle that had been photographed on the first pass of film through the camera. The lower portion of the black paper was then removed to reveal the rugged landscape below.

Finally, stagehands took the castle and its support out of the picture. The actors now moved across the barren landscape as a second exposure was made. The final shot, when developed, showed the miniature castle as a far off structure with the actors moving in the foreground.

Right: The castle miniature as seen on film with matte for the lower half.

Far right: Castle with foreground now exposed, as seen in the final film.

CAMERA SPEEDS

It is sometimes hard for people to understand what we mean when we say we film a scene at a "faster than normal" or a "slower than normal" speed. It is really quite simple if you remember that films are projected in the theater at a constant twenty-four frames per second; if we film a scene at double that speed, forty-eight frames per second, when it is projected at twenty-four frames per second, the action that in reality took ten seconds to occur will take twenty seconds when projected. "Slow motion" is achieved by filming at a faster than normal speed; conversely, if the desired effect is to speed up the natural action of a scene, the camera runs slower than normal, so when it is projected at twenty-four frames per second the action will appear to occur more rapidly. Chase and fight scenes often benefit from a slight increase in apparent speed, so they might be filmed at eighteen frames per second rather than twenty-four.

For example, the action of clouds for *Dragonslayer* was filmed at a slow camera speed so that when projected they appeared to be tumbling in a violent manner. For *Return of the Jedi,* the camera was literally walked through the woods while filming at a very slow speed of less than a frame per second. When projected later at twenty-four frames per second, the walk became an exciting race at an apparent 100 miles per hour.

The character Teek in *Ewoks: The Battle for Endor* moves about at hyperspeed. In fact, Teek was filmed at a rate of one frame each second, speeding up the action twenty-four times.

In MINIATURE PHOTOGRAPHY, high frame rates are often used to give a miniature action the appearance of more mass and

Far left, above: Production designer Joe Johnston listens while modelmaker Paul Huston explains how miniature vat will tip for a shot in *Indiana Jones and the Temple of Doom*.

Middle and below: The miniature set for the vat dump.

Left, above: Model supervisor Lorne Peterson fills the vat with water before flooding the mine tunnel in *Indiana Jones and the Temple of Doom*.

Middle: Modelmaker Paul Huston with the miniature vat.

Below: Miniature vat dumps water. This sequence was shot at faster than normal camera speed to make the action slow down.

size. Most explosions filmed at ILM are shot at speeds in excess of 100 frames per second; many are shot at speeds of 250 frames per second. Consider the effect of a small explosion that rips apart a miniature spaceship: the entire action may take a half of a second to occur when filmed, but if filmed at 240 frames per second this half-second event becomes a five-second explosion. When accompanied by a powerful sound, it is a convincing event.

There is a formula commonly given for the appropriate camera speed needed to give miniature objects in motion the proper apparent mass.

THE FORMULA FOR DETERMINING THE PROPER CAMERA SPEED WHEN PHOTOGRAPHING A MINIATURE

$$24 \times \sqrt{\frac{D}{d}} = f$$

D = Dimensions in feet of real object
d = Dimensions in feet of the miniature
photographed
f = Frames per second (camera frame rate)

If you were to photograph a spaceship that is supposed to be 20 feet long (D = 20) using a model 2 feet in length (d = 2), here is how the proper frame rate would be calculated:

$$24 \times \sqrt{20/2} = f$$
$$24 \times \sqrt{10} = f$$
$$24 \times 3.16 = f$$
$$76 = f$$

In theory, the proper frame rate for a tenth-size miniature is 76 frames per second, a little more than three times normal speed. This would make a one-second event slow down to 3.16 seconds.

Dennis Muren, however, does not rely on this formula; he prefers to use it only as a starting point for testing. In the end, after screening tests shot at many speeds, he uses his judgment.

Here are a few speeds that he remembers: The eighteen-inch Rancor Pit monster for *Jedi* was operated from below the set with direct hand control and cables to more articulated parts; it was shot at seventy-two to eighty-four frames per second. Richard Edlund placed a camera on a wire and crashed it into a set to simulate the crash of Luke's X-wing on Dagobah in *The Empire Strikes Back*; the camera was shooting at seventy-two frames per second when it hit. These speeds were not the product of a formula in a book but the result of experimentation.

When extremely high speeds are needed to achieve the effect desired, there is a technical complication: the faster the camera runs, the more light is needed to expose the film. The miniature landslide shot for *Dragonslayer* at 250 frames per second required more than ten times as much light to film as it would have

Jerry Jeffress stands next to the "Vista Cruiser", a motion control camera which he helped develop for *Return of the Jedi*. It is able to handle both eight and four perf 35mm film formats.

required at normal speed. In addition, a miniature is more effective when shot at a high f/stop in order to keep both close and distant objects in sharp focus—again, the need for a great many lights. Sometimes the lights are so intense and hot that they can only be turned on a second or two before the shot is made, and then must be extinguished the moment the shot is over so the model doesn't melt!

One of the fastest frame rates ever used at ILM was for the film *Star Trek II: The Wrath of Khan*. Near the end of the film an incredible explosion is to take place as a planet called Genesis is formed. Jim Veilleux, co-supervisor of effects on this project, chose a special rotating prism camera to film a phosphorus explosion.

While a standard motion picture camera holds the film momentarily immobile during the exposure, camera speeds greater than 250 frames per second test

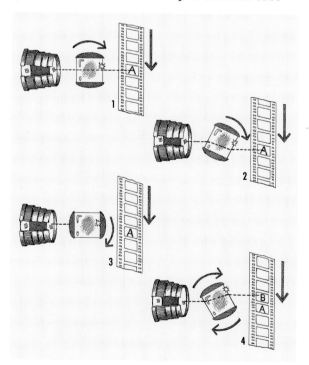

Above: Camera equipment and controllers built by ILM. The camera at left is housed in a soundproof blimp. The reflex (VistaVision format) camera in the center is capable of speeds up to 90 frames per second. The tripod head (camera support) is moved by computer-controlled motors. On the right, the "field recorder" built at ILM is capable of recording and playing back information that controls camera movement.

Below: Detail of the Quad optical printer. The camera and projector controls are in the lower foreground.

Left: ROTATING PRISM CAMERA
The film running through this camera does not stop to be exposed. A glass cube (shown in this simplified illustration) moves the image to follow the film as it races past. This kind of mechanism is used in ultra-high-speed cameras to record action in slow motion. Since image quality is poor, this type of camera is not used for normal speed photography.

Right: A pyro effect for *Star Wars*.

Below: A motion control set-up on the ILM stage. The computer and electronic controls are on the right and models being shot are in front of the bluescreen.

Far right: The field recorder with VistaVision camera on it, built at ILM.

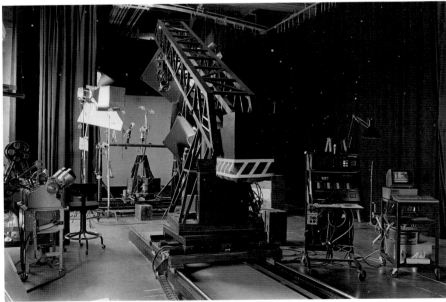

the capacity of even the best high-speed cameras. With a rotating prism camera, a prism bends the image to follow the film as it races past the lens. The film is never held immobile; therefore very high shutter speeds are possible.

The explosives for the *Star Trek II* shot were placed high above the floor of the Cow Palace in San Francisco. Black material was attached to the ceiling to provide the appropriate black space background, while the camera looked straight up at the falling phosphorus material. The special camera ran at *2,500 frames per second*. In real time it took one second to occur; on film it became a one-minute, forty-four-second event. Since the image from the rotating prism camera was not rock steady, each frame was repositioned and rephotographed in order to eliminate the shaky quality of the picture. The resultant effect was spectacular.

MOTION CONTROL

When one thinks of an ILM shot, probably the first thing that comes to mind is a spaceship roaring through a starry sky, and in fact, ILM has done a great deal of this kind of miniature photography. It probably comes as no surprise that these ships

Far left: The black background being hoisted at the Cow Palace in San Francisco. This was used for a high speed shot on *Star Trek II: The Wrath of Khan.*

Left: The explosion for the *Star Trek II* "Genesis Sequence." Pyrotechnic phospers cascade down on the camera.

Below: The beginning of the Genesis planet shot as it appeared from the camera's point of view.

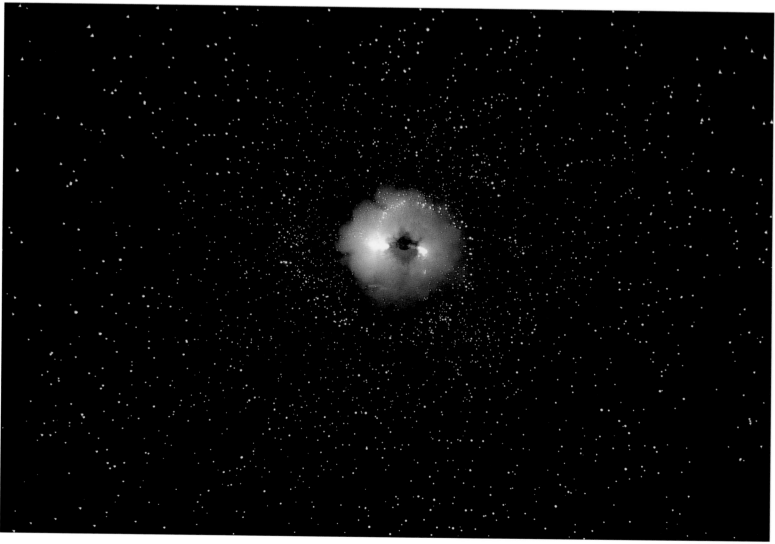

are miniatures and require a special photographic technique to make them look as real as they do.

Ken Ralston, one of the most versatile ILMers, has been involved with this special branch of photography since the early *Star Wars* days. Back in 1976 he and Dennis Muren worked the night shift at old ILM; now, as a supervisor of visual effects, he has used motion control extensively to film the models for *Star Trek II: The Wrath of Khan* and *Star Trek III: The Search for Spock.* For *Return of the Jedi,* Ken supervised most of the space battle photography, and won an Oscar for his work. His skill makes the job look easy, but it is much more difficult than it appears.

When a shot calls for a spaceship to race toward us, it is filmed using MOTION CONTROL. The camera moves down a long track toward a relatively stationary model ship. (ILM has several such cameras on tracks—one "rail line" is sixty feet long, permitting a mere speck of a model to race toward us and pass by inches from the camera.) The model, though quite restricted in its movements, is connected to a support that allows it to move a few feet to each side. However, most movements are provided by the camera, which is mounted on a crane. All of its functions, including focus, are controlled by a prerecorded computer program executed by the cameraman for each shot. When the scene is finished it may have several ships in it, but each one has been shot separately. Rarely are two ships filmed together; it would be a problem to keep them both in focus at the same time and the ships' movements would inevitably be interlocked, and appear as if they had been photographed together.

Right, top to bottom: Chris Evans paints a backing which will provide a background for a high speed explosion for *Return of the Jedi.* The Sail Barge with a painted backing behind it. The camera crew wears helmets, as they prepare to shoot an explosion for *Return of the Jedi.* The explosion of the Sail Barge as seen by the camera. The exploding barge filmed at high speed.

ships passed in front of each other, there would be a double exposure, making them look like ghosts.) The ship is then filmed one frame at a time. In order to get the maximum f/stop the camera exposures are usually longer than one second each, so a typical shot might take half a day to shoot. With each click of the shutter, the camera advances a fraction of an inch along its sixty-foot rail.

In *Explorers*, there was a sequence of shots with kids flying through the sky. This was done in two steps. First, we filmed backlit cotton on wires for clouds. Then,

Far left, above: Final shot of the radar dish for *Return of the Jedi*.

Middle: Art director Joe Johnston, visual effects supervisor Dennis Muren, supervising stage technician Ted Moehnke, and pyrotechnician Thaine Morris with a miniature of the radar dish.

Left: Visual effects co-supervisor Bruce Nicholson inspects the cloud effect for the opening sequence in *Explorers*.

Below: Visual effects co-supervisor Don Dow, behind the motion control camera, moves a cotton "cloud" into position.

When the second or third ship is filmed, a test is done on black-and-white film, which is then quickly developed in a small machine. The developed film is placed in a film viewer, along with the previous shots of the other ships; and all are run sandwiched together. The action of the ships is then studied to see if their relative movements are proper.

Once the camera move is decided, color film is threaded into the camera and the blue screen behind the model is illuminated. (This blue background will be used later in optical processes in order to isolate each element in the shot. Otherwise, as

the kids were filmed separately in front of a blue screen, lying on a blue support which moved during the shot to allow them to turn, bank, climb and dive like Superman. In the final optical composite shot, the support for the kids disappeared (since it was blue) and the kids appeared to be flying, unsupported, through clouds.

Once this shot is completed, another pass is done. This time only the ship's lights are turned on and everything else is dark. The separate light pass will be added to the model later in optical department processes.

The whole time-consuming operation requires a special kind of mind in order to visualize how it will all look when combined into a two-second shot. Fortunately, the motion control camera operators at ILM are good at this kind of thinking. When Ralston filmed the flying scenes for *Dragonslayer,* he not only had the usual problems of a motion control photographer, he was also flexing the dragon's

wings between exposures in order to make it look like it was flying. The results were quite realistic.

The job requires endless patience. In *Return of the Jedi,* there were some shots

Above: A miniature set for *Dragonslayer.* In the lower portion a dragon is being manipulated by an animator and in the upper portion, film of the actor is projected into the set.

Right: Ken Ralston, ILM visual effects supervisor for *Cocoon,* lights a bluescreen shot for the film.

Far right: An ILM VistaVision camera in the nose of an aircraft flies through real clouds. This scene was used as background for the flying dragon in *Dragonslayer.*

Far left, above: The miniature cave set which will be flooded with water for a special effects shot in *Indiana Jones and the Temple of Doom*.

Middle: The view inside the tunnel.

Below: Model supervisor Lorne Peterson modifies the tunnel.

Left, top to bottom: The Nikon camera rides on miniature rails in the mine set for *Indiana Jones and the Temple of Doom*. Its small size allows it to move through the tunnels. Cameraman Micheal McAlister checks the Nikon camera. Dennis Muren and Kim Marks line up water tunnel shot. Exterior of the tunnel set for *Temple of Doom*. The tower on the left contains water to be released by a trip valve.

Right: Camera assistant Toby Heindel sets up for a mine car shot in *Temple of Doom*.

Far right: The miniature mine car with puppets for *Indiana Jones and the Temple of Doom*.

Below: Indiana Jones looks back at the wall of water rushing through the mine tunnel.

where scores of ships were seen at the same time. Needless to say, it was *very* complicated and painstaking work. Once Ken got so frustrated by all of the ships in *Jedi* that he took off his tennis shoe and put it in the film as part of the Rebel fleet. The shoe actually ended up in the final film,

though you have to know exactly where to look in order to see it.

It is very difficult to film a reflecting object in front of the blue screen used for the traveling matte photography; if blue light from the screen is reflected by the model in the final composite shot, that por-

Above: Final shot in *Indiana Jones and the Temple of Doom* uses mine car miniatures.

Left: Cameraman Micheal McAlister builds the special Nikon camera used for miniature photography in *Temple of Doom*.

tion of the model will be seen as transparent wherever the blue or even a hint of blue is reflected. This problem even has a name given to it by people who work in special effects. They call it "Blue Spill."

For this reason, most spaceships are painted with non-reflective paint and are rarely white. (The great exception to the rule is, of course, the all white Star Destroyers from the *Star Wars* films. These ships have always presented a serious "blue spill" problem, which has plaqued every *Star Wars* project.)

When John Carpenter came to ILM to do the effects for *Star Man*, he posed a difficult problem for us, potentially the worst blue spill case we could think of.

In the climax of the film, he wished to have a large spaceship land in a desert crater. We could handle that, but it was the look of the ship that caused the trouble. It was to be a silver, mirror finished sperical object. Essentially, a large shiny silver ball! It would reflect all that surrounded it. This was "blue spill city." At this point in the film, there were helicopters buzzing about and, as the ship descended into the crater, Carpenter wanted to also see reflections of the crater's edges along with the choppers.

This visual riddle puzzled us until we came up with a possible solution. It worked and was successfully applied to the final shots with this unusual space ship. The "reflections" were provided by filmed scenes of helicopters and the cra-

ter, *projected* onto a large, white sphere. The natural distortion provided by the curved surface of the white ball gave the impression that what we were seeing were reflections from objects around the ship. The ship, in fact, looked as if it were a silver sphere. Just what John Carpenter wanted.

Miniature photography requires a multitude of skills to solve the wide variety of problems. It is quite remarkable that so many talented and highly skilled people in the field have all gathered at one place to practice their craft—Industrial Light and Magic.

DENNIS MUREN

Some people in visual effects have fallen into the job and find it hard to remember how or why they are in it. This is not so with Dennis Muren, visual effects supervisor at ILM. He traces his interests in visual effects almost as far back as he can remember. When he was six years old, he was making scratches on slides and projecting them. He was fascinated by films like *War of the Worlds*, *King Kong*, and other special effects spectaculars. He loved the excitement and look of them, but he did not understand that these films were actually made by people until he was eight or nine years old. When he finally made this connection, he realized that he wanted to make films himself. Using a ten-dollar Keystone 8mm movie camera, he began to make his own little spectacles at age ten. He didn't have a projector, only an editing viewer, but that didn't seem to matter to him; it was the making of the films, not the showing of them that fascinated him.

His parents, realizing that his interest was more than a passing childish phase, bought him a better camera when he was fourteen. With his new toy (a through-the-lens viewing reflex model), he experimented with stop motion and rear screen projection. He joined others with similar interests and haunted the used book stores for literature on the subject of special effects. He especially liked the English publications on the subject; by studying the still photos taken on the sets, he tried to decipher how the cinematography and special effects were actually done in the big movies.

After graduating from high school, he decided not to study film in college. He didn't want his films to be judged by anyone or have to pass judgment on the work of others, so he majored in business with a special interest in advertising, but he pursued his "hobby" anyway. During his first year in college he set out to make a very ambitious film, a sci-fi adventure film

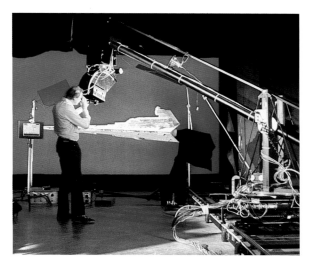

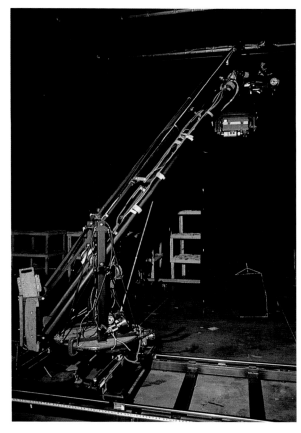

Far left: Dennis Muren programs a shot of the Star Destroyer with the Dykstraflex camera.

Left: The Dykstraflex camera in the raised position.

Below: Dennis Muren photographs a Star Destroyer.

called *The Equinox*. Assisted by his friends, including the established stop-motion expert Jim Danforth (*When Dinosaurs Ruled the Earth*), he invested all his energy and savings in this 16mm epic. However, unlike most such Walter Mitty projects, Dennis's film did get completed and was picked up by a small distributor who added forty minutes to it, had it blown up to 35mm, and released it. Dennis felt a special achievement when the picture played in a theater on Hollywood Boulevard, just like the hundreds of films he had seen there in his youth. It proved to him that it was now a "real" film.

The total cash investment for *The Equinox* was around $8,000. Most of it came from Dennis's savings, with the rest borrowed from friends and investors; though it wasn't a box office smash, he did get most of his money back. Dennis did not particularly enjoy the directing experience, but he did have fun shooting the special effects—it became clear to him that he wanted to pursue a career in film with a special focus on special effects.

While in college, he worked part time filming television commercials. At Cascade, a commercial production house in

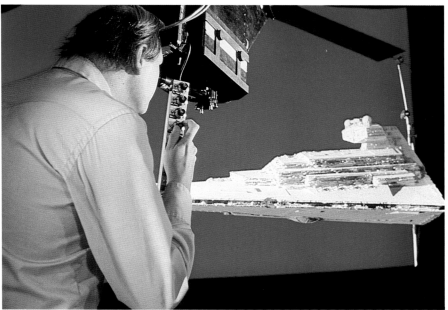

Top to bottom: Visual effects supervisor Dennis Muren (center) adjusts the model Ford trimotor built for *Indiana Jones and the Temple of Doom* by Mike Fulmer (right). Stagehand Pat Fitzsimmons is on the left. A test shot of the trimotor as it crashes. A very simple camera dolly is used here. The miniature trimotor crashes into a snowy mountaintop. The camera crew races alongside. The final shot as seen by the camera as the trimotor rushes in toward the cliff.

Hollywood, he met two other young special effect specialists who would later join him at ILM: Jon Berg and Phil Tippett.

In the early 1970s, work in special effects was hard to get in Hollywood and Dennis came close to abandoning the whole idea. He and Jon Berg worked on an idea for a feature film but had little luck in getting it off the ground. He was, however, developing a network of friends in one branch of the special effects field. They used the simple old-fashioned techniques; ingenuity, artistry, and lighting were the strong features of their work. Meanwhile, there was another school of thought with which they had practically no contact: the Douglas Trumbull/John Dykstra school, where technology was liberally applied wherever possible. Dennis never had budgets high enough to permit this kind of technological application in special effects and he was curious to become involved with Trumbull and Dykstra to see how it worked.

So it was that when the opportunity arose to join John Dykstra at the newly formed ILM, Dennis seized it. Dykstra liked Dennis and felt that his experience in stop motion would be of use on *Star Wars*. It is a rare talent to be able to comprehend screen time while filming a scene a frame at a time, a sort of sculpting of time, pulling it apart to manipulate it and then compressing it back together to be inserted into the film. As for the new motion control technology at ILM, Dennis felt that there was too much emphasis on constructing hardware. In his opinion, many of the shots for *Star Wars* could have been done without the high-tech motion control system, but nevertheless he recognized it as a powerful tool when properly applied. He is particularly proud of one shot in *Star Wars* where he made good use of motion control—the final assault on the Death Star. The shot shows a fighter racing through the trench while being bombarded by defenders. Rather than film it with mechanically smooth camera move, Dennis used the motion control device to duplicate the feel of a hand-held shot, looking down on the assaulting ship. This hand-held effect has been used by Dennis on other films since, particularly in the *Return of the Jedi* land battle scenes.

After *Star Wars*, Dennis went on to work for Douglas Trumbull on *Close Encounters of the Third Kind* and later rejoined ILM as work began for *The Empire Strikes Back*. He has remained at ILM as a key figure supervising the effects for *Dragonslayer*, *E.T.: The Extra-Terrestrial*, *Return of the Jedi* (co-supervisor), and *Indiana Jones and the Temple of*

Doom. Among his peers, Dennis is regarded as perhaps the best cinematographer of miniatures in the world. His sense of lighting and atmosphere is developed far beyond that of most cinematographers, and he is at his best when challenged by constraints in budget and technology. He is perhaps best known for his work on *E.T.*, yet his most ambitious and innovative film was *Dragonslayer*. Although the film did not succeed at the box office, it is a classic of visual effects cinematography and animated puppetry. Dennis has won four Academy Awards, for *The Empire Strikes Back*, *Return of the Jedi*, *E.T.*, and *Indiana Jones and the Temple of Doom*. Ironically, his finest work, *Dragonslayer*, was nominated but lost to another ILM project supervised by Richard Edlund, *Raiders of the Lost Ark*.

KEN RALSTON

No other individual at ILM has the range and variety of talents that Ken Ralston has: he sketches, sculpts, animates, administrates, and is an accomplished cameraman. He supervised three films at ILM and won an Academy Award, all before his thirtieth birthday. This may seem like a lot for one person, but then he's been in the business for a long time. He started when he was five years old.

The precocious Ralston was an avid monster fan who dreamed of donning gruesome makeup and becoming the creature in some weirdly wonderful fantasy flick. He was fascinated with special effects and adored the work of master stop-motion animator Ray Harryhausen. On his own, Ken experimented with stop motion and other effects, using a simple little 8mm

camera that his parents had bought for him; the camera wasn't equipped to go one frame at a time but instead advanced unpredictably, which was a bit frustrating to the young filmmaker.

Famous Monsters in Filmland, edited by a man named Forrest J Ackerman, was his favorite magazine. Ken found out that Ackerman had an incredible collection of old fantasy film paraphernalia and other collectibles at his home. When he was thirteen, Ken called up Ackerman and, to his delight, he and a friend were invited to visit. At Ackerman's home the two boys met Jon Berg, who was working at Cascade Pictures at the time. The thirteen-year-old boys immediately took to Jon and the friendship blossomed.

Jon taught them how to build better

armatures for their stop-motion puppets, how to cast them, how to improve their animation technique. Ken soaked up all the information Jon could give him, then went out and began work on his own forty-minute 8mm epic, which he called *The Bounds of Imagination*. This kept him busy for more than a year. The film won honorable mention in a Kodak film contest. More importantly, it resulted in his getting a job with Cascade Pictures. Ken was now seventeen years old. Ken began working on commercials. For a short time, he went to Cal Arts, thinking he could learn a lot about film. But he quickly found that it wasn't so, and returned to work at Cascade.

He'd begun to do some work outside Cascade when, in 1975, his friends Jon Berg and Dennis Muren showed him the script for *Star Wars*. Ken remembers laughing his head off when reading it "because it was the script any effects lover would write if he could do anything he wanted." Still wondering if it were possible to do all the effects the script called for, he agreed to work on the film as a camera assistant to Dennis Muren.

Ken was just a little over twenty years old when he arrived for work at ILM. He and Dennis worked camera on the night shift.

By the time work began on *Return of the Jedi*, Ken's duties at ILM had branched outward and upward. He started the project doing designs for monsters—many of Jabba the Hutt's henchmen on the floating skiff were his creations—then, halfway through production, he was appointed co-supervisor of visual effects for *Star Trek II: The Wrath of Khan*.

After several months on this project, he returned to work on *Jedi*, where he was given the job of creating part of one of the most complicated sequences in the whole

movie: the initial space battle. In the sequence, scores of spaceships zoom crazily in and out and around one another as the Rebel Alliance confronts the evil Empire head on. Ken's excellent work on this scene earned him an Academy Award in 1983.

The art of animation is an art at which he excels, but Ken still finds it slightly strange because of its intensity. First of all, he feels, the artist must be acutely aware of how things move. Then, he must thoroughly understand the way people and creatures react in different situations. He must have an almost instinctive mathematical ability, to be able to divide movement into minute segments, and, finally, he must have "one hell of an ability to concentrate."

"You have to keep track of every axis that the body is moving," he says, "every little digit on a finger and what direction it's going. And not just simple things like what direction you are moving or how much you are moving, but you also have to remember what the movement is and what you are trying to say each second in what the body is doing. Like Ray Harryhausen used to say—and it's true, it's happened to me—the phone will ring and that's it. You start over."

His method for designing creatures sounds a little more relaxed. He likes to begin by thinking in human terms about the different characteristics of people, then he tries to extrapolate these characteristics into a more alien design. Starting with a very rough sketch, he'll refine it to the point where he feels intuitively right about his design; then he begins to sculpt a miniature prototype of the creature. The prototype will usually reveal the elements in the creature's design that will and will not work. Once all the "bugs" are eliminated, work on the full-scale creature can begin.

Ken has also served as visual effects supervisor on *Star Trek III: The Search for Spock* and *Cocoon*. Life as a supervisor is quite different from his work as animator-sculptor-cameraman; he is keenly aware of his role as mediator between the powers existing outside ILM, such as studio executives, and his own crew. The politics, the many decisions, and the juggling of time and tasks are, he finds, a large responsibility.

Ken says that ILM has been a "fantastic place in which to grow," with many opportunities. "If you really want to get something," he says, "if you work hard enough, at least you can get it in a good working relationship with all the people who've come here and work here. As far as I'm concerned," he adds, "I couldn't find a better place to be working."

For now, Ken is still busy expanding his skills at ILM. He was pleased with his work on *Cocoon*, done under Ron Howard's direction, and Ken feels that someday he might just like to get into directing himself. Not surprisingly, he would like to do a fantasy picture. He could be producer, director, and visual effects department all rolled into one.

CHAPTER 7

MATTE PAINTING: FROM BRUSH TO FILM

Above: The matte painting department during the filming of *The Empire Striks Back*. Left to right: Michael Pangrazio, Craig Barron, Ralph McQuarrie, Neil Krepela. Harrison Ellenshaw is seated.

Below: Matte painter Chris Evans paints a planet detail for *Return of the Jedi*.

At the end of the long corridor that forms the spine of ILM's 25,000-square-foot industrial building is a narrow staircase that goes up one flight to the matte painting studio. The faint odor of paints and the bright, diffused daylight from sky-lights are striking. Four young artists, perhaps the best gathering of matte painting talent in the world, sit painting on glass, fiberboard, or canvas. Twenty-seven-year-old Michael Pangrazio, the senior matte painter in the department; Chris Evans, a former art instructor from UCLA, paints at his easel; twenty-five-year-old Frank Ordaz works quietly, listening to cassette tapes on his earphones. Caroleen Green, the newest painter in the department and a product of the University of Southern California and the Art School of Design, mixes paints for her palette. These people are the photo-realists who create landscapes from other galaxies, architecture impossible to build, and subterranean worlds that

exist only in the director's imagination and matte painter's eye.

They paint in oils and acrylics. While acrylics dry more quickly, providing a certain convenience, they have the rather distressing quality of sometimes drying to a slightly different color. Since color matching is critical in matte-painting work, a shift of hue can have disastrous results, so the artists will often finish off a painting in oils though the first layout undercoating may be acrylic. Many of the painters at ILM also find oils easier to work with for other reasons: some say that certain colors are only found in oil, and Chris Evans asserts that oil-based paints apply more smoothly than acrylics.

In order to speed up the drying of oil paint, ILM matte painters use a "secret" solution that, when added to the oils, causes the paint to dry faster than it would normally. Michael Pangrazio claims the formula for this solution came to them from Albert Whitlock (a long-time master matte painter who works in Hollywood), though other artists dispute this claim, asserting that the quick-drying formula is really quite common and no secret at all. These kinds of "black magic" claims for formulas and mechanical inventions are common around ILM, but just when you think you have debunked a claim, it turns

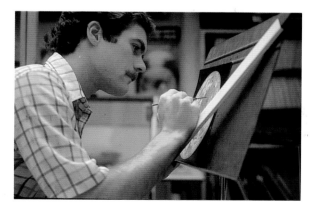

out that the secret alchemy and "trick" devices are, in fact, unique. One cannot discount these claims too quickly. . . .

The origins of matte paintings are a bit obscure, but most give credit to Norman Dawn, who first used paintings to enhance his still photographs in 1905. Max Handsheigl, his boss at the Thorp Engraving Company in Los Angeles, showed him how to improve on buildings to be photographed by placing a sheet of glass between the camera and the subject and painting the improvements on the glass. In 1907, Dawn put his skill to work on his first film, *California Missions*. He used the trick to repair the rather dilapidated appearance of some of the old mission structures. He went on to work for Universal, MGM, and Pathé, in a prolific career lasting over sixty-three years. He kept a record of 861 effects shots that he personally produced, and he also trained many artists who followed in his footsteps, creating thousands of paintings through the 1920s, 30s, 40s, and 50s.

This tradition continues today with the artists at ILM. Their paintings are for film, not museums, though many could hang alongside the great master landscape artists' work and not look out of place. It is remarkable how casually the matte artists treat their individual works. Magnificent painted backings thirty feet wide and twenty feet long that could easily sell as framable canvases have been painted over with a broad roller to create another scene or to provide a miniature background with a dark backing. Often a painting on glass is scraped entirely clean in order to paint another on the clear surface.

Michael Pangrazio can make a small photolike painting on white paperboard in less than an hour. Though it looks like a miniature masterpiece, he regards it simply as a working illustration. In one meet-

Above left: Michael Pangrazio paints a snowy background for *The Empire Strikes Back.*

Above right: Matte painter Caroleen Green paints foreground trees for *The Ewok Adventure.*

Below: Michael Pangrazio completes a matte painting for *Return of the Jedi.*

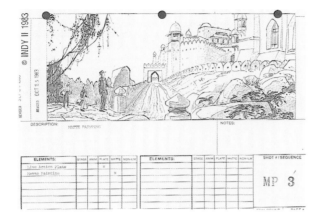

Above: A storyboard by ILM art director Joe Johnston, shows the exterior Pankot Palace shot as it was planned for *Indiana Jones and the Temple of Doom.*

Middle: Michael Pangrazio's matte painting of the same Pankot Palace scene. Live action will be inserted into the black areas. The entire shot was flipped right for left.

Below: The final composite shot from *Indiana Jones and the Temple of Doom* showing Indy, Willie, and Short Round approaching the Pankot Palace.

ing with a new young director, Pangrazio presented several of these small paintings as possible matte ideas. The director had been hypercritical of most of the other proposals at the meeting, but he could barely hide his respect for the beauty of these small works. Nonetheless, to retain his reputation as "difficult to please," he suggested several minor changes: "Lower this mountain line and enlarge that cloud." Pangrazio took the paintings and drew on them with a ballpoint pen, making the rough changes requested. The director's face dropped as the pen cut across the delicately painted surface. This was not a theatrical display by the artist; it simply demonstrated the way he regarded the pictures—as working documents, not fine art. Artists working in motion pictures in general, and at ILM in particular, must be willing to discard work and start all over again when changes are made in a film. It is the finished film that matters, not its artifacts.

Despite the artists' attitude, others in the Lucasfilm organization recognize that real art is being created and try to preserve it whenever possible. For that reason, Lucasfilm has an archivist whose function it is to collect finished work and store it properly. She is excellent at her job, yet is sometimes frustrated when paintings are altered or lost by the artists before she can catalog and store them behind the locked doors of the archive. During the making of *The Ewok Adventure*, Michael Pangrazio decided that he could modify an old painting for use in this new film. He asked the archive department if they could return one of his paintings from *Return of the Jedi*, a scene showing a full shot of an Ewok village. The archivist was hesitant to release the painting for she knew Pangrazio felt no qualms about painting over his previous work. She asked George Lucas if it was all right to release the painting; George gave his permission and the painting was reluctantly returned to the matte painting department. Pangrazio couldn't understand why there was a problem. "After all," he said, "if we can't use them again to paint over for a new movie, what good are

they?" The archivist asked if he was going to alter the painting. Pangrazio admitted he would probably change it, but said he would be happy to paint over the changes when he was finished with the new film, and make it look again as it had for *Return of the Jedi*.

When a scene in a film requires a set or location that is impractical or even impossible to find or build, it is time to consider the special effect MATTE PAINTING. If it is done to perfection, an audience can be completely deceived into thinking the image on the screen is real one. When poorly designed or executed, a matte painting is embarrassingly artificial in appearance; many directors reject the concept because they remember the bad ones they have seen elsewhere in other films and think the problem is common to all such effects. Yet these same individuals have probably been fooled many times

Above left: Michael Pangrazio completes a matte painting for *Young Sherlock Holmes.*

Above: The Pangrazio painting when added to the live action "plate."

Gatefold: A matte painting of the planet Vulcan from *Star Trek III: The Search for Spock.*

by a good application of the technique. *The Ewok Adventure* had forty matte paintings in it—an expert might be able to identify the majority of them but at least 10 to 20 percent would elude even the most astute observer. In fact, there may be paintings in this book that come as a surprise; when playing this game of "find the painting," experts often claim to have found matte paintings that in fact were actual full-scale objects or real scenery!

A major factor in the effectiveness of a matte painting is the skill of the painter. To be a matte artist, the painter must have the ability to duplicate actual scenes with near photographic realism. One of the tests given a prospective ILM matte artist is to paint a copy of a color photograph; when the painting and photo are subsequently held side by side, it is expected that the two will be nearly identical. From across the room, even the most discriminating observers should argue over which is the original.

A good matte painter, however, is more than an accomplished draftsman. Even though a surprising number of artists have this photo-realistic ability, they are often expected *not* to use it. Perfect photo-real-

Right: Details of an Ewok village matte painting by Chris Evans.

Below: Ewok village painting composited with live action for *Return of the Jedi.*

ism is not desired most of the time. Michael Pangrazio and Chris Evans (the two most experienced in the department) possess a looseness of style that blends perfectly with the rather coarse motion picture image. Pangrazio often stands back from the painting surface and holds the long brush handle at maximum length, stabbing at the painting. On close inspection a good matte painting seems to lack

such things as a tree or the edge of a road. Rough textures such as foliage or rocks also allow for a less visible matte line when the overlap occurs. Of course, the line must allow room for the action to take place without running into the matte painting; the line must also avoid clean, flat areas such as a clear blue sky. Achieving a perfect match of the shade and density of a live scene and a painting without some line or texture to separate the two would be quite difficult, if not impossible.

Even when the matte line is perfectly placed, matching the colors of the painting with those of the plate requires painstaking tests. A series of sample colors are painted on a board, which is then held next to the plate picture to be matched. The two are photographed, and the developed picture is studied to find the blend of colors that best matches the photographic plate; color as well as shades of light and dark must be perfect. Today's matte painter certainly has a more difficult job than his predecessor who worked only on black-and-white films.

*F*or another scene in *Raiders of the Lost Ark*, ILM was called upon to execute a very difficult painting. George Lucas and

Below: Executive Producer Howard Kazanjian (left), ILM general manager Tom Smith (center), and visual effects supervisor Dennis Muren (in German spy costume) on the set of *Raiders of the Lost Ark* in 1980.

Far right, top to bottom: The amphibious aircraft from *Raiders of the Lost Ark*, seen here in a cluttered boatyard. ILM cameramen prepare to film the aircraft using a VistaVision camera mounted on a tower. The aircraft, with actors positioned on the scaffolding, as photographed by the VistaVision camera. An unwanted background—an RV storage area—can be seen on the far left. The water plate for the amphibious aircraft scene, shot by cameraman Jim Veilleux.

Steven Spielberg wanted to show Indiana Jones boarding a 1930s amphibious clipper ship. The nearest plane of this type in operating condition was five thousand miles from Northern California, but less than ten miles from ILM, at the Richmond boatyard, sat the old hulk of a "Short Solent" amphibious plane. It was slowly being restored by a small group of dedicated amphibious aircraft devotees. Only one engine was in running condition; with large holes in its fuselage, the plane would sink like an anchor if it were put in the water. It also need a new coat of paint to keep it faithful to the period of the film. Obviously, this was a job for the "wizards" of ILM.

The scene was shot this way: A Vista-Vision camera was placed on a stabilized tower fifty meters from the plane, providing a full side profile. Shallow trays of water were set nearby to reflect ripples of sunlight on the fuselage, and a scaffolding was erected next to the passenger entry door to simulate a loading dock. After one day of preparation, the plane was ready to shoot. To a passing observer, the scene would

appear senseless: an old plane with holes in it parked in the middle of a field of junk being boarded by ILM employees dressed in period clothes! To make matters worse, behind the plane, in full view of the camera, was a recreational vehicle storage area with an array of trailers and mobile homes!

As the director called for action, the plane's only operating engine coughed to a start and the camera rolled. Stagehands below the plane paddled the water in large shallow trays to reflect the sun in an appropriate manner as distinguished-looking travelers boarded the plane. The next day, in another part of San Francisco Bay, an

ILM camera crew was filming another Vista-Vision "plate" to be used for this same shot. This second plate, the harbor water, would be added to the shot to fill out the picture and make it look like the plane was actually sitting in the water.

So much for the "real" action. Now came the hard part. At ILM, the director picked the best shot and Alan Maley, head

Far right: Artist Alan Maley does a matte painting for *Dragonslayer*.

Above: Photo doubles for Indiana Jones, Short Round, and Willie Scott on location. The Indian village matte painting will fill in the rest of the scene for *Indiana Jones and the Temple of Doom*.

Right: The matte painting composited with live action for the finished scene.

Below: Indian village matte painting by Michael Pangrazio for *Indiana Jones and the Temple of Doom*.

of the ILM Matte Painting Department at that time, went to work painting a background appropriate for the scene. The painting was on glass, so the "live" plates would be projected through it. The area where the recreational vehicles appeared was painted over with 1930s-style cabs and packing crates. The blue sky filmed above the plane in Northern California now became a hazy background of harbor cargo-loading cranes. Below the scaffolding a solid dock was painted in. Retouch work on the damaged fuselage made it look as flawless as the day it was built. Even the airline name, in an authentic type style, was painted on its side. The harbor water that had been filmed a day later sparkled beneath it.

In the finished film, this is the sequence of actions in the matte painting shot: The engine roars to a start, attracting the viewer's attention immediately to something real (and away from the painted parts of the frame). Next, the eye moves to the people as they file along the dock to board the plane. At this point, the shot ends and the story moves on to other scenes. In the first sneak preview of *Raiders*, the shot lasted for fifteen seconds. It was too much to ask that it sustain realism this long on the screen; the surrounding painted areas could not stand the scrutiny of the critical eye. When the shot was cut to its final eight seconds, it did exactly what was expected of it: few viewers could tell it was a painting the first or even the second time they saw the film.

Despite the fact that the goal is always the same—to blend real action with a painted environment—ILM uses several varieties of illusions to achieve this end.

REAR PROJECTION

Perhaps the simplest matte compositing system is a REAR SCREEN PROJECTION system. It works like this: A movie projector is placed behind a painting done on glass. If live action is desired in a portion of the shot, the paint is removed from that part of the glass, leaving a "window" in the painting, and a piece of frosted plastic (the translucent screen) is placed behind this "window." As the camera photographs the painting, the prephotographed live-action scene is projected on the translucent screen and is visible through the glass. Since the projector is behind the screen, the process is naturally called rear screen projection.

So much for terminology. Here's a more concrete example: Imagine a five-story building painted in great detail on a large sheet of glass, with one of the structure's windows left clear. Behind that clear space a diffused material, similar to a frosted shower curtain, is placed. A previously shot motion picture scene showing the interior of a room with people in it is projected onto this material. The scene is filled with

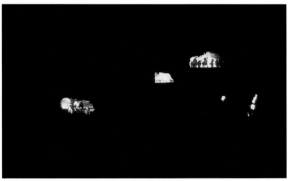

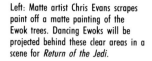
Left: Matte artist Chris Evans scrapes paint off a matte painting of the Ewok trees. Dancing Ewoks will be projected behind these clear areas in a scene for *Return of the Jedi.*

Below: The live-action dancing Ewoks, projected without the matte painting.

lively action. As the camera photographs the painted building, the live action scene on the translucent screen shows through the glass. The illusion of there actually being people inside a room in this "building" is complete.

Of course, the picture need not be limited to the projection of one scene in one window. Several projectors can be used to create many animated areas in the painting. In *Return of the Jedi,* twelve images were projected for the Ewok Village scene, each image showing a group of Ewoks celebrating around their huts in the trees. Additional projections added torches in the trees to illuminate the settings. Since the number of projection machines is limited, the film is exposed many times, with several projected images exposed one at a time. The film is then

Cameraman Neil Krepela sets up a front projection matte painting shot. The glass reflects the image from the projector onto the screen while the camera "sees" through the glass and photographs a composite image.

rewound inside the camera and re-exposed; each new exposure has a corresponding new projection exposure added while all else is kept dark.

FRONT PROJECTION

Practically all the matte paintings done for *The Empire Strikes Back* were photographed using front projection of action scenes over paintings on glass. Whereas rear projection puts the projector behind the screen, facing the viewer or camera, FRONT PROJECTION puts the projector on the same side of the screen as the camera—in front. It is similar to the standard movie theater where the audience and the projector are both in front of the screen and the screen is reflecting the image back to the viewer. In this case the viewer is the camera.

Front projection in matte painting special effects is a little more involved than normal film projection, but relatively easy to understand. Here is how it works: A scene is painted on a sheet of glass, and an unpainted area, perhaps in the center of the picture, is left clear—this is where the projected image will end up. A special screen is placed behind this part of the painting. Rather than the frosted material used for rear projection, this is a solid screen made of Scotchlite—a commercial product that reflects light back to its source, quite similar to a reflecting stop sign or roadside reflector. (This is the same material they put on dog collars to protect your pet's life on the road at night.) Since the projector and the camera are sharing the same side of the screen, the trick is to project an image on the screen without getting the camera in the way. Furthermore, to get the best results the camera and the projector should be exactly in line with one another, facing the screen from the same optical perspective. That is like saying they must share the same seat in the theater. How is this possible? In magic, nothing is impossible—you just use mirrors.

A partially reflecting mirror is put at a 45-degree angle to the camera lens. The projector is placed next to the camera and faces at a right angle to the direction the camera is pointed. If you were to place your eye right where the projector is pointing, you would see exactly what the camera sees. When the image is projected across the front of the camera, most of the light passes through the glass onto a black cloth at a 90-degree angle to the camera. Some of the light (and consequently the image) is reflected by the partial mirror onto the painting. The light projected onto the painting is of such low intensity that it is virtually invisible to the camera; but where the glass is clear and the Scotchlite material has been placed behind it, a bright image is reflected back to the camera. The camera now looks through the mirror, and a total composite image containing both the reflected photographic plate and the painting is visible.

Why go to all that trouble just to project an image onto a painting? Some feel that a front-projected image has advantages over a rear screen projection since it is sharper and more evenly illuminated from one side to the other than the rear-projected image.

ILM was certainly not the first to use the front projection technique—it has been around for years. Partially silvered mirrors (commonly called "one-way" mirrors or beam splitters) have been used by prestidigitators for more than a century, but in motion pictures front projection systems have only been popular since material like the Scotchlite screen has been available. It is most commonly used as a special process for projecting scenes behind actors, like car scenes, with front projection of the moving background. (It is interesting that when such scenes are shot, no one on the set but the camera operator looking through the camera lens can see the projection as it will appear on the final film. To anyone standing off-axis, the projected image appears dim or even invisible.) Still photographers working in a studio also use this system to place pre-photographed backgrounds behind studio set-ups. At ILM, however, front projection photography is mainly used for matte painting photography. Where actors require special backgrounds behind them, ILM prefers to use the blue screen "traveling matte" process in which backgrounds are optically added to the scene.

LATENT IMAGE MATTE PAINTING

The previously mentioned systems for the blending of actual plate photography with a painting both use some form of projec-

tion. In 1982, when work began on *E.T.: The Extra-Terrestrial*, ILM experimented with a technique they'd never used before: LATENT IMAGE MATTE PAINTINGS. I recall first seeing the result of the technique in the scene where Elliott goes out in the backyard at night and discovers E.T. hidden in the woodshed. The scene with the actor was shot in a studio and the matte painter was asked to add a night sky and moon over a cornfield. Though some difficulty was encountered in this first attempt, the process was so promising that since then the department had wanted to experiment further with it. Unfortunately, the opportunity never arose until three years later, when *The Ewok Adventure* was done at ILM.

The more frequently utilized techniques of front and rear screen matte paintings have a subtle defect that will sometimes show up when the film is transferred to television. Occasionally, the projected images used with the paintings take

Final composite shot of the adventurers mounting the steps of the Gorax's castle, from *The Ewok Adventure*.

on a slightly different hue than the painting itself. Everyone was concerned that the matte paintings for *The Ewok Adventure* look good—this was to be the first dramatic film ever made by Lucasfilm especially for television—so it was decided that the long-neglected latent image technique would be the preferred method for this film.

The latent image technique involves shooting a scene with a part of the picture blocked off; before the film is developed, a painting is made to fill in the area that was left unexposed. The final shot is a blending of both real and painted material, as with other techniques, but since the finished shot is on the original film and no extra projections are needed, the quality is outstanding. The colors of the painting and the real scene will most often match almost perfectly even when transferred to television.

In *The Ewok Adventure*, a shot was called for showing a caravan of Ewoks and children as they moved close to the mon-

ster Gorax's castle. The landscape was to be rough, the castle foreboding. It was unnecessary to build the twenty-story castle when ILM was available to provide the setting quite easily by painting. This is a typical situation in which matte painting technique is used, and the shot could have been done as a projection matte composite. However, this shot used the latent image method.

In this situation, the live-action scene was staged in a rock quarry a few miles from ILM. The matte camera crew set up the shot before the arrival of the actors with their horses. Viewing the shot through the camera, we sighted the trail where the caravan was to travel and blackened surrounding areas by placing tape over the matte box in front of the lens. These areas would be unexposed during the shot (matted out).

Before the first take with our Ewoks, we filmed a "dry run" in which twenty seconds of film were exposed prior to the real scene. (This test piece of film would become very important later on.) After the scene was filmed, this exposed film was removed from the camera and put in a labeled can. It is at this point that the latent image shot differs greatly from other methods: rather than developing all the

Right: Craig Barron gets a meter reading for a glass shot setup for *The Ewok Adventure.*

Below: Matte painter Frank Ordaz completes a matte painting for *The Ewok Adventure.*

film at once, only a few feet—the film shot before each take without action—were cut off and sent to the lab. When a print of the test piece returned from the lab, it was threaded into a camera with a light shining through the film. The camera acted as a projector, and the image was visible on a

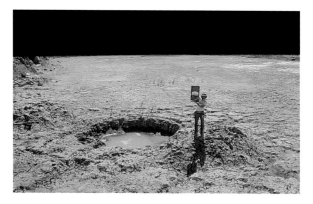

white screen that would soon become the matte painting. The exposed area showed the trail in the quarry where the Ewoks would soon travel; the rest of the picture was black where the camera lens had been covered with tape. Then the matte painter went to work. Tracing from the projection, the artist oulined the area that must be filled in. A tortured landscape was painted in the areas that were not exposed during the filming, and in this particular shot, the artist added a wonderful touch: a bright sun, breaking over the rough, rocky cliffs. After enough of the painting was completed for a test, it went back to the fixed camera, where, again, the small sample of developed film was projected through the camera. Next, the artist compared the two elements—the real picture and the paint-

Above: A latent image plate as it appears before the matte painting is added.

Left: Final composite shot of the adventurers trekking across a vast wasteland, from *The Ewok Adventure*.

ing being made to fill out the edges. It took several such comparisons before a test double exposure could be made. A piece of the remaining undeveloped film was loaded into the camera and a second exposure was made, combining the painting

with the image shot on location and already on the film. This small strip was then sent to the lab. The following day, the sample came back from the lab and was examined by the artist and the cameraman. The process was repeated again and again until the blend of the two images looked nearly perfect. Finally, the shot with the actors and horses was double-exposed with the painting, and a strikingly realistic matte shot resulted.

Although the results of the latent image process are generally superb, the risk of running out of test material is a major reason many matte artists would rather not attempt its use. During the early experiments with this process on the *E.T.* backyard shot, ILM almost ran out of test

Above: Latent image plate before painting is added.

Right: Final composite shot of the adventurers on a narrow mountain ledge, from *The Ewok Adventure*.

material and had great difficulty completing a shot. Had they ruined all the footage, it might have meant setting up the shot and doing it all over again at great expense, or editing around it. Fortunately, though, the last attempt worked. Another risk of the latent image process is that once a composition is planned and photographed, it is very hard to change the design after shooting the action plate. Even though George Lucas liked the looks of the latent image shots for the Ewok movie, he did not like the inflexibility. He also disliked the fact that he could not cut the action portion of the plate into the film while the painting was in progress. With this system you see nothing of the final shot until it is all done.

On the whole, however, the great advantage of the latent image matte painting process is that the picture is of first-generation quality. Other processes yield a picture at least one generation removed from the original. Rephotographing a photo does little except accent all the defects—colors become extreme, dark areas become very dark, light areas tend to burn out, and the graininess of the image increases. These deficiencies are further amplified when the film is shown on TV. I have often been disappointed to see small flaws in good special effects work magnified when transferred from film to video. The latent image process eliminates many of these problems.

CAMERA MOVEMENT WITH A MATTE PAINTING SHOT

Normally, the camera taking a matte painting shot must be extremely rigid, since even the slightest movement makes the shot a failure. Even the mechanical process that moves the film through the camera must get special attention; should

the machining be only several thousandths of an inch off, the camera cannot be used. As a result, one of the telltale signs of a standard matte painting is a lack of camera panning or tilting. Given the technical problems, it is a big challenge to make a matte painting shot that *does* pan or tilt. On the Ewok film, we asked for such shots and they were provided.

Rather than film the scene with a normal camera, a VistaVision camera was used, allowing us to expose twice the film area with each frame. The VistaVision shot was blacked out except for areas where the action would take place, stan-

Above: Latent image matte painting from *Return of the Jedi*.

Below: Final composite shot of R2-D2 and C-3PO from *Return of the Jedi*.

Gatefold: Final composite shot of the gantry in the heart of Cloud City from *The Empire Strikes Back*.

Right: Michael Pangrazio's matte painting of the Imperial Death Star hangar from *Return of the Jedi*.

Below: Final composite shot incorporating a matte painting and live action from *Return of the Jedi*.

The Imperial forces greet Darth Vader. Frank Ordaz's matte painting from *Return of the Jedi* without the live action scene added.

dard procedure for any matte shot. To add camera movement, however, the scene was rephotographed going from the large VistaVision format down to normal 35mm film. The camera panned across the VistaVision frame. In some cases, the camera did a horizontal pan and in others a vertical tilt, and the resulting scenes were quite effective.

With the latent image process, the only safe way of doing a camera move is to rephotograph a shot from a larger film format, putting a camera move into the second-generation shot. There are other options with other processes; when the action plate is projected from behind, for example, the camera can pan over the painting. This effect was used successfully in *Return of the Jedi* as the camera followed Vader's shuttle to its landing on the Death Star. There is a dream that one day a camera controlled by a computer will be able to have its movement recorded the first time it is used in the field and then played back so

exactly that the camera will be able to pan over a painting in the same manner without ever shifting out of line. ILM has a device called the *Field Recorder* that was designed to record moves in the field that could be duplicated in the special effects studio. But although it has provided some rather good effects (such as the toys flying around the room in *Poltergeist*), the Field Recorder has yet to accomplish the ideal of a studio shot locked together with a shot done outside.

Nevertheless, in most cases camera moves cannot be too extreme, for when the camera moves horizontally, perspective lines do not change on the flat painting and so the picture seems to retain a constant point of view. When the camera trucks in or out on a painting or photograph, the effect is simply one of cropping; it looks like a zoom lens, not a moving camera. Changes in perspective occur when a camera moves around a solid model. We know we are looking at a three-dimen-

Composite shot from *Return of the Jedi*, including the live action scene.

sional object, rather than a flat picture.

A good illustration of this difference is found in *The Empire Strikes Back* near the end of the film: a hospital ship is suspended in space; Luke Skywalker and Princess Leia are inside, sitting near a large window. The camera moves to the outside, where we see the exterior of the ship (a model) with the group inside the window (a projected scene). The ship passes the camera, right to left. The characters projected on the window of the ship move as the ship moves. However, the shot fails to succeed completely because the perspective inside the room *does not change as the model moves past us.* The effect is one of flatness behind the window, and it betrays the means used to achieve the effect; therefore, it doesn't work as well as it should have. We are so used to seeing things in the real world where perspective is taken for granted that we forget it is there, but when a picture is shown to us that is accurate in every detail except for perspective, it is amazing

how even an unsophisticated viewer can spot that something is wrong.

So although it can be very effective to move the camera over a painting containing projected images, there is always the danger that the shot will reveal itself to be flat and fake, because the lines of perspective do not change.

In a sense, the Matte Painting Department at ILM is a whole effects-shop-within-a-shop. The department is often called upon to create illusions that go beyond the limits of a painting: they may add miniature set pieces to a painting, or sculpt and properly light cotton on glass to simulate impressive cloud formations. They may also use models or paintings in several layers to achieve a feeling of depth. When coupled with the capability of the Optical Department, the Matte Painting Department adds even more power to ILM's abundant bag of tricks.

Despite all the technology and even the painter's artistry, the most effective matte paintings are those that are carefully planned and designed. No amount of draftsmanship or technology can save a poorly conceived shot. When properly executed and edited into the sequence for which it was intended, a well-planned shot can help keep the film within its budget and look spectacular on the screen as well.

MICHAEL PANGRAZIO

Michael Pangrazio had little formal training in painting. In fact, though he persisted in taking art courses in high school, he usually failed them because his teachers did not regard him as a cooperative student. He remembers one teacher, however, who was about to fail him until he turned in an extra-credit painting; after seeing the work, the astonished teacher gave Pangrazio an A in the course.

Before coming to ILM, Michael Pangrazio had limited professional experience as an artist. Out of high school, he worked briefly as a scenic artist for a TV network. He was first hired as a "bucket boy," and soon found out this meant that he was to wash out the paint buckets, clean the dirty brushes, and act as general flunky. He had been working conscientiously for about a week when he learned that union seniority rules required that he do this job for another seven years before he could have a chance to paint. One of the old-timers told him to stick with it because it was a wonderful opportunity to get into the union; Michael told them where to put their brushes, and quit.

The only thing he regretted about losing his job was the salary; he was earning pretty good money cleaning the buckets and brushes. His next job didn't pay so well: he went to work for a small special effects studio in Hollywood that offered starvation wages. He rode around Hollywood on a bicycle and wore old clothes. Then, in 1978, he met Joe Johnson, art director of ILM, who was looking for new talent to bring to ILM in Northern California. Michael was poorly dressed and only had a few dog-eared slides of his work in his shirt pocket. He showed the work to Joe, convinced that he would never hear from him again.

Later that year, after Michael's twenty-first birthday, he got a call from ILM. They wanted to hire him to work as an apprentice to Alan Maley, an established matte painter. Michael asked if there was much bucket cleaning involved, and Joe didn't understand what he was talking about. Michael joined ILM, only to find out that Maley himself had not been hired. He was an apprentice without a master.

Enter Ralph McQuarrie, gentle master artist, who saw in the young Pangrazio enormous raw talent. He took the youngster under his wing and began to teach him. Pangrazio watched McQuarrie work and questioned him like a precocious child. McQuarrie had limitless patience, and even when the pressure was on to turn out more work, he always had time to stop and instruct young Pangrazio. By the time McQuarrie left ILM after *The Empire Strikes Back*, Pangrazio was equalling the master. In less than three years, after proving himself again and again to be a

master of color and the brush, Pangrazio became the head of the Matte Painting Department at ILM.

When asked what he feels are the most important characteristics a matte painter must have, Pangrazio replies without hesitation, "Tolerance and the ability to keep your ego out of your work."

He advises would-be matte artists to prepare for a job such as his by copying color photographs and then submitting their work to the scrutiny of someone whose opinion they respect. In the planning of a matte painting shot, he feels it is most important to keep one's mind fixed on "the point of the shot!" He elaborates: "Think of what this shot is trying to say. It won't be on the screen for long, so the point must be made quickly. What you see first is the most important thing in the shot. If it's a painting of a tent at sunset, paint it so that you see the tent first, then as the eye moves around the painting perhaps you'll see a horse or stars in the sky. If the object of the painting is not quickly and clearly apparent, the shot will not be effective."

Michael Pangrazio is willing to tell of his failures as well as his successes. He feels he must remember things that go wrong so that he won't repeat old mis-

takes. On *Star Trek II*, he says that he was instructed to paint a shot he did not design. He called it the "Eden Cave" shot. There was no one focal point in the painting; no one knew what the point of the shot was to be. Consequently, the picture turned to "mush" on the screen. Though the ILM matte painting department came back and did a beautiful job for Paramount Pictures with the subsequent *Trek* film,

Above: Ralph McQuarrie works on a matte painting of Cloud City for *The Empire Strikes Back*.

Middle: Michael Pangrazio paints a background for *The Empire Strikes Back*.

Below: Artist Michael Pangrazio and photographer Neil Krepela discuss a matte painting for *Return of the Jedi*.

Star Trek III: The Search for Spock, for Pangrazio *Star Trek II: The Wrath of Kahn* was a low point in the career of the ILM mattte painting department.

What does he consider as an example of his best personal work? This causes him to ponder for a moment then he answers: "The warehouse shot at the end of *Raiders of the Lost Ark.*" This is a shot that is rarely identified by filmgoers as a matte painting, and has all the qualities lacking in the Eden Cave shot for *Trek II.*

Other high points in his career at ILM include his work for *Dragonslayer, E.T.: The Extra-Terrestrial, Return of the Jedi,* and *Indiana Jones and the Temple of Doom.*

Asked who he respects most in the matte painting business he answers, Albert Whitlock, the matte artist who has won countless awards for his work at Universal Studios. Whitlock is now retired from the brush trade.

When one closely examines a Pangrazio painting, the brush strokes are very loose; detail seems to be lacking, and the surface looks like someone has dabbed colors at random. Yet this is what makes the total work look more real—if the artist is "tight," the painting looks too con-

trolled. Looseness also allows for accidents to occur with the paint that look like natural elements of the composition. For Pangrazio it is a matter of intellect versus nature; loose work is more natural. Then he adds with a smile, "It is also faster, and speed is required to turn out the amount of work that must be done."

He does not visualize the finished work when he paints, it just seems to come from his hand automatically. He watches as the instinct to paint is let loose.

He claims to be a slob when he works. Chris Evans, the artist at the easel to his right, is immaculately neat. Pangrazio, on the other hand, places his paints on the palette in random order, splashes himself and sometimes the floor with color as he works and generally has an instinctive approach to his art. He also does not follow the traditional method of roughing out the work and then going into detail as the work progresses, preferring to go right for a finished product as he moves rapidly over the surface.

He holds Chris Evans in high esteem and claims that there is a friendly competition between them. In order to devote all his time to painting, Pangrazio stepped down as department head in 1984 and turned the administrative job over to Evans.

Right: Michael Pangrazio works on a painting for *The Ewok Adventure.*

Below: Michael Pangrazio (left) and Chris Evans (right) in the ILM matte painting studio. Here, the contrasting work styles of the two artists are evident!

Of the great directors he has worked with, Pangrazio has these comments. "George Lucas loves matte paintings and is very enthusiastic and fairly easy to please; but George piles on the work and when you get it done, he gives you more. Lucas hopes to use matte paintings more and more in the future. Steven Spielberg, on the other hand, is not so enthusiastic about what matte paintings can do. He is harder to please because of his suspicions about the matte painting medium."

In 1985, Michael Pangrazio decided to leave the high pressure of his position as head of the ILM matte painting department and turn back to a purer form of his first love: full days of just painting.

He has moved from California to a rustic home on a lovely quiet pond in southern Oregon. He paints in a studio over the garage and now creates paintings for sale to private collectors. His first show sold out in three weeks. He paints fanciful compositions showing elves and fairies in enchanted-looking forests. He plans to return to ILM perhaps once or twice a year to take on a film or two, working for Evans. He does not wish to continue as he had for the past six years, with a steady stream of films and the responsibility of running a department. Chris Evans enjoys the challenge of his new job as head of the department, so ILM's matte paintings are still in good hands.

Ironically, had Pangrazio stayed at the TV network to work as bucket boy, it would only have been recently that they would have let him take brush in hand to do his first painting.

CHRIS EVANS

Chris Evans, head of ILM's matte department, feels that artists get most of their training through experience. Unlike Pangrazio, Evans had a great deal of formal training. He majored in art at the University of California, Los Angeles, and he taught art at the university and gained a master's degree at UCLA. Despite this, he feels that he learned most from practical experience, since he has always regarded himself as a "realist" painter and realist painting was not fashionable in art school when he attended in the 1970s. Some of the faculty were not supportive and tried to dissuade him from painting in this style.

Before coming to ILM, he was earning a living doing commission portraits and landscapes. However, he didn't like the isolation of the job; he felt like a hermit, and wanted to get out and work with others. One day he went to the movies and saw *The Empire Strikes Back*. Noticing that there were paintings in the film, he was inspired to write to George Lucas and volunteer his services as an artist. A friend of his knew that Lucasfilm had an office near Universal Studios and volunteered to take his sample slides to the office for delivery to ILM. He had no idea how special effects were done; all he knew was that he wanted to do some paintings for a *Star Wars* movie. He found out that George himself was impossible to reach, but he was referred to ILM. When he came up for a job interview at ILM, he saw a matte painting for the first time. He was amazed that so many paintings had been done for the film; he had thought that many scenes were real, so

Opposite page: Composite shot of the Endor Imperial landing platform from *Return of the Jedi*.

it was a big revelation. He went home after the interview with instructions to read some copies of *Cinefex* magazine.

When he began studying the magazine, he saw how incredibly complicated the whole industry was. At the time of the interview he was not even sure that he wanted a job in the film business, but after reading about visual effects he began to get really excited and felt that he would be really upset if he didn't get the job.

In 1980, at the age of twenty-four, Chris Evans, to his delight and ILM's benefit, was hired to work in the matte painting department.

What are the qualities needed to be a good matte painting artist? Chris answers: "You have to be very observant of nature. We are creating illusions of the real world. So you have to know what the light, atmosphere, and shapes are.

"You have to know what a mountain looks like at the end of the day when it is back-lit, what the sun does when it shines on leaves. The colors of nature at different

times of day. These are the images that must go into the matte painter's store of memories. Beyond that, the artist must be able to spontaneously create images of the way nature looks. He must be the master of paint and brush."

To Evans, a good matte painting is one that the audience does not know is a painting. In effect, he feels he does his job best when no one knows he has done it. He enjoys the fact that a good matte painting expands the scope of the film. With a painting, a few actors wearing costumes in the parking lot can be made to look as if they are standing on a road in ancient Rome.

Evans feels that matte paintings require a more solid compositional structure than other shots in a film. They require a strong foreground element and a good live-action plate that draws the eye. He has a theory he calls "the pyramid of believability." He explains it this way: "The matte artist must concentrate on the two lower corners at the base of a pyramid and the apex of the pyramid. These are the areas that will receive audience scrutiny. The live-action plate should be in the center and base of the pyramid. If the painting is well designed, the eye will be drawn to the center of the picture and accept the surrounding areas as real."

Evans feels that matte shots should have a bold design. Since the viewer only has a few seconds in which to see the matte shot, the eye must be drawn immediately to the live-action plate. If there is no definite compositional element to draw the eye to the plate, the eye will scan the whole picture and give equal value to the entire image. When this happens, the artist is betrayed, and the trick does not work.

Evans's personal favorite is in *The Ewok Adventure*. It is one where the caravan of adventurers are leaving the Ewok

Matte painter Chris Evans sits in front of his painting of the landing platform from *Return of the Jedi*.

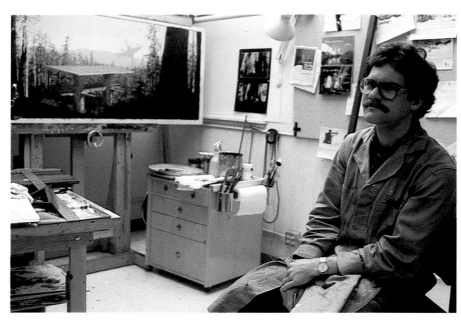

village and approaching the camera. This latent image shot shows the village in the trees; he was able to do this painting very quickly and it worked immediately.

His least favorite work, like Pangrazio's, was the Eden Cave scene done for *Star Trek II: The Wrath of Khan*. The live-action plate was too small and the camera did not move. Even if it were real, even if it had been actually shot in a "real" Eden Cave, Evans feels it still would have looked phony.

What the matte artist is trying to achieve is the *suggestion* of detail rather than the *description* of it. The realist painter might wish to paint every crack in a tree, but the matte artist does not have the time to do this. The matte artist suggests the cracks. For that reason, enlarged details of a matte painting invariably lack detail—the style is closer to impression-ism than realism. Evans uses the term "suggestion-ism." The artist paints tex-tures using the structure of the brush, sponge, or wad of paper; these textures and splashes of paint suggest realism that isn't actually there.

When Evans paints, he visualizes him-self as being "in the place" that is being portrayed. He asks himself: "Where is the light coming from? What is the quality of that light and the atmosphere?" Light and atmosphere guide the appearance of everything in the space being painted. He "sees" the location in his mind.

Evans worked only in oils before com-ing to ILM. He soon learned to deal with acrylics, cartoon colors, and airbrush (pri-marily for clouds).

Asked to compare the two directors Lucas and Spielberg, Evans states he has great admiration for both of them but finds them quite different in directorial style. "Lucas tends to understate a scene,

Spielberg always wants overstatement." He tells of Steven Spielberg enthusiasti-cally describing how the cliff in *Indiana Jones and the Temple of Doom* had to "drop away to infinity . . . very, very high . . . very dangerous." Evans said if George Lucas were asking for the same shot he would simply say, "They come out on this cliff."

He credits Michael Pangrazio as being the greatest influence on him as a matte artist. Alan Maley and Albert Whitlock are also artists whose work he respects and from whom he has learned a great deal.

He warns anyone wanting to get into this field to leave their ego at home. The work is not Art—the film is a work of art and the painting is simply one element in it. The work is also a team activity. The director, art director, and visual effects supervisor all have an input into the shot. The artist quite often has a great deal of freedom (especially when working for George Lucas), but nonetheless his per-sonal feeling is really not expressed in the painting. "After all," he adds, "most of the paintings have big holes in them where the live action plate is added."

However, Evans finds pleasure in thinking that what he does will be seen by millions. His work on *E.T.* yielded unex-pected rewards when "that little film we were all having fun with" turned out to be much bigger than anyone ever realized. It influenced millions, and Evans believes it had a positive message. He was proud to have played a part in the making of that film.

Evans's work is not totally impersonal; he adds his own private visual jokes in some of his paintings: The partially com-pleted Death Star in *Return of the Jedi* holds some hidden San Francisco sky-lines. The *E.T.* panorama at night shows a street with "every fast-food chain in America on it" and a drive-in movie theater screen running *Star Wars*. One shot in *The Ewok Adventure* has Winnie the Pooh painted in a tree.

Evans feels the real secret to successful matte painting is revealed in the ILM logo: the magician with the wand. "The magician moves the wand to divert your attention while the other hand does the trick. We don't see the trick because we are looking at the wand; we have been distracted. Well, the live-action plate is the diverting, moving wand and the painting is the trick hand. By the time we turn our attention to looking at the painting, the shot is all done and we're left with the impression that we saw something real, though it was only a painting."

CRAIG BARRON

At the age of eighteen, Craig Barron had graduated from high school and was attending classes at San Francisco State University. He had always been passionately interested in film and in fact had made a few experimental films of his own. Now he was taking classes to learn how to operate a professional film printer. While attending school, he had a chance to meet Neil Krepela, an assistant cameraman at the newly reassembled Industrial Light and Magic; Craig dreamed of working for the Lucas organization.

Through Krepela, he arranged for an interview with visual effects supervisor Richard Edlund. He knew that his youth and lack of experience would work against him so he lied about his age and went into the interview determined to succeed. Academy Award–winner Edlund received him in his small cluttered office just off the main stage, smoking unfiltered Camel cigarettes and talking enthusiastically about special effects hardware—even the brass lighter he used for the cigarettes was a "trick unit" of World War I design. Craig fielded Edlund's questions as best he could, while trying to hide his awe at the opportunity to speak to him. Barron noticed some old motion picture cameras

gathering dust on Edlund's shelves. When the interview began to close in on Craig's experience and age, he commented on the fine old cameras; he had read a little about them and asked several questions, revealing his interest in the antiques. Edlund, pleased to find an audience for his passion, began a long discussion of the mechanical merits of the old classics. When time had run out on the interview, Barron left ILM confident that if Edlund had any say in the matter, the young classic camera fan would get a job at ILM.

Sure enough, a month later, when the pressure was on to complete special effects photography for *The Empire Strikes Back*, at the tender age of eighteen Craig

Cameraman Craig Barron (left), and matte artist Chris Evans (right), with the Ewok village matte painting from *Return of the Jedi*.

Barron was hired to assist Neil Krepela with photography in the Matte Painting department. That was in the fall of 1979. Today, Craig is supervisor of all Matte Department photography, in charge of photography used in the creation of matte paintings both on location and in the ILM studio, and may be one of the best in the business.

Although Craig Barron may have been the youngest person ever hired at ILM, through persistent research and personal interviews, he has been able to bridge the gap of years that separate the ILM generation from the masters who dominated the craft four decades ago. During vacations and occasional weekends he travels to Southern California in order to meet and talk to retired special effects wizards from the 1940s and 50s. He has collected hours of videotaped interviews with these old-timers and continues to add to his library. The project has more than just historical value—he has picked up many tricks and secret processes from the old masters now living out their remaining years with memories of the golden days of Hollywood. They are impressed by the young man who actually knows of and appreciates their work.

HARRISON ELLENSHAW

At the age of thirty-two, Harrison Ellenshaw was the old man at ILM. During the long night shifts while *Star Wars* was being laboriously pieced together, the young bright-eyed technicians in their early twenties would gather around Harrison and ask what filmmaking was like in the old days. Harrison would strain to remember back to those halcyon days of 1970 and '71, when he began painting mattes at the Disney Studios—back when front-projection was just a gleam in Alan Maley's eye. . . .

Maley was head of the matte department at Disney when he hired the young Ellenshaw as an apprentice matte painter at $84 a week, to work on *Bedknobs and Broomsticks*. Ellenshaw's father had spent most of his life painting mattes at Disney, though young Harrison had not gotten his job through his father's influence.

"In the early 70s there wasn't that great an interest in special effects," he recalls. "There had been an opening in the department for six months. They had gone to art schools looking for painters and everybody said, 'What? Paint for films? Paint like a photograph? That's not art.' Of course, today if you'd put an ad in the paper for a matte painter, particularly at ILM, you'd get five hundred people lined up outside the door."

Ellenshaw's talent came naturally. His college work was in psychology, not art, and in fact he never had formal art training at all. Yet he can produce large-scale paintings of gallery quality in very short order—superrealistic as matte paintings must be—"but I try not to fall in love with them," he says. "It's easy to become attached to your work when you sit for days laboring on it. Someone will come in and make a comment like 'Gosh, that's really a blue sky,' and immediately something inside of you will say *blue* sky? What the hell's he talking about? It's not that blue. You tend to take paintings very personally, and that's why matte artists are crazy people. You have to keep a perspective on your work and understand people's comments on it—say to yourself, he didn't mean the sky was too blue; he wanted to say something nice, he's not a rotten person."

After four years at Disney, Alan Maley resigned as head of the department to begin painting gallery art. At his suggestion the studio promoted Ellenshaw to replace him, over the objections of some of the old-timers. Department heads are in their forties and fifties in most major studios like Disney, and a twenty-four-year-old newly trained matte painter is hardly a conventional choice.

But Harrison's talent and managerial ability were considerable, and he did well in his new position. Under his management the Disney matte department took on its first outside work—matte paintings for *The Man Who Fell to Earth*. Harrison personally did a number of them, and as a consequence in 1976 he got a call from Jim Nelson about some more outside work for a sci-fi film from a young filmmaker named George Lucas.

A few days later Nelson visited Ellenshaw with some production illustrations by Ralph McQuarrie for the new film. "They got me excited right away," Ellenshaw remembers. 'They were very, very nice—really great. He convinced me to do the mattes for *Star Wars* at a little place they were putting together in Van Nuys." The mattes would not go through the Disney studios, they decided, but Harrison would "moonlight" in their production.

Then followed months of silence. "I didn't hear anything from anybody," he recalls. "I figured they worked out some other arrangement—I'd lost out on the job." But out of the blue came another phone call. The film had finished its live-action shooting and was ready for Harrison's hand in its mattes. He was miffed, to

Harrison Ellenshaw works on a matte painting for *The Empire Strikes Back*.

say the least. "I'd never been handed cans of film before and told, 'Here, put some paintings on this.' At Disney matte artists always took part in the plates [the live-action filming]."

But he looked at the footage and was impressed. It was all in VistaVision—very large-format, high-resolution images—and it looked extremely promising. So he began spending his nights in the new, cramped quarters of ILM and continued managing and painting at Disney during the days.

Even after substantial work he had not met George Lucas or producer Gary Kurtz—they were too involved in pickup shots and editing to spend time at the special effects facility during Harrison's night shift. Much of his time was spent working with compositing shots with the old Bell & Howell camera used in ILM's infant facility. The team adopted a method of shooting mattes by bi-packing them, one element at a time: The VistaVision images, combined with special effects elements, would be squeezed down to normal 35mm anamorphic prints. For the purposes of creating effects the color film had been separated into its three individual parts—one roll of only the red components, one of only the blue, and one of only the green. These were then recombined onto 35mm film at the final stage.

A continuing problem was George Lucas's insistence on secrecy. Most people at ILM never saw a script, so technicians like Harrison didn't really know what the shots that they were creating were about. "One of my most embarrassing moments," Harrison remembers, "was during dailies, when my first shot came up on the screen. It was the *Millennium Falcon* by the Death Star. Everyone started laughing, and I thought, Oh my God, I've failed. I just wanted to crawl into a hole. But what I had done was to put a cockpit on both sides of the spaceship. It looked more symmetrical that way. George just didn't give me enough information, only a miniature storyboard panel. The actual model I was supposed to copy was locked up at night for security reasons, and since I worked at night I never saw it."

Because so little was known right up to the last week, few people at ILM understood the plot of the story they were creating. "The only scene I actually saw was a grainy black-and-white dupe of part of Reel 6 that an editor was working on. It was Han Solo and Princess Leia at the Death Star. Everybody thought, Well, it'll be a nice B movie. Maybe the science fiction people will look at it. Then, three days before the film was going to be released, we finally saw it—and the light hit."

The fantastic success of *Star Wars* was due at least in some degree to the extraordinary matte paintings that Harrison produced. When the project was over, all the ILM technicians went their ways. Harrison continued his work at Disney. In the meantime, Alan Maley had created mattes for another studio's film, *The Spy Who Loved Me*. The mattes were designed for a relatively new process, front projection. It was a considerable success, so Disney used the process on *The Black Hole*, for which Harrison painted the mattes. At the conclusion of his work on that film he received a call from Gary Kurtz in London, who told him there was to be a sequel to *Star Wars*, *The Empire Strikes Back*. He asked Harrison to completely take over the matte painting department for the film, give up his position at Disney, and create enough art for about seventy-five shots.

Harrison finished his work on *The Black Hole* on a Friday, and on Monday he was an hour north of San Francisco in the little town of San Rafael, ready to take over Lucas's brand-new facility.

"I met Neil Krepela in the middle of this big room," Harrison remembers, "with parts of space models and optical machinery scattered all over, and he said, 'Well, this is the set-up. If we can get it together we're going to do some wonderful things.' And I thought, Oh my heavens, I've been through all this before."

They had six months to create the seventy-five shots. Ellenshaw had a small and dedicated staff, with painter Ralph McQuarrie as his chief matte artist. "Ralph kept saying to me, 'I don't want to know anything about how things work around here, I just want to paint.' And I said, 'Fine, you paint. Any shot you want to start, you do it and let me worry about making it work.' Well, he started coming in eight, ten, fifteen hours a day, just painting, while I was lucky to spend half my time painting, what with looking at tests and handling personnel affairs."

The huge workload began to take its toll. Three months went by and still none of the seventy-five shots was complete. Planning and testing were taking a tremendous amount of time, and while the department crew knew they were still on schedule, it wasn't obvious to anyone else—particularly 20th Century–Fox, the distribution company for the film. They began pressuring Lucas to stop spending money and show some footage. "I have to say this for George," Ellenshaw says, "he supported us, and he didn't relay the pressure he was getting onto the matte department. Jim [Bloom, associate producer] would come in about once a day and say, 'Hi, how are ya? Need any help?'; then this kind of furtive look: 'Anything I can do for you? Mix your paints, maybe?'"

In the fourth month, the first completed shots appeared, and soon they were coming off the printer every day or two. The crew went on extended hours; with a swing shift the facility was operating twenty-four hours a day. At the end of the six months the last of the seventy-five shots was delivered—on time, magnificently detailed, and well deserving the second Academy Award given the effects of ILM. After *The Empire Strikes Back* was com-

pleted, Harrison left ILM and returned to work on a film for Disney.

What advice would he give to a teenager who is considering going into special effects art? "If you are an artist, *do* it—just practice, practice. Learn as much as you can, so that when the opportunity arises you can bring your work to the producer and really have something to show. And always remember, in special effects art, the point is to make a scene work, not to show off your painting talent. You never get extra points for being a good artist, you get extra points for making a scene come to life. Some matte artists will look at a painting and say, Boy, that guy can really paint clouds. But I'm not interested in what he can paint. The matte painter can only equal reality, never go one better on reality—and anything less than reality is failure. If you notice how good the clouds look, then they're not good enough. Look at that building over there. You don't see every little detail on it, you just see some tone values, where the windows are, some reflections. That's reality. When you start to put too much finish into it it gets what I call 'bitty.' It just kind of sits there and calls attention to itself. Painting for total reality is a different thing. It's not always possible to get a handle on the reality of a scene. Sometimes you never do. But if this is the business you want to get into, there's only one way to do it: make art, and lots of it."

CHAPTER 8

ANIMATION AND FX

People often ask us how we make our famous lightsabers. Well, the truth is these *Star Wars* laser swords don't really exist at all and, in any case, have nothing to do with lasers. The lightsabers we see on the screen are the work of a very important group of people at ILM: the special effects animators.

Most people associate animation with cartoon characters like Donald Duck or Bugs Bunny. So do most art schools. As a result, very few animators receive the "formal" training necessary to do the kind of work needed at ILM. Above all, such work must look real, not like cartoons, and the ability to make this happen is a rare talent indeed.

At ILM, animation is used for a number of tasks that can be divided into two general categories. The first involves creating

Luke Skywalker with lightsaber.

or enhancing objects that will appear as part of the final film image, including, for instance, putting the lightsaber into Luke Skywalker's hands, streaking the sky behind Indiana Jones with lightning, and making evil spirits fly out of a *Poltergeist* television set. There are other, more subtle applications of this kind of visible animation. If we want to strengthen the spatial relationship between models that have been filmed separately and then composited into one shot, we can do this with animation. An example: an X-wing fighter is zooming over the Death Star; to enhance the union of the two individually filmed elements we can add an animated shadow of the spacecraft onto the Death Star's surface, solidifying the impression that the two objects are and always have been part of the same image.

Still another subtle enhancement is the glow emanating from "magical" objects, like the rocks in *Indiana Jones and the Temple of Doom* or the enchanted spearhead in *Dragonslayer*. This is an extremely practical application of special effects animation; in order to achieve so bright a glow in live-action filming, objects would have to be lit so intensely that their heat would be a danger to the actors. Animation is much safer and more reliable.

These applications of animation have visible presence in the final film. A large portion of special effects animation, however, is of another type altogether, our second category. This animation erases things the filmmakers don't want their audience to see. Animation can eliminate the rods that are used to move a model, or block out the everyday parts of scenery that would destroy the illusion of an alien world. If done correctly, the results of such animation will be invisible in the final image projected on the screen. Obviously, this

Animation was used to create the "shocks" used by the Emperor in *Return of the Jedi*.

type of work is critical to the success of the finished film, but unfortunately it is rarely appreciated as much as it should be.

The ROTOSCOPE CAMERA is a tool crucial to much of ILM's animation work; without it, many of the tasks the Animation Department performs would be virtually impossible to do.

A rotoscope camera is set up, like most animation cameras, by being mounted in a firm position on a high pylon, pointing down at a flat work area. The artist works on a sheet of paper with special holes at the top; registration pegs go into the holes and hold the paper in place. After each frame is drawn, the paper is removed and a clean sheet is placed on the pegs. The camera can operate either as a camera or, when a light is turned on inside, as a projector. When creating the *Star Wars* lightsabers, for example, it functioned in the latter capacity. (Actually, the lightsabers haven't always been animated. In the first *Star Wars* film, the actors in the scenes were filmed using stick swords. A Scotchlite front-projection material was wrapped

around the sticks and light was reflected from them. This worked some of the time, but often it wasn't too convincing. Because of this we turned to animation—and our rotoscope camera—for *The Empire Strikes Back* and *Return of the Jedi*.

In order to achieve the effect of a bright, solid sword blade emanating a diffused laser glow, we still begin by filming actors with stick swords, but now we insert the developed film of each lightsaber scene into our rotoscope camera. Frame by frame, the camera, acting as a projector, projects each scene onto the work area. In near darkness, an animator positions an animation cel on the work area. Each cel is a clear plastic sheet onto which the animator traces the projected image of the lightsabers in pencil. After tracing the sabers from one frame, he will push a lever and advance the film in the camera to the next frame, which shows the swords in a slightly different position. This frame is now traced onto a new animation cel, which has been placed on the work area. The process is repeated until a stack of cels is produced corresponding to each frame of a particular scene.

Right: ILM rotoscope artist Barbara Brennan works at the easel, preparing artwork which will function as a detailed, articulated matte. The processed film matte will be sent to the optical department where it will become an element in a special effects shot. Though never seen on screen, hand-drawn mattes such as these are an important tool in special effects.

Below: Chuck Eyler uses an air brush to paint a missile.

Far right: *Mechanical Concepts* computerized animation stand used at ILM.

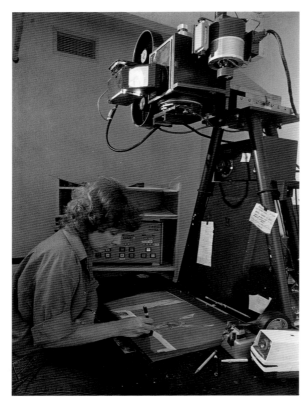

purpose is to blur the sharp image of the lines and give them a hazy appearance appropriate for a laser glow. (We will use either diffusion lens filters designed especially for this purpose or some more common material such as gauze.) The camera with the filtered lens photographs the cels one at a time against a black background; then the film is developed and turned over to the ILM Optical Department. They receive images of glowing colored sabers against a black background. The sabers appear in *precisely* the same positions as the stick swords that were used in the original live-action filming. The Optical Department now combines the animated image of the lightsabers with that of the live-action shot; on the screen, the lightsabers look as if they are actually being wielded by the actors. A similar method is used to put in lightning, like the storm in

Next, each tracing is painted with cartoon color acrylic so that the blade becomes either a red or blue line (depending on who wields the sword!). The painted cels are then put before a camera loaded with unexposed film. The camera lens is covered with a diffusing material whose

Raiders of the Lost Ark, or for adding electric "shocks," such as those the Emperor gives Luke at the climax of *Return of the Jedi*.

Although an animated image must often be distorted by using a diffusion filter, the same technique can also be used when diffusion is not required. In *Raiders of the Lost Ark*, when the Ark was being opened and the Nazis' power generator began to sputter, sharp electrical sparking was desired, so diffusion was not used.

In contrast to these dramatic and highly visible examples of animation, the invisible work of special effects animators occurs most often in the making of mattes whose purpose is to erase images or portions of images that are not meant to be a part of the finished film. Here again the rotoscope process is of the utmost import-

Left: Animation cameraman A.J. Riddle programs a movement for a shot on an ILM animation camera. This versatile system, built by *Mechanical Concepts*, with electronics by Bill Tondreau, is capable of photographing in both the standard 35mm four perforation and the eight perforation VistaVision formats.

Below: A frame blowup from *Raiders of the Lost Ark*. To create the effect of the Nazis being "zapped," the actors' shirts were rigged with lightbulbs set to go off at one-second intervals.

Right: *Oxburry* animation stand used at ILM.

Below: Bruce Vecchitto works on the *Oxburry* animation stand.

Far right top: Mike Lessa animates a special effect light blast for *Poltergeist*.

Far right middle: Animator Bruce Walters reviews work for *Explorers*.

Far right below: Barbara Brennan draws a frame for an animated laser blast on the "animation disk" easel.

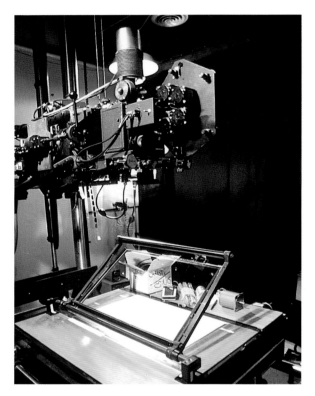

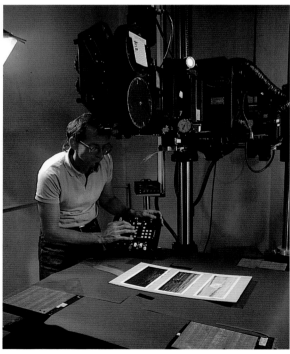

Animation is used here to create the "lightning" striking the dragon in this finished composite shot from *Dragonslayer*.

ance. During the filming of *Dragonslayer*, for instance, a special device was developed to move the dragon's legs. However, the device involved the use of rods at the base of the dragon. Obviously, the rods had to be eliminated from the picture. This was a job for the Animation Department.

As before, the animators inspected the image of the moving dragon frame by frame. Wherever the rods were visible, the animator traced their shape in pencil on the white animation paper. These pencil tracings were then covered with a transparent acetate cel, and used as guides for black painted areas, which correspond to the pencil tracings. Again, the cels are photographed and the developed film sent

to the Optical Department. This time, however, the film wouldn't become part of the final image, but would be used instead to make mattes that allow the spots where the rods were visible to blend in with the rest of the background.

The Animation Department can also create a kind of traveling matte using the rotoscope process. This is particularly helpful on those occasions when objects are filmed that cannot have a blue screen behind them. One instance of this occurred in *Return of the Jedi* when Jabba the Hutt's sail barge explodes. The explosion was actually filmed on the rooftop of a building next to ILM, so a blue screen was out of the question. However, a matte was cre-

Right: Ellen Lichtwardt, supervising rotoscope artist, loads the roto camera.

Below: Bruce Walters tests an animation concept on the Lion Lamb television animation device. This TV system allows the artist to make a frame-by-frame video tape of the scene to be animated, in order to test it prior to committing it to film.

problem with this technique, though, is that while garbage mattes work well in the theater, they tend to show up on television. Indeed, when seen on TV, both *The Empire Strikes Back* and *Star Wars* have telltale garbage mattes that occasionally show up as gray square boxes around flying spaceships. The reason is that television lacks the full range of colors and densities found on film. When the film is transferred to TV, this deficiency results in an inferior picture. Television also strips the picture of subtleties that disguise some elements such as garbage mattes. This is a problem at present, but an effort is being made to overcome this drawback to the technique.

ated using our rotoscope technique—in this case, the animators painted the entire cel black *except* for an area within tracings of the explosion that was left clear. As before, the cels were shot and the resulting film used by the Optical Department to make a matte.

Even when live action does take place before a blue screen, the Animation Department may still be called in because often the blue screen occurs only behind a moving object in the scene. Surrounding this area of the image, the Animation Department may provide a "garbage matte," which will allow the Optical Department to deal with the image's perimeter area separately from the blue-screened area. GARBAGE MATTES are used to block out areas of the screen containing unwanted objects, such as stage lights or even technicians operating equipment in the edges of the frame. A garbage matte is usually a large, roughly done area matte. It does not require the articulation of a matte that is done to block out a specific detailed object in the frame. The

*T*he movie *Poltergeist* contains some of the most complicated animation that ILM has ever done, and it is a good example of the many visible and invisible tasks performed by the Animation Department. Many things, like lightning and shock waves, were put in by rotoscoping, and a number of mattes, like that of the imploding house, were created to "place" the house in the neighborhood.

Animation can enhance reality by putting glow in a magic object or a shadow where none really exists; *Poltergeist* also

has a number of effects that demonstrate how reality can enhance animation. For example, in one scene a malevolent spirit materializes from a television set, flies across a bedroom, and implants itself in a wall. To make the spirit (which was animated) appear more real in the final composite image, light was cast on the actors during filming to correspond to the passing of the spirit overhead. At the same time, a pneumatic cannon was set off that blew a vast amount of air through the actors' hair, further helping to create the impression that something had actually passed over their heads.

Animators in visual effects spend much of their time covering up the deficiencies of other processes. But they can look forward to a day when, through the use of digital technology, they will be given more and more responsibility for the creation of special effects shots in their entirety.

CHARLES MULLEN

Unlike many ILMers, Charley Mullen's childhood was not filled with dreams of one day working in films. The former head of the ILM animation department, now promoted to the job of ILM Production Supervisor, became interested in film after he had received a college degree in English and served as a VISTA volunteer in the low-income neighborhoods of Los Angeles. Only when he returned to college for an advanced degree in corporate communications was he drawn by the seductive lure of television and film.

Charley's first opportunity to work in animation occurred at a small New York studio that had installed a new, computerized animation system. The boss asked him if he knew how to load the camera or work an animation stand. Charley, always very direct and honest, confessed that he had never done it before but would be willing to learn. The boss was pleased—he had found what he was looking for, someone with no prior traditional-animation experience. He had tried several "experienced" operators on the new device and found that they couldn't adapt to the computerization of animation and continued to try to run the

machine like the earlier mechanical models, so he was looking for someone with no prejudices who could learn to use the computer-controlled camera as intended. Charley got the job.

He easily mastered the new machine and quickly learned to create interesting animation effects. But there was another passion in Charley's life that would take him away from his work in New York. He was, and still is, an avid outdoorsman. He enjoyed hiking, mountain climbing, and boating in wilderness areas, and wanted to live near tall mountains and wild rivers. He decided that he should move west.

He asked the company making the new computerized animation system if they had sold any of their machines out west. They told him of a sale to a company called Alpha Cine in Seattle, Washington. Charley wrote to Alpha Cine and applied for a job; he even flew, at his own expense, to Seattle and met the company's owner, Wes Davis. He then returned to New York and waited to hear if he got the job. Weeks passed and he heard nothing; he finally abandoned the idea of working in film on the West Coast and took an offer to run

Right: The "L.S." optical printer, named for ILM optical cameraman John Ellis, who built the device.

Below: Final composite shot of the *USS Enterprise* and an enemy ship from *Star Trek II: The Wrath of Khan*.

machinist who literally built the printer with his own hands. The "Anderson" is named after an old-timer in Hollywood, Howard Anderson, who built this printer for use on the 1956 Cecil B. De Mille classic, *The Ten Commandments*. The "Work Horse" was built in 1982 when budgets were being cut in every department at ILM and the rationalization that this printer would pay back its cost was important to get administrative approval for its

development. The "Quad" was designed for *The Empire Strikes Back* by Richard Edlund, with camera and projector movements by George Randle; David Grafton designed the special optics; the electronics interface was the project of Jerry Jeffress and Michael MacKenzie, with Bruce Nicholson providing his expertise. It has won several Academy Awards for itself, and one of them sits atop the machine looking a bit out of place in this high-tech environment. Though the Quad was originally built as a sort of double printer with four projectors (most printers have two projectors), prior to *Return of the Jedi* it was dismantled and two of the projecters were used to make the Work Horse. But the name Quad stuck and is still used.

There are a couple of important features that make the Quad and the Work Horse very special pieces of equipment. First, their lenses were custom designed and built for ILM. They produce an image so sharp and clear that the only limitation to the picture clarity is the film grain. Second, all of the printers are run with highly sophisticated computerized control systems. These systems speed up the optical processes enormously. Without the computer-driven printers, ILM would not have enjoyed its prolific stream of special effects projects—they would still be working on *The Empire Strikes Back*!

So what do the Optical Dogs do with all this equipment? And what makes their work so important? It's easier to understand what is involved in optical photography by examining a specific example.

Princess Leia is racing through the forest on the moon of Endor astride a stolen Imperial speeder, hovering above the ground and traveling at great speed through the heavily forested woods. (This is, of course, an actual scene from *Return*

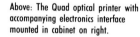

Above: The Quad optical printer with accompanying electronics interface mounted in cabinet on right.

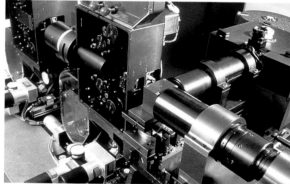

Left: Close-up of the Quad printer, showing projectors (left), beam splitters (center), 4-perf camera (right), and anamorphic lens (lower right). This unit was built by ILM.

Below: ILM's original Quad printer, which was later modified and rebuilt.

of the Jedi.) Since it was impossible to actually build such a bike and shoot this scene, it became a special effects problem, which was solved as follows: The scene was essentially composed of two main elements—Princess Leia riding the bike, and a background of trees speeding past us. Dennis Muren's crew provided the trees by walking a camera through the woods while shooting a frame every few seconds, so when projected at the normal twenty-four frames per second, the walk became faster than an out-of-control dune buggy, increasing the apparent speed more than 5000 percent! So much for the background. Meanwhile, the Princess (played by Carrie Fisher) was filmed in front of a large blue screen as she pretended to drive the vehicle, hair blowing in the wind of electric fans, which added to the impression of great speed.

Ultimately, the two pieces of film were delivered to Bruce Nicholson in the Optical Department. It was his job to combine the shots to make it look as though the Princess was really racing past the trees. This is where the TRAVELING MATTE optical process comes in. The term "traveling matte" refers to the fact that the matte moves with each successive frame. A traveling matte blocks out areas around an object in motion, whereas a garbage matte

is more static and simply covers an unwanted area of the screen. If a double exposure of the two scenes were made, we would have been able to see *through* the foreground Princess, which wouldn't have looked right at all. The challenge was to combine the two shots and avoid this problem.

By rephotographing the foreground Princess on her bike with a special red filter, the blue screen that was behind her turned black; this background would be used when the picture of the Princess was exposed before the optical camera. Now, using a reverse of that black area, a black silhouette of the Princess is created; when the shot of the trees is rephotographed, the silhouette is used to matte out the area of the picture that will be filled during the exposure of the foreground Princess. This eliminated the double exposure and successfully isolated the two objects in the final composite picture.

The actual process employed more than ten pieces of film, but the principle was essentially one of creating silhouettes using the special blue light coming from the blue screen. The pictures and their mattes are run on the printer's projector while the camera rephotographs the scene; each projection exposes a part of the image. The electronically controlled camera is

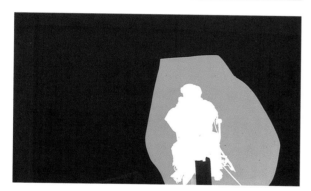

then rewound to the starting position, and new elements are threaded into the projectors. Again, another exposure is made and more of the image is revealed. After all the elements have been used and the picture is complete, the film containing the final composite picture is unloaded from the camera and sent to be developed. This scene was an easy one; many of the composited scenes are not so simple, sometimes taking several days of tedious work before the film can be removed and sent for development. With one mistake all of the previous work is often ruined and the operator must start all over again from the beginning.

The blue screen process can also be used to enhance more subtle effects. In *Cocoon*, the script called for the aliens to pull off their "human" outer skin to reveal their true alien forms. The "skin pull back" of Kitty was photographed at ILM using the blue screen process. This provided more control than attempting to do the shots on the actual locations would. Greg

Far left, top to bottom: Actors for the speeder bike scene are filmed in front of a bluescreen. The background forest plate for the same scene. A matte blocks out the background. A matte blocks out the riders on the speeder bike.

Below: Final composite shot of Princess Leia in the speeder bike chase scene, from *Return of the Jedi*.

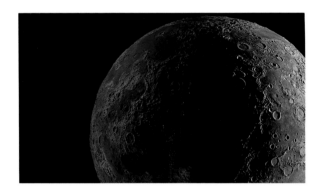

Cannon, a free-lancer hired by the production company, was the special effects artist that sculpted the rubber outer skin. Under the rubber skin was an extremely thin actress wearing a white full body stocking. A VistaVision plate was shot on the set to establish the room in which the action takes place. Later, the shot of the woman was added to the setting. By separating the two elements, a glow could be added to the alien form.

One other problem involves color. If the scenes were in black-and-white, all the camera operator would have to worry about would be the exposure of the elements. However, since all of our films are in color, each picture element must be carefully tested to determine the exact color filtration needed to keep it in balance with the other elements in the picture. It is this color balance that requires most of the re-shoots in the Optical Department.

The memory of one particular sequence from *The Empire Strikes Back* still gives the optical camera operators nightmares—the Asteroid Chase scene.

Opposite page: Composite shot of the final space battle in *Return of the Jedi*.

Left: Here are four of the elements which combine to form the final composite shot on the right.

Below: The final composite shot from *Star Trek II: The Wrath of Khan*.

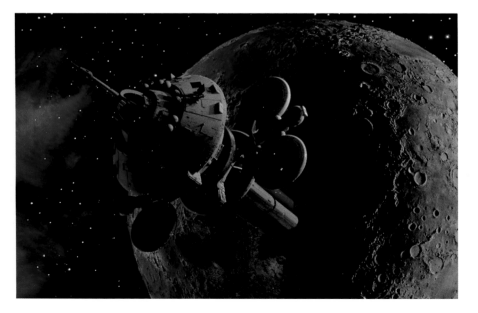

One shot in this notorious collection of optical mindbenders required over 200 individual pieces of film and took more than seven days to line up and shoot on the printer! The *Millennium Falcon* was escaping from pursuing TIE fighters. Han Solo chose to enter the asteroid field where his skill as a pilot allowed the *Falcon* to escape while the Imperial fighters collided with the rocky asteroids and were destroyed. The shot involved filming many separate elements: the *Millennium Falcon*; several large foreground asteroids; midground asteroids; distant asteroids; *very* distant asteroids; the star field; and animated laser blasts. As the *Falcon* raced along, certain asteroids were matted to appear in front of it while others were matted to appear in the background. Each element (a large asteroid, for example) was reduced to three black-and-white pieces of film, representing the primary colors of red, green, and blue. In addition, a positive and negative matte were made, totaling five strips of film for one asteroid. Though the Optical Dogs often feel that their work is not appreciated or understood, when a complicated shot such as the Asteroid Chase is successfully shown at the next morning's dailies, the entire room full of colleagues from other departments will break into applause.

Up to now we've focused on the optical camera operator, whose job is quite important and very difficult. But it couldn't be done without a little help from several of his co-workers sitting nearby at a row of clean editing tables: the line-up people. They provide the instructions for the camera operator concerning which matte should be shot with which image; they essentially place objects either in front of or in back of

other objects. The principle is quite simple: if object A blocks out object B, we assume A is in front of B. But in this fabricated world of elements that were shot at different times and places, it isn't always so easy to sort out the pieces—most of the time it isn't just A and B, it's A-1 through Z-97. And once it is clear which elements should go where, the line-up operator has to convert this information into foot and frame numbers, to match the right matte with the proper picture.

Adjoining the optical room are two smaller rooms, each containing a large film processor. Although all of the work done at ILM is in color, these machines develop only black-and-white film. When a blue-screen shot, filmed in color, enters the Optical Department, it is rephotographed through filters and converted into black-and-white separation negatives— one copy represents the red record, another the green, and a third the blue— which allows better control of the color. The traveling mattes, which are extracted from the blue screen, are also in black and white. When the elements are rephotographed on the optical printer, filters are used to return the three colors to their appropriate shades. When the black-and-white film strip representing red, for example, is rephotographed onto color film, a red filter is used to recreate that color. Then the color film in the camera is rewound, and the blue element is photographed with a blue filter. Breaking the colors down into black-and-white elements results in a less grainy image than if intermediate color elements were used, and the black-and-white film also allows for more control over color contrast. Finally, after all the black-and-white elements with their corresponding color filters have been exposed onto the film in repeated passes through

Gatefold: The mothership from *Cocoon* draws up space travelers on a small fishing boat.

Composite shot from *Return of the Jedi*.

the camera, the exposed color film is sent to a laboratory for developing and making a print.

Although in its time *The Empire Strikes Back* was the most ambitious film ever made, three years later *Return of the Jedi* required a 50 percent increase in effort. There were more special effects shots, all more complex than before. One space-battle shot for *Return of the Jedi* used over *300 elements*! Each element was exposed with the appropriate filter onto the undeveloped film of the printer's camera. Three hundred exposures later, the color film was removed from the camera and sent to the lab for development. Though this was the most complex of the shots, most had between 20 and 80 elements to keep track of. *Return of the Jedi* as a whole had more than 500 optical shots done at ILM.

"LAZY EIGHT": EIGHT PERFS ON THEIR SIDES

In most esoteric environments, people develop their own language, a jargon that becomes so familiar to them they are sometimes surprised that others in related fields do not know what they are talking about. "Eight perf" and four perf" are such words for ILM. But they are more than an esoteric term; they describe the heart of the cameras that have made possible the clarity of image now associated with ILM's special effects.

Special effects rely on rephotography in order to manipulate images. If the intermediate film format is larger than a standard 35mm film frame, the final special effects shot will have greater clarity. Many effects have been done using 70mm film, but it has the disadvantage of a limited variety of film stock. So what was needed was a significantly larger image size that still used the standard 35mm film format. We started looking for a solution to this problem in the history of film technology.

Since its beginning, the motion picture industry agreed that 35mm film with a certain type of perforation should be the international standard—so a film made in the United States, for instance, can be projected in a neighborhood theater in a rural town in India or Russia, and films produced in China can be shown without difficulty at theaters in San Francisco. In the 35mm feature-film format, there is a space for the picture and next to it a strip reserved for the sound track. (35mm film has 4 sprocket holes per frame.) Surprisingly enough, the picture area is about the size of an average postage stamp, yet the image it projects is often larger than a house. The only exception to this common 35mm standard is in certain special first-run theaters where 70mm film is used. This film is twice the width of the 35mm and has space reserved on it for six tracks of magnetic sound. Still, all the films shown in 70mm nowadays are originally filmed in 35mm and then optically enlarged to 70mm.

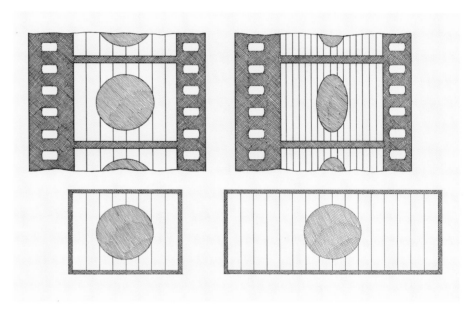

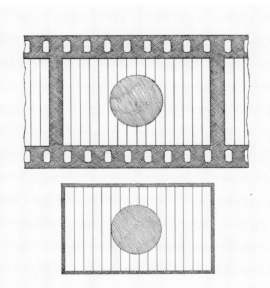

Above: FILM FORMATS
The film on the left shows the image just as it will project on the theater screen. On the right, the film image is optically "squeezed." When projected, it will be "un-squeezed" and become a wide screen picture.

Left: VISTAVISION FRAME
In the VistaVision format, the image is not squeezed. The film runs horizontally. It has more than twice the film area, providing a sharper and less grainy image. This unusual format is used at ILM to get better quality special effects.

Above: The ILM crew sets up the bluescreen shot of Mark Hamill riding a speeder bike for *Return of the Jedi*. The TV monitor on the right allows the director to see what the camera sees.

Right: Visual effects supervisor Dennis Muren takes a light meter reading on Luke Skywalker and Princess Leia; George Lucas is on the far right.

Far right above: Princess Leia and Luke Skywalker puppets on the speeder bike, from *Return of the Jedi*.

Far right below: Camera operator Micheal McAlister works on the Vista Cruiser, lining up a bluescreen shot of Princess Leia and Luke Skywalker puppets, for *Return of the Jedi*.

and rather than the normal four perforations between pictures, VistaVision doubled the size of each picture and measured eight perforations per frame. Obviously, the bigger the film area, the clearer the film will be. It wasn't a bad idea; the picture certainly looked good. But the problem was that only certain theaters went along with the new concept—after all, they had to buy new projectors. At its peak, less than twenty theaters were equipped to show the full-size VistaVision film. In addition, the cameras required to photograph in this special format were specially built and quite expensive. You may have seen films shot in VistaVision and not realized it; a few famous ones are Alfred Hitchcock's *North by Northwest*, C. B. De Mille's *The Ten Commandments*, and the Bing Crosby hit *White Christmas*. However, the idea did not survive, and by 1961 Paramount Pictures made its last VistaVision picture,

There was another film format that flourished back in the 1950s when the big Hollywood studios were battling each other for the dwindling attention of TV-crazed Americans. 20th Century–Fox introduced wide-screen Cinemascope, and Paramount Pictures introduced VistaVision, a new motion picture format. The theaters only had to add a cinemascope lens to show the Fox films, but a special projector was required to show the VistaVision films in their original format. VistaVision put the 35mm film on its side,

One-Eyed Jacks, a western directed by Marlon Brando.

What does all this have to do with ILM and special effects? While most of the VistaVision projectors were junked and many of the cameras with the famous eight-perf heart were torn apart and discarded, there were still some perfectionists who felt that this larger negative had its merits. A quarter of a century later, when George Lucas was setting up his Industrial Light and Magic studio, the ghost of the VistaVision format was resurrected and put to use filming special effects for *Star Wars*.

Though the cameras and projectors were scarce, they were quite cheap; used-camera dealers in Hollywood thought they had unloaded real white elephants when young ILMers paid good money for the old eight-perf VistaVision parts. Some dealers hesitated to remind the young buyers that the parts they were buying were not "standard" 35mm, since it might have killed the sale. An entire printer (now in use at ILM and known as the Anderson) was bought for a mere $11,000. Following the success and publicity surrounding *Star Wars*, not even the film movements could

The mother ship from *Cocoon*.

Above: The final composite shot of the Fyrene IV planet from *Enemy Mine.* Notice that the brightly exposed sun has flared enough to make it seem more realistic than if it had been simply a painted element.

Right: Assistant cameraman Wade Childress prepares to photograph the painted portion of the scene.

Below: Childress prepares to expose the bright sun element for the composite shot. This element will be over-exposed, causing a bright flare which will "bleed over" into successive exposures of other elements.

be purchased for $11,000—the entire unit is now worth over $300,000! Richard Edlund reported that after *Star Wars* came out, he returned to some of the "junk" dealers that had supplied him with the original VistaVision parts. They were now advertising the precious remaining pieces in their inventory as if they were part of the crown jewels. Mechanical exiles relegated to a dark corner of the back room were now given felt-lined boxes and center stage in the shop window, and the prices soared astronomically. In recent years ILM has given up trying to find VistaVision cameras from the original Paramount inventory. For its part, Paramount owns little of the original VistaVision equipment; what little remains, they rent at appropriate prices.

At ILM, almost all film that ends up as elements in the Optical Department is shot in VistaVision, and most of the cameras have been custom-built by ILM.

When a big production is in process, cameras are always scarce, sometimes resulting in spats between crews competing for the same camera.

Because of the eight-perf camera with its double-sized film area, the optical effects at ILM have a special clarity quite impossible to achieve with a simple 35mm four-perforation half-scale camera. But even more important than the cameras and lenses is the skill and dedication of the ever-faithful Optical Dogs of ILM.

BRUCE NICHOLSON

Bruce Nicholson was in his second year at the University of California at Berkeley when he developed an interest in cinematography. He couldn't fit it into his regular social services major so he took an extension course on the subject. It was love from the word "roll," and before long he was shooting his own super-8mm films.

After graduating, he decided to make cinematography his career. He moved to Los Angeles and began looking for a job in film—which is as easy to come by as a spare piece of meat in a lion's den. The closest he could get to a job in film production was some work at a film processing laboratory. His duties were repetitive and boring, but elsewhere in the lab Bruce found something that made his life there worthwhile. The lab had an optical printer, and whenever he had time, he would play around with it. With the aid of some kindly co-workers, he learned the basics of how to operate it. This large mechanical toy marked the beginning of Bruce's career in optical effects.

After a couple of years, he had had enough of the film lab and moved on to a job at a small optical house in East Hollywood. The shop was in a quiet residential neighborhood outside the normal Hollywood commercial areas, located in a remodeled barn-like building tucked behind a home on the street.

The location had its drawbacks. Optical printers require absolutely rock solid grounding to assure the steadiest possible picture, but the optical printers in this shop were on the second floor of the old wooden building. Whenever printing was in progress, everyone near the machine had to freeze in their tracks to keep the floor from jiggling and upsetting the machinery.

It was here, under the tutelage of an experienced old-timer, that Bruce began to broaden his knowledge of optical printing. Despite the primitive operating conditions and the relative ease of most of the assignments (mainly putting in fades, dissolves, and titles for TV shows and educational films), Bruce learned a lot about optical work and looked forward to a good future with the company. Unfortunately, the number of orders started to dwindle, and one day Bruce found himself laid off and looking for work.

It was 1976. Things were slow all over Hollywood, and prospects for new employment were not good. Luck, however, was on Bruce's side. Just two weeks after his layoff, he was contacted by a new company in Van Nuys called Industrial Light and Magic. The company didn't sound like anything spectacular, but it beat unemployment and so Bruce took the job.

Robby Blalack was the head of the optical department for ILM on *Star Wars*; he and John Dykstra hired Bruce as an optical camera assistant. In the final film credits Bruce's name appears a modest third among the assistants in the optical section. In retrospect, this seems a modest spot, considering what his contribution would be on subsequent films in the *Star Wars* saga.

Following *Star Wars*, ILM was shut down. Bruce went to work first on *Battlestar Gallactica*, then on *Star Trek: The Motion Picture*. When ILM was reborn to do the effects for *The Empire Strikes Back*, Bruce was offered the job of supervisor on the biggest optical effects project ever attempted. His previous work had shown his aptitude for the job; it was time now to prove that he had the ability to handle the responsibility of supervising an entire department.

As *Empire*'s optical supervisor, he had to start from the ground up; some of the equipment had to be built from scratch. The department needed a new kind of printer to do the big job ahead, and it could

Bruce Nicholson's work bench, showing an optical densitometer (a complex exposure meter used in optical work) in the upper right-hand corner.

not be bought anywhere. A team of optical, mechanical, and electronic specialists, including visual effects supervisor Richard Edlund (who is a first-class engineer), joined Bruce in the task of assembling a revolutionary printer, which was dubbed "The Quad." Because of the uniqueness of the VistaVision format it was impossible to purchase an off-the-shelf optical printer, so until this machine was operating, no shots could be composited. Meanwhile, spacecraft were being designed and filmed awaiting the printer's completion. When it was finally finished, the race to get everything done for the May 1980 release date was on. The pressure was tremendous.

I first met Bruce in early 1980, when the workload on the ILM optical department was at its worst. The full shop of more than twenty people was working at top speed, with twelve- and fourteen-hour days the norm. People were staggering around the building like soldiers at the end of a long, rough battle. On top of the sheer volume of work, there were new challenges to overcome that had not been faced in the original. In *Star Wars*, the special effects work was not simple but dealt mainly with spaceships in dark, starry space. When, as sometimes happened, there were black outlines around the ships (caused by the optical matting process), they were not easy to see as the craft streaked across the black void of space. But in *The Empire Strikes Back*, there were to be two major sequences that would not be in black space at all but in the white snow of a planet in the Hoth System and in the pastel-colored skies around Cloud City. In either place, a black matte line would make the spaceships look like paper cutouts. A way had to be found to blend the ships with the light background.

On the snow planet, the early results

were discouraging. The ships didn't look like they were really in the picture; they looked fake and pasted on over the white snow and blue sky. Then Bruce tried something new: he double-exposed a spaceship flying over the surface of the planet with a section of the same scene photographed in the Norway snow. The trick worked. It desaturated the ship and made it look like it really belonged in the scene. When it was shown to George Lucas, he was astounded. "How did you do that?" he asked. Bruce replied that they used "a Norway Filter" on the shot. It wasn't until later that Bruce explained to George how he'd really saved the snow battle from looking unnatural.

The job of Optical Supervisor at ILM requires not only attention to the minutiae of optical photography, but also a talent for managing people and establishing high standards that the whole shop will respect. It was gathering and, in many cases, training the kind of crew needed to take on the job. Before *The Empire Strikes Back* was completed, Bruce had certainly earned the respect of his crew. I can think of no other department as disciplined and loyal to its supervisor as the optical department. In 1982 he won an Academy Award for his work on the visual effects for *Raiders of the Lost Ark*, reaching a new level of achieve-

ment for himself and gaining the admiration of his peers outside of Lucasfilm.

Sometimes Bruce must have felt the proverbial loneliness of command. He was truly the key figure in a multimillion-dollar film venture. But Bruce's plight did not go unnoticed. At one point, as we neared the end of a critical optical-effects deadline for *Return of the Jedi*, executive producer George Lucas, in an uncharacteristically vocal mood, lectured me at some length about the importance of getting the opticals done on time. As he raised his voice my co-workers crept out of the room, leaving us alone. Bruce had not heard any of this, and I suggested that George tell him directly. George stopped mid-sentence, lowered his voice, and said, "Oh, I wouldn't tell Bruce. He's under too much pressure already."

Bruce is now taking on additional responsibilities at ILM by going into the field. He co-supervised the effects for the John Carpenter film *Starman*, along with cameraman Micheal McAlister. Though he has little spare time, Bruce is attempting to return occasionally to the thing that first brought him to optical work, his love of cinematography. After *Return of the Jedi*, he shot his own 16mm film, which deals with the graceful movements of a ballet dancer. He has done nearly all of the film on his own. Not surprisingly, it makes extensive use of optical effects.

CHAPTER 10

DIGITIZED MOVIES: A SCENARIO FOR THE FUTURE

*T*he artists and managers of Industrial Light and Magic realize that they are part of an industry that is being rapidly transformed by modern technology. In order to keep its place as a leader in special effects, Lucasfilm must continue to develop new methods of creating effects as well as new uses for effects.

There are those who would argue that such concern is uncalled for, that high-tech effects are simply a fad of the 80s that will soon pass. But that flies in the face of the actual history of film. Visual effects have been around for far more than the last decade; they have been an integral part of motion pictures since the early 1900s and have always been used whenever an exotic or totally imaginary setting has been required in a script. There is little reason to believe that future audiences will not want such settings, and so little reason to believe that effects will lose their importance. It is more likely, in fact, that their role in filmmaking will expand as future technology improves the quality of effects and makes them increasingly affordable.

When we think of visual effects today, the term tends to evoke visions of starships racing through space or of ethereal ghosts hovering in the air. This perception is common to many in the movie audiences and even to many filmmakers. It must be remembered that special effects are also used in places where few suspect they have been applied; matte paintings that have replaced real but expensive scenery; miniatures that have been used to cut the costs of vehicles or of set construction. Imaginative filmmakers use special effects to expand the possibilities of their medium. Directors such as Alfred Hitchcock and Cecil B. De Mille and producers such as David Selznick and Darryl Zanuck used visual effects to thrill audiences.

The myriad uses of special effects will most certainly assure them a place in tomorrow's film world; however, it is also certain that those effects will have to be considerably more sophisticated than the effects of today. Just as audiences now would not accept special effects done in the style of the old Buck Rogers serial,

Part of the digital effects used in the Rebel briefing room from *Return of the Jedi*.

future audiences will not accept effects that now seem wonderfully advanced.

Part of the reason for increasing expectations lies in the old show-business problem of topping yesterday's show. But more than that, every new generation of filmgoers is more visually sophisticated than the previous one. When audiences of 1904 saw Méliès' films, they were truly mystified by visual effects that would now seem simplistic and crude. But today, because of television, audiences have achieved a very high level of visual sophistication. The audience's ability to perceive ever more acutely offers special effects practitioners the greatest challenge, a challenge computer technology is helping to meet.

Star Wars was the first feature film to use a computer to control the effects camera. This made the process more reliable and allowed the camera shutter to be controlled, thereby creating a blurring that permitted rapid camera moves without creating distracting strobing of the picture. It also allowed for repeatability. The camera operator could get precisely the camera move desired and could then use successive camera passes to add light or engine-glow effects to the models.

The computer technology used on *Star Wars* in 1976 was borrowed from other industry applications, yet it required an imaginative mind to put it to use in the special effects field. Since that time, many other roles for the computer have been found in special effects work, especially with artists, since a computer helps to relieve them of some of the repetitive drudgery in their work. Computers are now used in practically every department at ILM, from production coordination to film filing. It is not unreasonable, therefore, to expect that the creation of

special effects will be increasingly influenced by the ever-expanding capabilities of computers.

The next big jump in technology is taking place as the computer manipulates images that exist only in digitized memory, and paints those images directly onto film. This permits the filmmaker to do such things as create the image of an object from new perspectives directed by the operator's "joy stick," much as is done with computer video games. Through the use of a paint station with an electronic stylus, a full range of colors is available to the matte painter. Models can be built on a monitor screen; the modelmaker/designer will assemble shapes into the forms and colors desired, and when sufficient parameters are provided, the computer can display the model from any angle, with perfect perspective. As it moves in space, lighting will be simulated so that reflections and shading are all appropriate to the object's orientation.

As it happens, effects for some television commercials and even a few films have already been generated by digital means. Quite often, though, we see them as tasteless station-break logos, or spinning titles for a television program.

A more interesting demonstration of COMPUTER-GENERATED IMAGES occurred in ILM's "Genesis Sequence" for the film *Star Trek II: The Wrath of Khan.* In this film, a lifeless moonlike body in space was changed into a beautiful lush planet resembling an idealized Earth. The sequence begins as a white-hot missile is fired from the Starship *Enterprise* toward the barren body. The camera follows it through space. The missile quickly strikes the surface. We then orbit around the planet as it metamorphoses into a realistic-looking, lush, living world, com-

This sequence of shots from *Star Trek II: The Wrath of Khan* was entirely made up of digital images. No tangible images or artwork were used—it all came from the mind of Lucasfilm's computer, programmed by artists from Sprocket Systems. This is the first time such an extensive digital image sequence was used in a film.

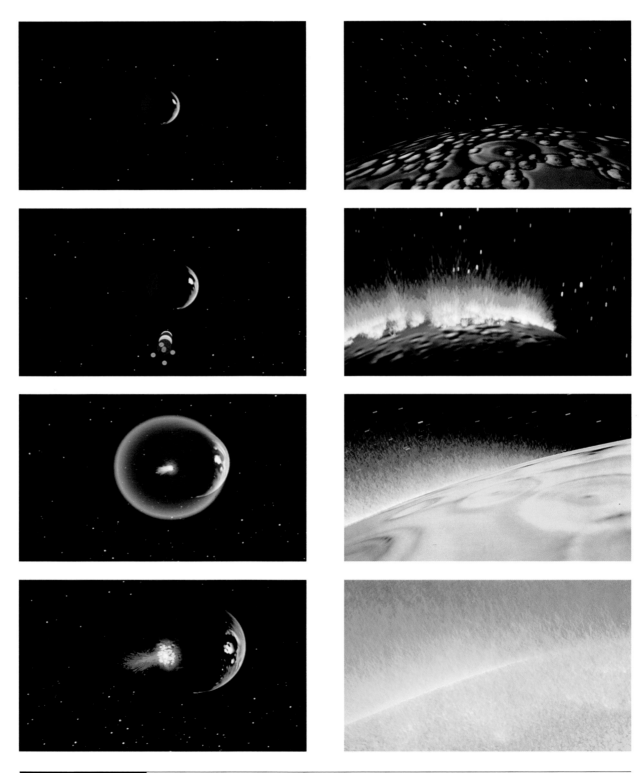

plete with white clouds, blue oceans, and snow-covered mountains. There were, of course, no models of the planet and no solid art work—all the images existed only in the workings of the computer. The effect was astounding in its realism. It did not look like a computer-generated image; it looked quite real. I sometimes wonder whether audiences who saw this sequence in 1982 realized what a historic moment they were witnessing: it was the first public use of a technology being developed by the Lucasfilm Computer Division headed by Ed Catmull.

As Ed explains it, "The computer revolution itself (of which special effects applications are a part) is based on a printing revolution."

The most sophisticated computers are largely made up of thousands of circuits of great complexity—enough circuits that if they were made of copper wires with solder and capacitors and so on they would occupy large rooms, buildings, and whole city blocks of circuit boards. And if that were the case, they wouldn't work: the miles of copper wire, the sheer distance that current would have to travel, would defeat the machines, make impossible the rapid calculation of millions of formulations in the blink of an eye. Heat would build up, critical timings drift into the chaos of knotted wire and radiating power.

But an extraordinary revolution in photographic reduction techniques has made it possible to reproduce photographs of these circuits onto tiny, nearly microscopic chips of crystal and other materials, so that the power operating the circuits drops to fractions of what it was, the distance traveled by electrons is measured in millimeters and less, not feet or yards. Formulations based on parallel operations become possible, and in the smallest

space, millions, billions of computations can be accomplished dependably and relatively economically.

Furthermore, substantial amounts of data can be stored in small spaces—spinning disks read by lasers, for instance—and because of the all-around miniaturization of components, the data can be quickly and continuously retrieved and stored by the machine, making possible the most delicate and subtle of data manipulation.

Such data as picture elements, for instance.

A TV set creates an image through the action of cathode rays striking a phosphorous screen. The tube emitting the cathode rays responds to electric impulses, which deflect electrons striking the screen and thus create patterns that form the image we see. In the same way, when a photograph is stored in a computer, the machine "reads" it by scanning a narrow beam back and forth over the entire image, translating every tiny section into a dot of light or shadow, black, white, reddish, greenish—turning it into the thousands of dots of a TV picture. The computer interprets all these colored dots as numbers, and stores them exactly as it does any other string of numbers.

Any photograph can be scanned and then stored by a large computer in this manner. That's how photographs are received from space. Whether the camera is on Mars or a weather satellite, it sends a television picture down as a stream of dots that can be reassembled into a television picture. The dots are transmitted by a radio transmitter near the space-borne camera, sending them as a string of numbers.

It follows that a strip of photographs such as a motion picture can also be scanned and stored. There are many advantages to storing a movie in a computer's memory: it will be less likely to become lost or damaged; it can be projected directly by the computer through a television projector; if motion picture prints are needed the computer can create a projection print onto fresh film directly from its databank.

But, at least presently, there are also several limitations. The images of the individual film frames will only be as sharp and clear as the fineness of their scanning: if the computer breaks up a film frame into ten thousand dots, then it will come out looking like a crude photograph from a pulp magazine. If it records the frame in a hundred thousand dots, the effect will be not unlike your home television set—not exactly the image you pay $5 to watch in a gleaming movie palace. In fact, the computer must break up each film frame into well over *ten million dots* to approximate the look of 35mm motion picture film, and that is a large order, particularly with over two hundred thousand frames in a typical two-hour movie.

But in order to commit film to a computer databank this must be done, and already in a number of special effects houses across the United States companies are scanning and storing short films—mostly the elements of television commercials, and some brief sequences for sci-fi flicks.

At Lucasfilm the goals are somewhat more ambitious. An image computer device named Pixar has been developed by the Lucasfilm Computer Division, and it already figures prominently in ILM's special effects program.

The Pixar image computer actually manipulates the film images once they

Digital effects for *Return of the Jedi* are added to a scene with actors.

have been scanned. The scanning itself is a relatively slow process: the Lucasfilm computer people recently completed and delivered to ILM a scanner that takes just forty seconds to scan a full color picture— or sixteen hours to scan and store one minute of film.

When Steven Spielberg saw the Genesis sequence that ILM did for *Star Trek II: The Wrath of Khan*, he asked if it would be possible to do a whole film using this technology. I cautioned him that those few shining moments he saw on screen were the product of a great many dull hours of computer time. It did not mean that we had conquered the scanning process; we were limited by current computer technology. Later, Walt Disney Productions released *Tron*, a film that publicized the fact that computer images were used in abundance. Observers of the film industry watched closely to see if this meant a new chapter in film history was about to unfold. Some predicted that if computer images caught on, it would be as big a revolution as the advent of sound with *The Jazz Singer* in 1927. Unfortunately for Disney, the film did not make much of a mark—it was not a success at the box office and did not mark a sudden revolution in special effects com-

Right: Ed Catmull stands among the memory disks in Lucasfilm's main computer room.

Middle: Bill Reeves sits at a computer terminal where he calls up a new program for a digital image project.

Below: Bill Reeves uses the paint station.

puter applications. Indeed, it seems unlikely to me that there will ever be a time when, overnight, computer-generated images will sweep over the visual effects field; there is too much technological development involved. Still, a quiet computer revolution is underway.

Storing the images presents one of the largest problems. The limitations are in computer hardware technology. More memory is needed, and greater random access of that memory is necessary if we are to use it as a serious tool in feature films. At one point during the production of the effects for *Return of the Jedi*, we calculated that if the effects had been done in a digital form rather than the traditional manner, it would have required a good-sized warehouse simply to store the data representing the scenes on which work was being done. The cost, of course, would be prohibitive.

Simple floppy disks do not have enough capacity to store even one image, and the smaller hard disks cannot hold more than a few frames of film. So far the best storage medium is a thin, optically read digital disk that can store up to forty seconds of black-and-white images, or ten seconds of color. Such a disk costs under $200 (versus $7000 for a large hard disk that stores less), and because it spins very fast

and is read by a laser, retrieving the stored pictures is faster.

On the other hand, it takes 720 disks to store a two-hour movie, without its soundtrack, at a total disk cost of just under $140,000—plus the technicians' and machine time. That's 150 times more than an ordinary projection print costs, so obviously there have to be compelling reasons to scan and store movies on computer disks, rather than just keeping standard prints.

The compelling reasons lie with Lucasfilm's Pixar. Images that are stored in a computer can be manipulated in any number of ways: stretched and distorted, matted one into another, selectively color-altered, and so on. These are all effects that are common to television at much cruder levels of resolution and color

A frame from the experimental digital film, *Andre and Wally B.*

dynamics. The Pixar makes similar effects possible in the high-definition world of motion pictures.

Just how much difference there is between television and movies is shown by the different computers that each must use to create their effects. A powerful television image manipulator is the Quantel, an impressive machine with many knobs and displays that processes TV images with an ordinary commercial mini-computer inside it. On the other hand, for "The Adventures of Andre and Wally B.," a 1.8-minute Lucasfilm animated short, it was necessary to use two of the largest computers in the world, the Cray XMP-2 and XMP-4, along with no less than fourteen high-speed VAX computers, to process data for several months. The Lucas production involved the actual creation of animated images, not merely the manipulation of existing ones, though a substantial part of computer time was spent in precisely the kinds of manipulation that a TV network's Quantel does on low-resolution TV images.

One of the first places that the computer will assist special effects technicians will be in the COMPOSITING of images—taking elements from one picture and putting them inside another. Pictures filmed in a traditional manner will be converted into digital form and then blended and manipulated into new composites. The filmmaker will be able to see the composite on a television-type monitor before it is made. Ultimately, the optical department will look like a TV control room, with techni-

John Lasseter, interface designer (animator), lays out the design for a wireframe figure.

cians making adjustments that register instantly on a screen rather than having to wait until the film comes back from the lab.

The most common visual effects involve compositing: for instance, placing an image of Luke Skywalker inside a model spaceship, along with Darth Vader and perhaps a dozen technicians in the background or under a bridge, and also a few hundred stars and a spiral galaxy out "giant" windows. We might also want to put animated laser swords in Luke's and his dad's hands, and maybe the ghost of Obi-Wan Kenobi peering down from above, while on distantly seen television screens we surely will insert a few choice computer graphics and an approaching starship—with, of course, more inserted stars around it. Your basic ILM shot.

Now each element, before it is composited, is a full-fledged motion picture scene. In a computer it is made of about four to ten million dots per frame. To composite several elements that are contained in a databank, we can either give them to large computers such as the Cray to play with for months, or we can give them to the much smaller Pixar—which only processes images, and in that single regard is faster and more efficient than anything else. Though for all its speed and accuracy in compositing images, the Pixar is still more costly at compositing shots than the old-fashioned optical printers that all special effects companies use. In time the Pixar will be more cost efficient, but that time will not come until a substantial leap is taken in the technology of scanning and particularly of storing large amounts of data in small, cheap spaces.

*F*or the time being, when used merely to supplant optical printers, the Pixar is a rich kid's toy. But it also has another, more interesting, potential for which there is presently nothing more cost effective. The Pixar can be used in the actual manufacturing of picture images—images that have never been taken by a camera, but exist from the first as strings of numbers inside computers. This is, in fact, the function for which it was designed.

Video games—the kind you see in arcades and on kids' computers—were among the first users of computer-generated images, though in their incipient forms some computer-made digital images were around in the 1950s, at Bell Labs and some universities. But the idea of high-resolution COMPUTER-GENERATED IMAGES is much more recent; it came from flight simulators (the machines that pilots train on) built into model cockpits, with computer-created images outside the windows. They are now so realistic that a pilot can get a license to fly a 767 without ever having flown one, only demonstrating his knowledge of it in a simulator.

Simulators actually create images of clouds, cities below, airport towers, and all the details of runways and adjacent rocky fields, entirely at the prompting of

A background for the digital film,
Andre and Wally B.

the pilot who is moving the controls and reading the dials. A simulator creates a synthetic environment based on the real world. How can a filmmaker use a computer simulation to create environments for his films? With great difficulty, as it turns out, but it is possible. And the results can be spectacular.

It isn't enough to suppose that a computer can make synthetic scenes by making up series of colored dots, like a TV does. After all, the TV doesn't invent the programs that are on it; it only transmits them. A computer must first create the idea of a picture, see it in its broadest outlines, supply it with architectural and organic details, light it, color it, shade it, then determine how to analyze what it has made as so many hundreds of thousands or millions of dots, and express its two-dimensional synthetic image that way.

Of course, a computer image is created in its essential outlines by programmers, and all detailing is made at their direction. The initial outlines of the scene—often called the "model"—can be created in three ways. The simplest is to "draw" it with a device called a data tablet—the term for any one of a number of machines that take a basic blueprint and translate it into numbered coordinates. With this data the computer can manipulate the lines of the blueprint by turning them three-dimensionally or distorting them any number of ways.

A second way of getting an image started in a computer is to imagine its basic outlines as made up of simple geometric forms—spheres, cones, cylinders, ellipsoids, etc.—all cut up and fit together; then to describe them in formulas that can be fed into the computer. This gives the computer a more detailed, sophisticated starting point in its manipulations.

The third method of model building is called developing a "procedural" model: telling the computer what it must do to create the basic shape. Perhaps it begins with a line, sweeps it through space in a given direction, then rotates the resulting plane in a certain way; extends a point into a road toward the horizon, introduces hills and valleys to a flat plain. . . . The computer then analyzes the surface it has drawn, and translates it into series of numbers each corresponding uniquely to one point in that surface. Now, it is ready for the next step.

Almost all computer images are made up of polygons. The basic model, or outline of the scene, is filled out by covering it with a skin of small, flat, geometrical shapes—triangles, squares, polyhedrons of various kinds. A computer can define and deal with a mass of geometric shapes because it sees them as simple strings of numbers; what it can't deal with is a tumblin' tumbleweed, unless it's reduced it to simple pattern.

The smaller these polygons, the smoother and more detailed the surface of the model will look. Of course, most surfaces are not smooth and seamless. We see the world almost entirely as texture, shading, and hue, but surfaces are actually rough, dirty, cracked, pockmarked, woven, grained, reflective—on and on. And in a computer image of any complexity, virtually every surface will have a different texture.

Such textures are difficult to describe geometrically, so other techniques have been developed to insert them into a scene. The simplest is texture mapping: various

textures (tweed, leather, sand, bark) are described in a separate set of instructions in the computer—described as small patches, but in full three-dimensional detail—and then applied to the appropriate surfaces in a computer image by multiplying the texture, stretching it, flexing it, and so on.

In a similar method, the programmer can "paint" a texture onto a computer model in real time, using a stylus with variable color control.

A more realistic kind of texturing is to introduce a photograph of a surface—rock or leather or whatever—into the computer, have it scan and analyze the texture, then apply it to the model. Again, though it cannot be rotated, it is cost-effective for static shots.

A particularly sophisticated kind of texturing was invented at the Jet Propulsion Laboratory in Pasadena by J. F. Blinn. It's called "bump mapping," and does not actually store any textures; instead it's an analysis of how light is reflected off different, unique surfaces. Then, when the computer "lights" its image, it makes the light bounce off the various surfaces according to the ways it naturally does off their particular textures. This kind of texturing can be moved and rotated, though it takes *many* more computations to achieve.

Realism can be greatly enhanced by improving the light source. In the earlier computer images, all the light came in a kind of flood from one side or another. Instead, light should come from one or more sources of a definite size, and furthermore, reflective surfaces within a scene should bounce light according to their reflectivity. While such secondary lighting sources are subtle, their effect is considerable; we see secondary lighting all around us all the time and we are exceedingly sensitive to it, even if we're not consciously aware of its presence.

In 1980, researchers at Bell Labs and Cornell University developed the most believable method yet of texturing and lighting computer models, though it is a method that takes an enormous amount of computational time. It is called "ray tracing," and it accomplishes nothing less than following every ray of light that falls on a scene, tracing it from its point of origin to some part of the scene, bouncing (perhaps) back and forth within the picture, then finally bouncing back to the image plane and to us, the viewers. The concept is very sophisticated, and the effect is electrifyingly real, photographically exact. It makes possible such effects as transparency, the refraction of images, mirrored surfaces, and optically exact shadows.

In order to simplify the procedure, the rays are actually traced backward, from the viewer's eye to the light source, so rays that would bounce off in some other direction are not computed. The rays are traced strictly according to the laws of optics: shiny objects reflect rays according to their reflectivity; translucent materials transmit rays; refractive surfaces (such as water, thick coats of wax, heavy glass) bend the transmitted ray. Calculations may be carried out up to ten "bounces" per ray, before it strikes the image plane as a single dot of the picture. Thus many billions of calculations must be carried out for every image.

A serious problem with ray tracing is in rendering objects of such diffuse surfaces as carpets and moss, since rays scatter off them in unpredictable ways. But a more serious problem for film work is the tremendous amount of computer time it takes for each individual frame. A number of researchers, including those at Lucasfilm, are working on alternative solutions in laboratories around the world.

Another important area of research at Lucasfilm is in creating the shapes of natural objects by a wholly new kind of mathematics, called fractal geometry. The brainchild of IBM's Benoit Mandelbrot, fractal geometry is fundamentally different from the Euclidean geometry we learn in high school. It is based on the observation that some natural shapes simply cannot be accurately measured; that the measurements we come up with depend on how finely divided our measuring sticks are and how close we are to the object we're measuring.

Consider a coastline, for instance: the closer we get to it, the more indentations and bumps we notice, and the "longer" it becomes, until we literally have our nose at ground level and we're having to measure around every pebble. And closer still, to every molecule and particle . . .

Thus every natural surface—coastlines, mountain horizons, trees, leaves, waterfalls—has more detail, and greater linear dimension, the closer we get to it. With fractal geometry this is taken into account, and from it comes a way of computer-animating landscapes. Some surfaces such as the shape of a mountain repeat themselves the closer we get to them: boulders and soil along a mountain ridge are mountain shaped, and so are the pits and valleys in the surfaces of the boulders. Likewise, the branches and leaves of many trees are miniature trees in themselves. Fractal geometry acknowledges these patterns, and from them supplies the mathematics of almost infinitely detailed computer models.

If a computer knows what basic shapes a mountain horizon will break up into, and what shapes those smaller units break up into, then the computer can move in any direction toward the edge of a mountain and no matter how close it gets there will always be more detail revealed. Likewise, computer-made forests can be entered and explored, as long as the basic formulations of the surfaces of bark and brush and berries are known. So too with grassy fields and the most convoluted of caves.

Of course, the more completely we describe micro-details in a scene, the more interesting and unexpected close-up views will become. But the point is that with a minimum of information, a scene can be entered at any point and always the greatest detail will be revealed, no matter where or how close we look.

An intriguing application of fractal geometry has come from Lucasfilm's Games Group, which has created a game for Atari and other computers called "Rescue From Fractalus!" It involves an interplanetary rescue mission in which players

try to save fellow pilots and avoid enemy Jaggi attacks. The entire landscape of an imaginary planet, Fractalus, is in the game's memory, along with descriptions of its micro-structure, so that players can travel over thousands of "miles" of landscape, and nose down close at absolutely any point, and never run out of detail to see . . . all within the limited memory of an Atari home computer.

Another aspect of fractal surface generation is the way irregular shapes can be created. For instance, a mountain can be developed beginning with a basic triangle shape. At each stage the new triangles are joined at random points within the existing ones, and their dynamic interaction distorts the shapes more and more, until the incoming triangles are so small their edges cannot be distinguished any longer.

As we said, most shapes used in computer pictures are polygons that are "dressed up" in textures. In a typical aircraft simulator, the computer generates about seven thousand polygons in real time. However, in Digital Productions' film *The Last Starfighter*, typical frames of the spacecraft and giant starship consisted of 600,000 polygons, with some much larger. Thus the shapes were able to be impressively detailed and well modeled, though the textures were distinctly uniform: semi-glossy metal for virtually everything, with only a nominal degree of surface character.

ILM's newest Pixar mechanism is capable of handling *80,000,000* polygons at a time, when practical computer storage and computational speeds are achieved, so that the degree of surface detail can approach that of 35mm motion picture film.

Ed Catmull examines the laser image scanner.

Until now, computer-generated images have been displayed on TV screens and converted to film by simply filming the screen. The resolution of the image can be made far better than the picture on your home TV set by increasing the number of lines used on the screen, yet the tonal and color range available with a TV-style image is still greatly inferior to that found in a normal motion picture film image. The blacks are not as profound nor the whites as brilliant from a cathode ray tube, and the color palette is also limited. The computer is capable of providing the data needed to create a full range of grays and colors, but the cathode-ray tube, the singer of its music, so to speak, is not able to deliver. To solve this problem, engineers are turning to another scientific miracle of our time: the laser.

In motion picture film there are about 300 distinctly different gradations visible in every color, from palest hue to totally vibrant saturation. (This is the potential of the original film as it comes from the camera; by the time it has gone through several generations and reached your local theater, its ability to differentiate colors is less.) Good network television can manage no more than twenty-five variations of a color's range—and they're all somewhere in the color's middle hues, excluding the extremes that really give surfaces their character. Current home video projectors are downright gruesome, with color ranges of no more than 10 to 1. The Pixar has a dynamic range of 4000 to 1. However, the images must still go through the laser, which has a control of only 250 to 1. Computer-generated images have better color dynamics than television, but they're still far from motion picture film. Researchers are currently exploring the abilities of the laser to lessen this gap.

Up to now, digitized images have usually been put onto film by photographing them off a high-resolution CRT (television) tube; but a far more efficient source of light than a beam of electrons is a laser light—as fine a point of light as there is, color-perfect, fast, powerful, but extremely difficult to direct. While a beam of electrons from a CRT can be deflected in a coherent scanning pattern back and forth across a field by the action of an electromagnet, a magnetic force has little effect on laser light. Nonetheless, development bravely plows ahead on ways to scan-read pictures with a laser light. At Lucasfilm's Computer Division a method has been devised for directing the laser with a small mirror and a moving prism arrangement that zips back and forth, tilting in microscopic degrees for each upcoming line and scanning an entire frame. The technique works, though everyone would prefer a method that involves fewer moving parts.

In *Young Sherlock Holmes*, supervised by Dennis Muren, most of the difficult visual effects deal with hallucinations caused by an evil enemy of Holmes (when he was a lad). These were done using traditional stop motion techniques. One scene, however, called for a church stained glass window to come to life. A sword-wielding character, made of glass from the window, comes down and chases a priest out of the church and into the street. Muren decided that this was a perfect application of digital image techniques. First, the stained glass character was "painted" using a cathode ray tube and an electronic paint station. Artists applied a stilus to an electronic canvas. Little-by-little the image appeared on the TV screen as they worked. The data was then stored in a computer and rearranged so that the drawn character would appear from differing per-

Right: Visual effects supervisor Dennis Muren coaches modelmaker Jeff Mann (in white suit). This model of the desired action for the stained glass man in *Young Sherlock Holmes* will be used by the computer image animators for reference as they develop the computer animated image.

Middle: A "wire frame" figure used in the early stages of image development.

Below: The computer graphic system animator's work area. This is the image displayed by the computer as the animator sits down to do a day's work.

spectives and seem to move.

When all the images were drawn and played back on a TV monitor, they had to be put on film. (The traditional way of photographing digital images is to film them off a cathode ray tube—something like a TV set. However, Lucasfilm has been working on a method of scanning the images with a laser *directly* onto the film! The result is an image of much greater detail and more vivid color, that does not look like the typical computerized shot we are used to seeing.) The digital image was then composited with the scene of the priest in the church. The final results were unique and startling. In this regard, *Young Sherlock Holmes* entered the history book of special effects as the first feature film whose effects were painted directly on the film with a laser. The interface between the computer and film is finally close to being conquered.

How computer-drawn images move is an entire, extremely complicated field of study. The position of moving objects can be specified by programmers for each frame; or their position at key points in space and time can be specified, leaving the computer to trace their paths from point to point by a mathematical procedure called "spline algorithm"; or the camera can be imagined as moving through a coordinate system and its path computed by a related algorithm.

In computer animation, it is often the case that scenes are worked out as fully three-dimensional models, with all surfaces, whether they will ultimately be seen or not, fully detailed. As a final step, once the computer knows how everything will move in a sequence, it re-images the scene into a two-dimensional view—the camera's view—lights it from one or more sources, and blocks out

everything (including the backs of things) that will not be seen.

For the time being, digitized images are impractical for anything but short special effects sequences and television commercials. On television they make some sense, in a medium with low resolution and color dynamics; but in theatrical motion pictures, impractical amounts of data storage space and computer time are necessary, so only shots that would be outrageously difficult to achieve by any other means can be considered for digital manipulation.

The situation is changing even as this is written, however, and with the intensive work at Lucasfilm Computer Division and many other research facilities around the world, breakthroughs in the technique are inevitable.

Though early research in laser scanning will have application in the special effects field, the most significant application will be seen in the final exhibition of films. Imagine a day when an entire film can be "projected" by laser in your local theater. The "film" need not be shipped in heavy and expensive print form, but will be transmitted by satellite. A new *Star Wars* film could be exhibited in tens of thousands of theaters simultaneously, all over the world. Its laser images would be brighter and sharper than traditional images. The potential is enormous.

We must always be careful not to limit our thinking to the more obvious and traditional applications of visual effects. When the technology allows us the freedom to create objects and settings through the mind of the computer, entire environments can be created in which real actors will move freely; a film's decor could be the

Left: Graphic system programmers Eben Ostby and Bill Reeves discuss further refinements of the animated church window scene, shown on the monitors behind them.

Below: Two details of the final digital element as it appears in *Young Sherlock Holmes*.

The final digital element (the Stained Glass Knight) as it appears in *Young Sherlock Holmes*.

the past to play new roles. Who knows what will happen in the exciting decade to come? Will John Wayne and Humphrey Bogart play together in some new production in the next century?

However, I feel that it will not be long before an entire film will be made of computer-generated images. The film may not look completely realistic, as the closer we get to realism the more computer effort and time are involved; it will look more like an animated film. Perhaps, at some later time, we will also see realistic visual presentations in which the story is directed by the viewer. The possibilities of the future are tremendously exciting. As research continues, those possibilities will become realities. It is not surprising that Lucasfilm should be so intensely involved in the development of these ideas for tomorrow's special effects.

figment of a computer's imagination. I would like to think that at least actors will be real for a long time to come, but I could be wrong—financial constraints could conceivably tip the scales in the computer actor's favor. Imagine a matinee idol in the twenty-first century who is merely a computer image and not real at all! It may even be possible to recall some of the greats of

After all, Lucasfilm is a company whose business has long been the making of fact from fantasy.

WARREN FRANKLIN

As a teenager, Warren Franklin started creating light shows for rock performances being given near his home in the San Francisco Bay Area. In order to give the light shows some extra pizzazz, Warren also started making animated films for use with the lighting effects. It was at that point that animation and filmmaking captured his interest.

Still in high school, Warren did a film called "Light Dance" that won the Kodak Teenage Movie Award. He also became apprenticed to documentary filmmaker Rondal Partridge. By the time he was nineteen, he and a good friend had formed their

own production company, which specialized in doing logos and animation for local television commercials. While studying animation at San Francisco State University, he simultaneously worked as a cameraman for Colossal Pictures, an animation studio in the city.

When *Star Wars* came out in 1977, Warren was fascinated by the high-tech special effects that were used in the picture. He began to learn more about special effects on his own and through his work for Colossal. By the time George Lucas's Industrial Light and Magic moved from Southern California to its new location north of San Francisco, Warren was qualified and ready to apply for a job.

He joined the ILM Optical Department in March of 1979 while work was going on for *The Empire Strikes Back*. The department still didn't have much of its equipment when he joined, and Warren helped to set things up. He then worked on the optical line-up for composited shots for the remainder of the picture.

Steady and conscientious, Warren began to work his way up through the ranks. On *Dragonslayer,* he was made Optical Coordinator. He was next promoted to Production Coordinator on *Star Trek II: The Wrath of Khan*. This is a job he also held on *E.T.: The Extra-Terrestrial* and *Return of the Jedi*. He worked as Production Supervisor on *Indiana Jones and the Temple of Doom* and on *Star Trek III: The Search for Spock*. Finally, in April 1984, Warren became general manager of ILM, the position he currently holds.

Among his other duties as general manager, Warren acts as spokesman for ILM. He also is largely responsible for finding and selecting projects for the company that will challenge and interest his talented and highly accomplished staff.

Between the making of *Empire Strikes Back* and *Return of the Jedi,* ILM began to take on outside film projects. The first of these was doing the special effects for *Dragonslayer*. Warren feels the addition of these non-Lucasfilm productions to the workload of ILM is gradually changing the character of the company. He says that during the making of the *Star Wars* movies, ILM's identity was still largely bound to that of the Lucasfilm company as a whole. Now, as ILM continues to work on more and more films separately from the rest of Lucasfilm, it is beginning to have an identity and reputation that is all its own.

Based on its previous work, that reputation is an extremely strong and positive one. It makes it very easy, Warren says, to interest other productions in using ILM to do their special effects work.

Warren wishes to assure Lucasfilm fans that working on outside productions doesn't mean ILM isn't looking forward to future work on further *Star Wars* and Indiana Jones adventures, but he feels it does mean that the outlook of the company will, through variety in its work, be kept fresh and original.

There are two areas of involvement that Warren feels will be of major importance to ILM in the future. One is in the expanded use of special effects in movies outside of the science fiction and fantasy genres; the other is in the development and application of digital special effects techniques.

As the expense of filming in exotic locations and of building massive or intricate sets increases, Warren thinks that filmmakers will turn increasingly toward special effects as an alternative means of showing real but unusual settings. In some ways, this may be more challenging than doing effects for films with purely imaginary stories, because it will be crucial that the effects completely convince the audience of their reality.

As a new area of involvement, Warren says, the use of digital techniques will in turn lead to still further uses of special effects that we haven't even dreamed of yet. He does not believe, however, that special effects will ever completely take over the movies. To ILM's benefit, effects are playing an increasingly central role in film production, though they will never, he says, completely do away with the importance of a good story and good acting.

CHAPTER 11

ILM: THE FIRST TEN YEARS

STAR WARS

MINIATURE AND OPTICAL EFFECTS UNIT

SPECIAL PHOTOGRAPHIC EFFECTS SUPERVISOR
JOHN DYKSTRA

FIRST CAMERAMAN RICHARD EDLUND

SECOND CAMERAMAN DENNIS MUREN

ASSISTANT CAMERAMEN DOUGLAS SMITH,
KENNETH RALSTON,
DAVID ROBMAN

SECOND UNIT PHOTOGRAPHY BRUCE LOGAN

COMPOSITE OPTICAL PHOTOGRAPHY
ROBERT BLALACK (PRAXIS)

OPTICAL PHOTOGRAPHY COORDINATOR PAUL ROTH

OPTICAL PRINTER OPERATORS DAVID BERRY,
DAVID McCUE,
RICHARD PECORELLA,
ELDON RICKMAN,
JAMES VAN TREES, JR.

OPTICAL CAMERA ASSISTANTS CALEB ASCHKYNAZO,
JOHN C. MOULDS,
BRUCE NICHOLSON, GARY SMITH,
BERT TERRERI, DONNA TRACY,
JIM WELLS, VICKY WITT

PRODUCTION SUPERVISOR GEORGE E. MATHER

MATTE ARTIST P. S. ELLENSHAW

PLANET AND SATELLITE ARTIST RALPH McQUARRIE

EFFECTS ILLUSTRATION AND DESIGN
JOSEPH JOHNSTON

ADDITIONAL SPACECRAFT DESIGN COLIN CANTWELL

CHIEF MODELMAKER GRANT McCUNE

MODEL BUILDERS DAVID BEASLEY, JON ERLAND,
LORNE PETERSON, STEVE GAWLEY,
PAUL HUSTON, DAVID JONES

ANIMATION AND ROTOSCOPE DESIGN ADAM BECKETT

ANIMATORS MICHAEL ROSS, PETER KURAN,
JONATHAN SEAY, CHRIS CASADY,
LYN GERRY, DIANA WILSON

STOP MOTION ANIMATION JON BERG, PHIL TIPPETT

MINIATURE EXPLOSIONS JOE VISKOCIL, GREG AUER

COMPUTER ANIMATION AND GRAPHIC DISPLAYS
DAN O'BANNON, LARRY CUBA,
JOHN WASH, JAY TEITZELL, IMAGE WEST

FILM CONTROL COORDINATOR	MARY M. LIND	SPECIAL MECHANICAL EQUIPMENT	
FILM LIBRARIANS	CINDY ISMAN, CONNIE McCRUM, PAMELA MALOUF		JERRY GREENWOOD, DOUGLAS BARNETT, STUART ZIFF, DAVID SCOTT
ELECTRONICS DESIGN	ALVAH J. MILLER	PRODUCTION MANAGERS	BOB SHEPHERD, LON TINNEY
SPECIAL COMPONENTS	JAMES SHOURT		
ASSISTANTS	MASAAKI NORIHORO, ELEANOR PORTER	PRODUCTION STAFF	PATRICIA ROSE DUIGNAN, MARK KLINE, RHONDA PECK, RON NATHAN
CAMERA AND MECHANICAL DESIGN	DON TRUMBULL, RICHARD ALEXANDER, WILLIAM SHOURT	ASSISTANT EDITOR (OPTICALS)	BRUCE MICHAEL GREEN

1977

THE EMPIRE STRIKES BACK

MINIATURE AND OPTICAL EFFECTS UNIT

SPECIAL VISUAL EFFECTS	BRIAN JOHNSON, RICHARD EDLUND
EFFECTS DIRECTOR OF PHOTOGRAPHY	DENNIS MUREN
EFFECTS CAMERAMEN	KEN RALSTON, JIM VEILLEUX
CAMERA OPERATORS	DON DOW, BILL NEIL
ASSISTANT CAMERAMEN	SELWYN EDDY, JODY WESTHEIMER, RICK FICHTER, CLINT PALMER, MICHEAL McALISTER, PAUL HUSTON, RICHARD FISH, CHRIS ANDERSON
OPTICAL PHOTOGRAPHY SUPERVISOR	BRUCE NICHOLSON
OPTICAL PRINTER OPERATORS	DAVID BERRY, KENNETH SMITH, DONALD CLARK
OPTICAL LINE-UP	WARREN FRANKLIN, MARK VARGO, PETER AMUNDSON, LORING DOYLE, THOMAS ROSSETER, TAM PILLSBURY, JAMES LIM
OPTICAL COORDINATOR	LAURIE VERMONT
LABORATORY TECHNICIANS	TIM GEIDEMAN, DUNCAN MYERS, ED JONES
ART DIRECTOR—VISUAL EFFECTS	JOE JOHNSTON
ASSISTANT ART DIRECTOR	NILO RODIS-JAMERO
STOP MOTION ANIMATION	JON BERG, PHIL TIPPETT
STOP MOTION TECHNICIANS	TOM ST. AMAND, DOUG BESWICK
MATTE PAINTING SUPERVISOR	HARRISON ELLENSHAW
MATTE ARTISTS	RALPH McQUARRIE, MICHAEL PANGRAZIO
MATTE PHOTOGRAPHY	NEIL KREPELA
ADDITIONAL MATTE PHOTOGRAPHY	MICHAEL LAWLER
MATTE PHOTOGRAPHY ASSISTANTS	CRAIG BARRON, ROBERT ELSWIT
CHIEF MODELMAKER	LORNE PETERSON
MODEL SHOP FOREMAN	STEVE GAWLEY

MODEL MAKERS — PAUL HUSTON, TOM RUDDUCK, MICHAEL FULMER, SAMUEL ZOLLTHEIS, CHARLES BAILEY, EASE OWYEUNG, SCOTT MARSHALL, MARC THORPE, WESLEY SEEDS, DAVE CARSON, ROB GEMMEL, PAT McCLUNG

ANIMATION AND ROTOSCOPE SUPERVISOR — PETER KURAN

ANIMATORS — SAMUEL COMSTOCK, GARRY WALLER, JOHN VAN VLIET, RICK TAYLOR, KIM KNOWLTON, CHRIS CASADY, NINA SAXON, DIANA WILSON

VISUAL EFFECTS EDITORIAL SUPERVISOR — CONRAD BUFF

EFFECTS EDITOR — MICHAEL KELLY

ASSISTANT EFFECTS EDITORS — ARTHUR REPOLA, HOWARD STEIN

APPRENTICE EDITOR — JON THALER

PRODUCTION ADMINISTRATOR — DICK GALLEGLY

PRODUCTION SECRETARY — PATRICIA BLAU

PRODUCTION ASSOCIATE — THOMAS BROWN

PRODUCTION ACCOUNTANT — RAY SCALICE

ASSISTANT ACCOUNTANTS — GLENN PHILLIPS, PAM TRAAS, LAURA CROCKETT

PRODUCTION ASSISTANT — JENNY OZNOWICZ

TRANSPORTATION — ROBERT MARTIN

STILL PHOTOGRAPHER — TERRY CHOSTNER

LAB ASSISTANT — ROBERTO McGRATH

ELECTRONICS SYSTEMS DESIGNER — JERRY JEFFRESS

SYSTEMS PROGRAMMING — KRIS BROWN

ELECTRONIC ENGINEERS — LHARY MEYER, MIKE MACKENZIE, GARY LEO

SPECIAL PROJECT COORDINATOR — STUART ZIFF

EQUIPMENT ENGINEERING SUPERVISOR — GENE WHITEMAN

DESIGN ENGINEER — MIKE BOLLES

MACHINISTS — UDO PAMPEL, GREG BEAUMONTE

DRAFTSMAN — ED TENNLER

SPECIAL PROJECTS — GARY PLATEK

SUPERVISING STAGE TECHNICIAN — T. E. MOEHNKE

STAGE TECHNICIANS — WILLIAM BECK, BOBBY FINLEY, LEO LOVERRO, EDWARD HIRSH, DICK DOVA SPAH, ED BREED

MINIATURE PYROTECHNICS — JOSEPH VISKOCIL, DAVE PIER, THAINE MORRIS

OPTICAL PRINTER COMPONENT MANUFACTURER — GEORGE RANDLE CO.

CAMERA AND MOVEMENT DESIGN — JIM BEAUMONTE

SPECIAL OPTICS DESIGNER — DAVID GRAFTON

SPECIAL OPTICS FABRICATION — J. L. WOOD OPTICAL SYSTEMS

OPTICAL PRINTER COMPONENT ENGINEERING — FRIES ENGINEERING

HIGH SPEED CAMERA MOVEMENTS — MITCHELL CAMERA CORP.

ULTRA HIGH SPEED CAMERA — BRUCE HILL PRODUCTIONS

1980

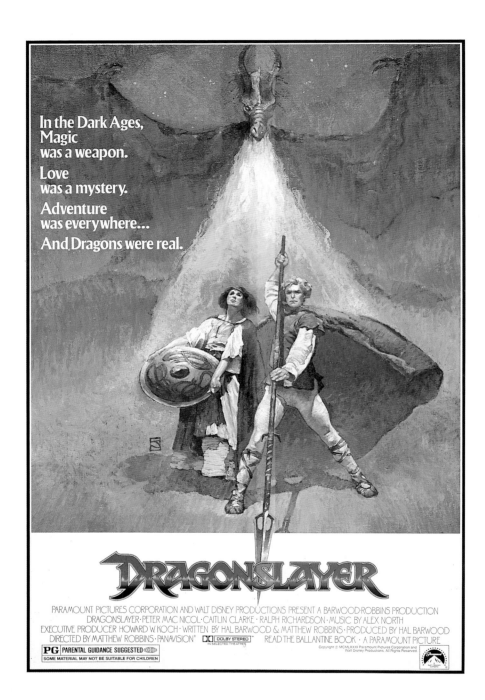

DRAGONSLAYER

PHOTOGRAPHIC EFFECTS PRODUCED AT
INDUSTRIAL LIGHT & MAGIC, INC.
MARIN COUNTY, CALIFORNIA

SUPERVISOR OF MINIATURE AND OPTICAL EFFECTS
DENNIS MUREN

DRAGON SUPERVISORS PHIL TIPPETT,
KEN RALSTON

DRAGON MOVERS CHRISTOPHER WALAS,
TOM ST. AMAND, STUART ZIFF,
GARY LEO, JON BERG

MINIATURE SET DESIGNS DAVE CARSON

OPTICAL PHOTOGRAPHY SUPERVISOR
BRUCE NICHOLSON

OPTICAL COORDINATOR WARREN FRANKLIN

OPTICAL PRINTER OPERATORS KENNETH SMITH,
JOHN ELLIS, DAVID BARRY

OPTICAL LINE-UP TOM ROSSETER, MARK VARGO

MATTE PAINTING SUPERVISOR ALAN MALEY

MATTE ARTISTS CHRISTOPHER EVANS,
MICHAEL PANGRAZIO

MATTE PHOTOGRAPHY NEIL KREPELA

MATTE PHOTOGRAPHY ASSISTANT CRAIG BARRON

EFFECTS CAMERAMEN RICK FICHTER,
MICHEAL McALISTER,
JIM VEILLEUX

EFFECTS CAMERA ASSISTANTS SELWYN EDDY III,
JODY WESTHEIMER

ANIMATION SUPERVISOR SAMUEL COMSTOCK

ANIMATORS DIETRICH FRIESEN,
GARRY WALLER, LORING DOYLE,
JOHN VAN VLIET, KIM KNOWLTON,
JUDY ELKINS, SYLVIA KEULEN,
SCOTT CAPLE

ADDITIONAL ANIMATION PETER KURAN,
VISUAL CONCEPT ENGINEERING

ANIMATORS SUSAN TURNER, KATHRINE KEAN,
PAM VICK, CHRIS CASADY,
LEN MORGANTI

ANIMATORS CAMERAMAN ROBERT JACOBS

OPTICAL CAMERAMAN JAMES HAGEDORN

ADDITIONAL OPTICAL COMPOSITES
RGB FILM PROCESSING,
LOOKOUT MOUNTAIN FILMS,
MODERN FILM EFFECTS

ULTRA HIGH SPEED CAMERA
BRUCE HILL PRODUCTIONS

EFFECTS PRODUCTION SUPERVISOR   THOMAS SMITH

EFFECTS PRODUCTION COORDINATOR
LAURIE VERMONT

MODEL SHOP SUPERVISOR   LORNE PETERSON

SUPERVISING STAGE TECHNICIAN   T. E. MOEHNKE

DRAGON ASSISTANTS   ERIC JENSEN,
MARC THORPE, WESLEY SEEDS,
PETER STOLZ

PYROTECHNICS   THAINE MORRIS

STILL PHOTOGRAPHER   TERRY CHOSTNER

EFFECTS EDITORIAL COORDINATORS   ARTHUR REPOLA,
HOWARD STEIN

EFFECTS EDITORIAL ASSISTANT   PETER AMUNDSEN

EQUIPMENT ENGINEERING SUPERVISOR
GENE WHITEMAN

MACHINISTS   UDO PAMPEL,
CONRAD BONDERSON

ELECTRONICS SYSTEMS DESIGNER   JERRY JEFFRESS

COMPUTER ENGINEER   KRIS BROWN

ELECTRONIC ENGINEER   MIKE MACKENZIE

ELECTRONIC TECHNICIANS   MARTY BRENNEIS,
MELISSA CARGILL,
CRISTI McCARTHY

1981

Indiana Jones—the new hero
from the creators of JAWS and STAR WARS.

PARAMOUNT PICTURES Presents A LUCASFILM LTD. Production
A STEVEN SPIELBERG Film
Starring HARRISON FORD
KAREN ALLEN · PAUL FREEMAN · RONALD LACEY · JOHN RHYS-DAVIES and DENHOLM ELLIOTT
Music by JOHN WILLIAMS · Executive Producers GEORGE LUCAS and HOWARD KAZANJIAN · Screenplay by LAWRENCE KASDAN · Story by GEORGE LUCAS and PHILIP KAUFMAN
Produced by FRANK MARSHALL · Directed by STEVEN SPIELBERG Filmed in Panavision® DOLBY STEREO NOVELIZATION FROM BALLANTINE BOOKS ORIGINAL SOUNDTRACK ON COLUMBIA RECORDS & TAPES
PG PARENTAL GUIDANCE SUGGESTED
SOME MATERIAL MAY NOT BE SUITABLE FOR CHILDREN
A PARAMOUNT PICTURE
TM Copyright © Lucasfilm Ltd. (LFL) MCMLXXXI All Rights Reserved

RAIDERS OF THE LOST ARK

SPECIAL VISUAL EFFECTS PRODUCED AT	INDUSTRIAL LIGHT & MAGIC MARIN COUNTY, CALIFORNIA
VISUAL EFFECTS SUPERVISOR	RICHARD EDLUND
OPTICAL PHOTOGRAPHY SUPERVISOR	BRUCE NICHOLSON
PRODUCTION SUPERVISOR	THOMAS SMITH
ART DIRECTOR—VISUAL EFFECTS	JOE JOHNSTON
MATTE PAINTING SUPERVISOR	ALAN MALEY
VISUAL EFFECTS EDITORIAL SUPERVISOR	CONRAD BUFF
PRODUCTION COORDINATOR	PATRICIA BLAU
PRODUCTION ASSOCIATE	MIKI HERMAN
ANIMATION SUPERVISORS	SAMUEL COMSTOCK, DIETRICH FRIESEN
EFFECTS CAMERAMAN	JIM VEILLEUX
CAMERA OPERATORS	BILL NEIL, DON DOW
ASSISTANT CAMERAMAN	CLINT PALMER
OPTICAL PRINTER OPERATORS	DAVID BERRY, KENNETH SMITH, JOHN ELLIS
OPTICAL LINE-UP	MARK VARGO, WARREN FRANKLIN, TOM ROSSETER
ASSISTANT ART DIRECTOR	NILO RODIS-JAMERO
ILLUSTRATOR	RALPH McQUARRIE
MATTE ARTIST	MICHAEL PANGRAZIO
MATTE PHOTOGRAPHY	NEIL KREPELA
MATTE PHOTOGRAPHY ASSISTANT	CRAIG BARRON
MODEL SHOP FOREMAN	LORNE PETERSON
MODELMAKERS	STEVE GAWLEY, MIKE FULMER, WESLEY SEEDS, PAUL HUSTON, CHARLIE BAILEY, SAM ZOLLTHEIS, MARC THORPE, BRUCE RICHARDSON, EASE OWYEUNG
ANIMATORS	JOHN VAN VLIET, KIM KNOWLTON, GARRY WALLER, LORING DOYLE, SCOTT CAPLE, JUDY ELKINS, SYLVIA KEULEN, SCOTT MARSHALL
ASSISTANT EFFECTS EDITORS	PETER AMUNDSON, HOWARD STEIN
ASSISTANT FILM EDITOR	DUWAYNE DUNHAM
PRODUCTION COORDINATOR	LAURIE VERMONT

CLOUD EFFECTS	GARY PLATEK
SPECIAL MAKE-UP EFFECTS	CHRISTOPHER WALAS
LABORATORY TECHNICIANS	TIM GEIDEMAN, DUNCAN MYERS, ED JONES
STILL PHOTOGRAPHER	TERRY CHOSTNER
ADMINISTRATION ASSISTANT	CHRISSIE ENGLAND
PRODUCTION ACCOUNTANTS	DAVID KAKITA, SHIRLEY LEE, LAURA KAYSEN
STILL LAB TECHNICIANS	ROBERTO McGRATH, KERRY NORDQUIST
ELECTRONIC SYSTEMS DESIGNER	JERRY JEFFRESS
COMPUTER ENGINEERING	KRIS BROWN
DESIGN ENGINEER	MIKE BOLLES
ELECTRONICS ENGINEERS	MIKE MACKENZIE, MARTY BRENNEIS, GARY LEO
ELECTRONIC TECHNICIANS	CRISTI McCARTHY, BESSIE WILEY, MELISSA CARGILL
EQUIPMENT ENGINEERING SUPERVISOR	GENE WHITEMAN
MACHINIST	UDO PAMPEL
SPECIAL PROJECTS	WADE CHILDRESS
SUPERVISING STAGE TECNICIAN	T. E. MOEHNKE
STAGE TECHNICIANS	WILLIAM BECK DICK DOVA SPAH, BOBBY FINLEY III, EDWARD HIRSH, PATRICK FITZSIMMONS, JOHN McLEOD, PETER STOLZ
PYROTECHNICS	THAINE MORRIS
ULTRA HIGH SPEED CAMERA	BRUCE HILL PRODUCTIONS

STAR TREK II: THE WRATH OF KHAN

SPECIAL VISUAL EFFECTS PRODUCED AT
INDUSTRIAL LIGHT & MAGIC,
A DIVISION OF LUCASFILM LTD.

SPECIAL VISUAL EFFECTS SUPERVISORS
KEN RALSTON & JIM VEILLEUX

EFFECTS CAMERAMEN DON DOW, SCOTT FARRAR

CAMERA OPERATOR STEWART BARBEE

ASSISTANT CAMERA OPERATORS SELWYN EDDY III,
DAVID HARDBERGER,
MIKE OWENS, MICHAEL SANTY,
ROBERT HILL

OPTICAL PHOTOGRAPY SUPERVISOR
BRUCE NICHOLSON

OPTICAL PRINTER OPERATORS DAVID BERRY,
KENNETH SMITH, MARK VARGO,
JOHN ELLIS, DONALD CLARK

OPTICAL LINE-UP THOMAS ROSSETER, ED JONES,
RALPH GORDON

OPTICAL LABORATORY TECHNICIANS TIM GEIDEMAN,
DUNCAN MYERS, BOB CHRISOULIS

GENERAL MANAGER, ILM TOM SMITH

PRODUCTION SUPERVISOR PATRICIA ROSE DUIGNAN

PRODUCTION COORDINATOR WARREN FRANKLIN

MATTE PAINTING ARTISTS CHRIS EVANS,
FRANK ORDAZ

MATTE PHOTOGRAPHY NEIL KREPELA

MATTE PHOTOGRAPHY ASSISTANT CRAIG BARRON

SUPERVISING MODELMAKER STEVE GAWLEY

MODELMAKERS WILLIAM GEORGE, SEAN CASEY,
LARRY TAN, JEFF MANN,
STEVE SANDERS, BRIAN CHIN,
BOB DIEPENBROCK, MIKE FULMER

MODEL ELECTRONICS MARTY BRENNEIS

ANIMATION SUPERVISOR SAMUEL COMSTOCK

ANIMATORS KIM KNOWLTON, SCOTT CAPLE,
JIM KEEFER, KATHRYN LENIHAN,
JUDY ELKINS, JAY DAVIS

ADDITIONAL ANIMATION
VISUAL CONCEPT ENGINEERING

SUPERVISING EFFECTS EDITOR ARTHUR REPOLA

EFFECTS EDITOR PETER AMUNDSON

COMPUTER DATABASE MANAGEMENT
MALCOLM BLANCHARD

COMPUTER GRAPHICS
LOREN CARPENTER,
ED CATMULL, PAT COLE,
ROB COOK, TOM DUFF,
ROBERT D. POOR,
THOMAS PORTER,
WILLIAM REEVES,
ALVY RAY SMITH

STARFIELD EFFECTS BY
EVANS & SUTHERLAND,
DIGISTAR SYSTEM

TACTICAL DISPLAYS BY
EVANS & SUTHERLAND,
PICTURE SYSTEM,
BRENT WATSON,
STEVE McALLISTER,
NEIL HARRINGTON, JERI PANEK

MOLECULAR COMPUTER GRAPHICS BY
COMPUTER GRAPHICS LABORATORY
UNIVERSITY OF CALIFORNIA
SAN FRANCISCO
DR. ROBERT LANGRIDGE

STILL PHOTOGRAPHER   TERRY CHOSTNER

STILL LAB TECHNICIANS   ROBERTO McGRATH,
KERRY NORDQUIST

SUPERVISING STAGE TECHNICIAN   T. E. MOEHNKE

STAGE TECHNICIANS   DAVE CHILDERS,
HAROLD COLE, DICK DOVA SPAH,
BOBBY FINLEY III,
PATRICK FITZSIMMONS,
EDWARD HIRSH, JOHN McLEOD,
PETER STOLZ

PYROTECHNICS   THAINE MORRIS

EQUIPMENT COORDINATOR   WADE CHILDRESS

ULTRA HIGH SPEED CAMERA
BRUCE HILL PRODUCTIONS

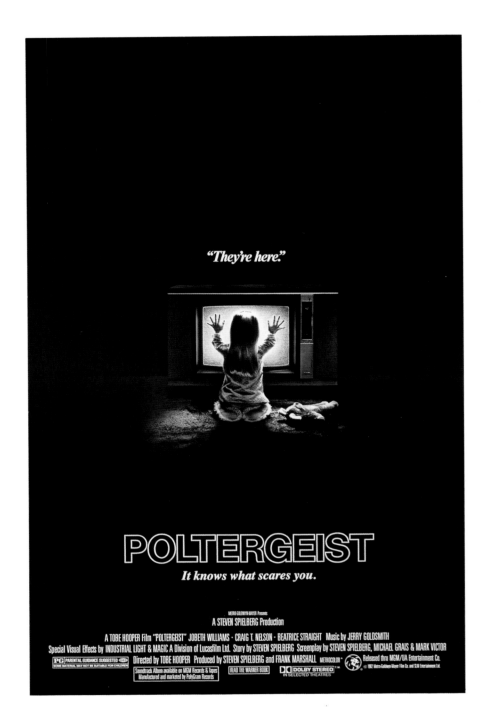

POLTERGEIST

SPECIAL VISUAL EFFECTS PRODUCED AT
INDUSTRIAL LIGHT & MAGIC,
A DIVISION OF LUCASFILM LTD.
MARIN COUNTY, CALIFORNIA

VISUAL EFFECTS SUPERVISION	RICHARD EDLUND, A.S.C.
OPTICAL PHOTOGRAPHY SUPERVISOR	BRUCE NICHOLSON
VISUAL EFFECTS EDITORIAL SUPERVISOR	CONRAD BUFF
EFFECTS ART DIRECTOR	NILO RODIS-JAMERO
EFFECTS CAMERAMEN	RICK FICHTER, BILL NEIL
PRODUCTION SUPERVISOR	TOM SMITH
PRODUCTION COORDINATOR	LAURIE VERMONT
MATTE PAINTING SUPERVISOR	MICHAEL PANGRAZIO
MATTE PHOTOGRAPHY	NEIL KREPELA
ANIMATION SUPERVISOR	JOHN BRUNO
LASER AND CLOUD EFFECTS	GARY PLATEK
MODEL SHOP SUPERVISOR	LORNE PETERSON
CHIEF MODELMAKER	PAUL HUSTON
TECHNICAL ANIMATION SUPERVISOR	SAMUEL COMSTOCK
FIRST ASSISTANT CAMERAMEN	PETER ROMANO, ROBERT HILL, GARRY WALLER, KIM MARKS
SECOND ASSISTANT CAMERAMAN	RAY GILBERTI
CAMERAMAN-ADDITIONAL SCENES	JIM VEILLEUX
OPTICAL PRINTER OPERATORS	JOHN ELLIS, MARK VARGO, DON CLARK, DAVID BERRY
OPTICAL LINE-UP	ED JONES, TOM ROSSETER, RALPH GORDON
OPTICAL TECHNICIANS	TIM GEIDEMAN, DUNCAN MEYERS, BOB CHRISOULIS
MODELMAKERS	EASE OWYEUNG, BARBARA GALLUCCI, MARC THORPE, SEAN CASEY, CHARLIE BAILEY, DAVE SOSALLA, BRUCE RICHARDSON, STEVE GAWLEY, GRANT SMITH, LARRY TAN, JEFF MANN, SCOTT MARSHALL, MARGHE McMAHON, TOBY HEINDEL
KEY ANIMATOR	ART VITELLO
ANIMATORS	JOSÉ ABEL, MILT GRAY

LAYOUT	TERRY WINDELL	SPECIAL WIRE PERFORMANCE	PAULA PAULSON
ANIMATION CAMERA SUPERVISOR	JAMES C. KEEFER	SPECIAL WARDROBE	LISA JEAN MOWER
ANIMATION ASSISTANT SUPERVISOR	RENÉE HOLT	PRODUCTION ACCOUNTANT	LAURA KAYSEN
KEY ASSISTANT	MICHAEL LESSA	ADMINISTRATIVE SUPERVISOR	CHRISSIE ENGLAND
ASSISTANT ANIMATORS	JACK MONGOVAN, PEGGY TONKONOGY, SCOTT CAPLE, ROB LaDUCA, ELLEN LICHTWARDT	PRODUCTION SECRETARIES	MARY LOU HALE, KATHY SHINE
		PRODUCTION PROCURERS	ED BREED, PAULA KARSH
MATTE ANIMATION	KATHRYN LENIHAN, KIM KNOWLTON, JAY DAVIS, JUDY ELKINS	ELECTRONIC SYSTEM DESIGN	JERRY JEFFRESS
		ELECTRONIC SYSTEM SOFTWARE	KRIS BROWN
ASSISTANT MATTE PHOTOGRAPHY	CRAIG BARRON	ELECTRONIC ENGINEERS	MICHAEL MACKENZIE, GARY LEO, MARTY BRENNEIS
ADDITIONAL MATTE PHOTOGRAPHY	MICHAEL SHANNON	ELECTRONIC TECHNICIANS	BESS WILEY, MELISSA CARGILL
VISUAL EFFECTS EDITOR	HOWARD STEIN	ELECTRONIC COORDINATOR	CRISTI McCARTHY
ASSISTANT VISUAL EFFECTS EDITOR	PETER AMUNDSON	DESIGN ENGINEER	MICHAEL BOLLES
SUPERVISING STAGE TECHNICIAN	TED MOEHNKE	DRAFTSMAN	ED TENNLER
STAGE FOREMAN	PATRICK FITZSIMMONS	EQUIPMENT ENGINEERING SUPERVISOR	GENE WHITEMAN
STAGE TECHNICIANS	DICK DOVA SPAH, BOBBY FINLEY III, EDWARD HIRSH, JOHN McLEOD, PETER STOLZ, THAINE MORRIS, DAVE CHILDERS, HAROLD COLE	MACHINISTS	UDO PAMPEL, CONRAD BONDERSON
		APPRENTICE MACHINISTS	DAVID HANKS, CHRIS RAND
STILL PHOTOGRAPHY	TERRY CHOSTNER, ROBERTO McGRATH, KERRY NORDQUIST	EQUIPMENT MAINTENANCE	WADE CHILDRESS, MICHAEL SMITH

E.T.: THE EXTRA-TERRESTRIAL

VISUAL EFFECTS PRODUCED AT
INDUSTRIAL LIGHT & MAGIC,
A DIVISION OF LUCASFILM LTD.,
MARIN COUNTY, CALIFORNIA

VISUAL EFFECTS SUPERVISOR   DENNIS MUREN

EFFECTS CAMERAMAN   MIKE McALISTER

CAMERA OPERATORS   ROBERT ELSWIT, DON DOW

CAMERA ASSISTANTS   PAT SWEENEY,
KARL HERRMANN,
SELWYN EDDY III, MIKE OWENS

OPTICAL PHOTOGRAPHY SUPERVISOR
KENNETH F. SMITH

OPTICAL PRINTER OPERATOR   DAVID BERRY

OPTICAL LINE-UP   RALPH GORDON

OPTICAL TECHNICIANS   DUNCAN MYERS,
TIM GEIDEMAN, BOB CHRISOULIS

GO-MOTION FIGURES   TOM ST. AMAND

MODEL SHOP SUPERVISOR   LORNE PETERSON

CHIEF MODELMAKERS   CHARLIE BAILEY,
MIKE FULMER

MODELMAKERS   SCOTT MARSHALL,
EASE OWYEUNG, MIKE COCHRAIN,
SUZANNE PASTOR,
MICHAEL STEFFE, JESSIE BOBERG,
RANDY OTTENBERG

SPACESHIP DESIGN   RALPH McQUARRIE

MATTE PAINTING SUPERVISOR   MICHAEL PANGRAZIO

MATTE PAINTING ARTISTS   CHRIS EVANS,
FRANK ORDAZ

MATTE PHOTOGRAPHY   NEIL KREPELA

MATTE PHOTOGRAPHY ASSISTANT   CRAIG BARRON

EFFECTS EDITORIAL SUPERVISOR   CONRAD BUFF

EFFECTS EDITOR   HOWARD STEIN

GENERAL MANAGER, ILM   TOM SMITH

PRODUCTION COORDINATORS   WARREN FRANKLIN,
LAURIE VERMONT

ANIMATION SUPERVISOR   SAMUEL COMSTOCK

ANIMATORS   PEGGY TONKONOGY,
GARRY WALLER, TERRY WINDELL,
JACK MONGOVAN

STILL PHOTOGRAPHER   TERRY CHOSTNER

STILL LAB TECHNICIANS	ROBERTO McGRATH, KERRY NORDQUIST	*PRODUCTION ACCOUNTANT*	LAURA KAYSEN
SUPERVISING STAGE TECHNICIAN	T. E. MOEHNKE	*EQUIPMENT MAINTENANCE*	WADE CHILDRESS, MICHAEL SMITH
STAGE TECHNICIANS	DAVE CHILDERS, HAROLD COLE, DICK DOVA SPAH, BOBBY FINLEY III, PATRICK FITZSIMMONS, EDWARD HIRSH, JOHN McLEOD, THAINE MORRIS, PETER STOLZ	*ELECTRONIC SYSTEMS DESIGN*	JERRY JEFFRESS
		MODEL ELECTRONICS	GARY LEO, MARTY BRENNEIS
		OPTICAL PRINTER ENGINEERING	GENE WHITEMAN, JOHN ELLIS

RETURN OF THE JEDI

MINIATURE AND OPTICAL EFFECTS UNIT	INDUSTRIAL LIGHT & MAGIC
VISUAL EFFECTS	RICHARD EDLUND, A.S.C., DENNIS MUREN, KEN RALSTON
MAKE-UP AND CREATURE DESIGN	PHIL TIPPETT, STUART FREEBORN
ART DIRECTOR-VISUAL EFFECTS	JOE JOHNSTON
OPTICAL PHOTOGRAPHY SUPERVISOR	BRUCE NICHOLSON
GENERAL MANAGER, ILM	TOM SMITH
PRODUCTION SUPERVISOR	PATRICIA ROSE DUIGNAN
MATTE PAINTING SUPERVISOR	MICHAEL PANGRAZIO
MODELSHOP SUPERVISORS	LORNE PETERSON, STEVE GAWLEY
ANIMATION SUPERVISOR	JAMES KEEFER
SUPERVISING VISUAL EFFECTS EDITOR	ARTHUR REPOLA
EFFECTS CAMERAMEN	DON DOW, MICHEAL J. McALISTER, BILL NEIL, SCOTT FARRAR, SELWYN EDDY III, MICHAEL OWENS, ROBERT ELSWIT, RICK FICHTER, STEWART BARBEE, MARK GREDELL, DAVID HARDBERGER
ASSISTANT CAMERAMEN	PAT SWEENEY, KIM MARKS, ROBERT HILL, RAY GILBERTI, RANDY JOHNSON, PATRICK McARDLE, PETER DAULTON, BESSIE WILEY, MARYAN EVANS, TOBY HEINDEL, DAVID FINCHER, PETER ROMANO
PRODUCTION COORDINATORS	WARREN FRANKLIN, LAURIE VERMONT
OPTICAL PRINTER OPERATORS	JOHN ELLIS, DAVID BERRY, KENNETH SMITH, DONALD CLARK, MARK VARGO, JAMES LIM
OPTICAL LINE-UP	TOM ROSSETER, ED L. JONES, RALPH GORDON, PHILIP BARBERIO
LAB TECHNICIANS	TIM GEIDEMAN, DUNCAN MYERS, MICHAEL MOORE
PRODUCTION ILLUSTRATOR	GEORGE JENSON
MATTE PAINTING ARTISTS	CHRIS EVANS, FRANK ORDAZ
MATTE PHOTOGRAPHY	NEIL KREPELA, CRAIG BARRON

STOP MOTION ANIMATOR	TOM ST. AMAND
CHIEF MODELMAKERS	PAUL HUSTON, CHARLES BAILEY, MICHAEL GLENN FULMER, EASE OWYEUNG
MODELMAKERS	WILLIAM GEORGE, MARC THORPE, SCOTT MARSHALL, SEAN CASEY, LARRY TAN, BARBARA GALLUCCI, JEFF MANN, IRA KEELER, BILL BECK, MIKE COCHRANE, BARBARA AFFONSO, BILL BUTTFIELD, MARGHE McMAHON, RANDY OTTENBERG
HEAD EFFECTS ANIMATORS	GARRY WALLER, KIMBERLY KNOWLTON
EFFECTS ANIMATORS	TERRY WINDELL, RENEE HOLT, MIKE LESSA, SAMUEL COMSTOCK, ROB La DUCA, ANNICK THERRIEN, SUKI STERN, MARGOT PIPKIN
VISUAL EFFECTS EDITORS	HOWARD STEIN, PETER AMUNDSON, BILL KIMBERLIN
ASSISTANT VISUAL EFFECTS EDITORS	ROBERT CHRISOULIS, MICHAEL GLEASON, JAY IGNASZEWSKI, JOE CLASS
SUPERVISING STAGE TECHNICIAN	TED MOEHNKE
STAGE TECHNICIANS	PATRICK FITZSIMMONS, BOB FINLEY III, ED HIRSH, JOHN McLEOD, PETER STOLZ, DAVE CHILDERS, HAROLD COLE, MERLIN OHM, JOE FULMER, LANCE BRACKETT
PYROTECHNICIANS	THAINE MORRIS, DAVE PIER
SUPERVISOR-STILL PHOTOGRAPHY	TERRY CHOSTNER
STILL PHOTOGRAPHERS	ROBERTO McGRATH, KERRY NORDQUIST
ELECTRONIC SYSTEM DESIGNERS	JERRY JEFFRESS, KRIS BROWN
ELECTRONIC ENGINEERS	MIKE MACKENZIE, MARTY BRENNEIS
COMPUTER GRAPHICS	WILLIAM REEVES, TOM DUFF
EQUIPMENT ENGINEERING SUPERVISOR	GENE WHITEMAN
MACHINISTS	UDO PAMPEL, CONRAD BONDERSON
APPRENTICE MACHINISTS	DAVID HANKS, CHRIS RAND
DESIGN ENGINEER	MIKE BOLLES
EQUIPMENT SUPPORT STAFF	WADE CHILDRESS, MICHAEL J. SMITH, CRISTI McCARTHY, ED TENNLER
ADMINISTRATIVE STAFF	CHRISSIE ENGLAND, LAURA KAYSEN, PAULA KARSH, KAREN AYERS, SONJA PAULSEN, KAREN DUBE
PRODUCTION ASSISTANTS	SUSAN FRITZ-MONAHAN, KATHY SHINE

1983

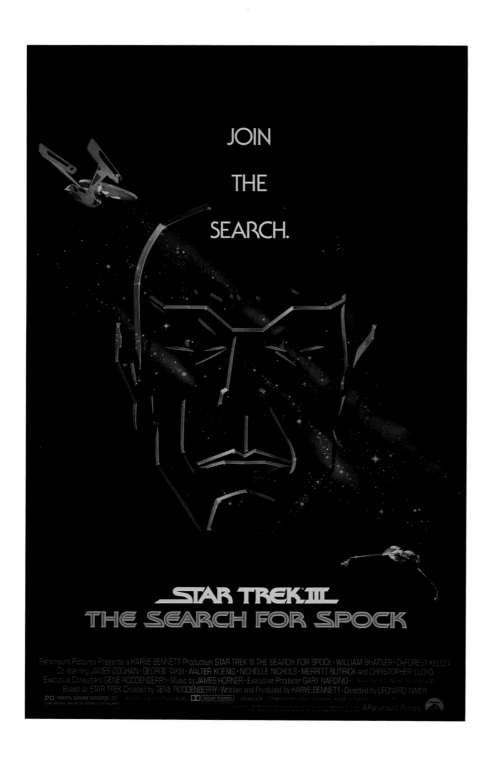

STAR TREK III: THE SEARCH FOR SPOCK

VISUAL EFFECTS PRODUCED AT
INDUSTRIAL LIGHT & MAGIC,
MARIN COUNTY, CALIFORNIA

SUPERVISOR OF VISUAL EFFECTS   KENNETH RALSTON

EFFECTS ART DIRECTORS   NILO RODIS-JAMERO,
DAVID CARSON

VISUAL EFFECTS CAMERAMEN   DONALD DOW,
SCOTT FARRAR, SELWYN EDDY III

ASSISTANT CAMERAMEN   PETER DAULTON,
ROBERT HILL, PATRICK McARDLE,
RAY GILBERTI, DAVID HANKS,
TOBY HEINDEL

OPTICAL PHOTOGRAPHY SUPERVISOR
KENNETH F. SMITH

OPTICAL CAMERA OPERATORS   JAMES LIM,
DONALD CLARK

OPTICAL LINE-UP   RALPH GORDON, DAVID BERRY

GENERAL MANAGER, ILM   TOM SMITH

PRODUCTION SUPERVISOR   WARREN FRANKLIN

PRODUCTION COORDINATOR   LAURIE VERMONT

SUPERVISING MODELMAKER   STEVE GAWLEY

ADDITIONAL SPACECRAFT DESIGN   WILLIAM GEORGE

MODELMAKERS   WILLIAM BECK,
MICHAEL FULMER, IRA KEELER,
JEFF MANN

CREATURE SUPERVISOR   DAVID SOSALLA

MATTE PAINTING SUPERVISOR   MICHAEL PANGRAZIO

MATTE ARTISTS   CHRIS EVANS, FRANK ORDAZ

MATTE CAMERA SUPERVISOR   CRAIG BARRON

ANIMATION SUPERVISOR   CHARLES MULLEN

EFFECTS ANIMATORS   BRUCE WALTERS,
PHILLIP NORWOOD,
RICHARD SCHULZE

CHIEF VISUAL EFFECTS EDITOR   BILL KIMBERLIN

VISUAL EFFECTS EDITOR   JAY IGNASZEWSKI

STILL PHOTOGRAPHY SUPERVISOR   TERRY CHOSTNER

MINIATURE PYROTECHNICS AND FIRE EFFECTS
ILM STAGE CREW

1984

INDIANA JONES AND THE TEMPLE OF DOOM

VISUAL EFFECTS PRODUCED AT	INDUSTRIAL LIGHT & MAGIC, MARIN COUNTY, CALIFORNIA
VISUAL EFFECTS SUPERVISOR	DENNIS MUREN
CHIEF VISUAL EFFECTS CAMERAMAN	MIKE McALISTER
OPTICAL PHOTOGRAPHY SUPERVISOR	BRUCE NICHOLSON
GENERAL MANAGER, ILM	TOM SMITH
PRODUCTION SUPERVISOR	WARREN FRANKLIN
MATTE PAINTING SUPERVISOR	MICHAEL PANGRAZIO
MODEL SHOP SUPERVISOR	LORNE PETERSON
STOP MOTION ANIMATION	TOM ST. AMAND
SUPERVISING STAGE TECHNICIAN	PATRICK FITZSIMMONS
ANIMATION SUPERVISOR	CHARLES MULLEN
SUPERVISING VISUAL EFFECTS EDITOR	HOWARD STEIN
VISUAL EFFECTS CAMERAMAN	MIKE OWENS
ASSISTANT CAMERAMEN	KIM MARKS, PAT SWEENEY, RANDY JOHNSON, JOE FULMER
PRODUCTION COORDINATOR	ARTHUR REPOLA
STAGE COORDINATOR	EDWARD HIRSH
OPTICAL CAMERA OPERATORS	JOHN ELLIS, DAVID BERRY, DONALD CLARK
OPTICAL LINE-UP	TOM ROSSETER, ED JONES, PEG HUNTER
LAB TECHNICIANS	TIM GEIDEMAN, JEFF DORAN, LOUIS RIVERA
EFFECTS CREATIVE CONSULTANT	PHIL TIPPETT
STOP MOTION TECHNICIANS	DAVID SOSALLA, RANDY OTTENBERG, SEAN CASEY
MATTE ARTISTS	CHRISTOPHER EVANS, FRANK ORDAZ, CAROLEEN GREEN
MATTE CAMERA SUPERVISOR	CRAIG BARRON
MATTE PHOTOGRAPHY	DAVID FINCHER, DEBORAH MORGAN
STORYBOARD ARTISTS	STAN FLEMING, PHILLIP NORWOOD
CHIEF MODELMAKERS	PAUL HUSTON, BARBARA GALLUCCI, CHARLIE BAILEY, EASE OWYEUNG, MICHAEL FULMER

MODELMAKERS	WESLEY SEEDS, BARBARA AFFONSO, LARRY TAN, MARC THORPE, SCOTT MARSHALL, CHUCK WILEY, PETE RONZANI, JEFF MANN, IRA KEELER, RICHARD DAVIS, WILLIAM GEORGE, MIKE COCHRANE
HEAD EFFECTS ANIMATOR	BRUCE WALTERS
EFFECTS ANIMATORS	BARBARA BRENNAN, JACK MONGOVAN, ELLEN LICHTWARDT, REBECCA PETRULLI, SEAN TURNER, SUKI STERN
VISUAL EFFECTS EDITOR	MICHAEL GLEASON
ASSISTANT EFFECTS EDITOR	MICHAEL MOORE
ADDITIONAL PHOTOGRAPHY	RICK FICHTER
STAGE TECHNICIANS	BOB FINLEY III DICK DOVA SPAH, JOHN McLEOD, DAVE CHILDERS, HAROLD COLE, LANCE BRACKETT, MERLIN OHM, MIKE SPEAKMAN

MINIATURE PYROTECHNICS	TED MOEHNKE, PETER STOLZ, BOB FINLEY, Jr.
STILL PHOTOGRAPHY	TERRY CHOSTNER, KERRY NORDQUIST, ROBERTO McGRATH
ENGINEERING	MICHAEL MACKENZIE, WADE CHILDRESS, GREG BEAUMONTE, JERRY JEFFRESS, KRIS BROWN
MACHINE SHOP	UDO PAMPEL, CHRISTOPHER RAND
LOCATION COORDINATOR	PATTY BLAU
ADMINISTRATIVE STAFF	CHRISSIE ENGLAND, CHERYL DURHAM, SUSAN MONAHAN, PAULA KARSH, KATHY SHINE, KAREN AYERS, KAREN DUBE, NED GORMAN, GEOFFREY de VALOIS

THE EWOK ADVENTURE

(CARAVAN OF COURAGE: AN EWOK ADVENTURE)

VISUAL EFFECTS PRODUCED AT
INDUSTRIAL LIGHT & MAGIC

VISUAL EFFECTS SUPERVISOR MICHAEL PANGRAZIO

POST PRODUCTION EFFECTS SUPERVISOR
DENNIS MUREN

OPTICAL PHOTOGRAPHY SUPERVISOR JOHN ELLIS

MATTE PAINTING SUPERVISORS CRAIG BARRON,
CHRIS EVANS

SUPERVISING VISUAL EFFECTS EDITOR HOWARD STEIN

ILM CREATURE SHOP SUPERVISOR DAVID SOSALLA

GENERAL MANAGER, ILM WARREN FRANKLIN

PRODUCTION SUPERVISOR JACK FRITZ

PRODUCTION COORDINATOR
SUSAN FRITZ MONAHAN

OPTICAL CAMERA OPERATORS DAVID BERRY,
KENNETH SMITH

OPTICAL LINE-UP RALPH GORDON, ED L. JONES,
TOM ROSSETER

LAB TECHNICIANS JEFF DORAN, TIM GEIDEMAN

MATTE ARTISTS FRANK ORDAZ,
CAROLEEN GREEN

MATTE PHOTOGRAPHY DAVID FINCHER,
WADE CHILDRESS, PAUL HUSTON

ASSISTANT EFFECTS EDITOR MICHAEL MOORE

CREATURE ANIMATORS MARGHE McMAHON,
RANDY OTTENBERG

ILM STILL PHOTOGRAPHY KERRY NORDQUIST

ENGINEERING EQUIPMENT SUPERVISOR
MICHAEL MACKENZIE

STARMAN

SPECIAL VISUAL EFFECTS BY
INDUSTRIAL LIGHT & MAGIC,
A DIVISION OF LUCASFILM LTD.

SUPERVISOR OF SPECIAL EFFECTS	BRUCE NICHOLSON
DIRECTOR OF VISUAL EFFECTS PHOTOGRAPHY	
	MICHEAL McALISTER
SUPERVISING MODELMAKER	EASE OWYEUNG
MATTE PAINTING SUPERVISOR	MICHAEL PANGRAZIO
ANIMATION SUPERVISOR	CHARLIE MULLEN
CHIEF VISUAL EFFECTS EDITOR	MICHAEL GLEASON
PRODUCTION COORDINATOR	PATRICIA BLAU
GENERAL MANAGER, ILM	WARREN FRANKLIN
VISUAL EFFECTS CAMERAMEN	PAT SWEENEY, SCOTT FARRAR
ASSISTANT CAMERAMEN	TOBY HEINDEL, PETER DAULTON, BOB HILL, JOE FULMER
OPTICAL CAMERA OPERATORS	JAMES LIM, KENNETH SMITH
OPTICAL LINE-UP	RALPH GORDON, ED JONES, TOM ROSSETER
MATTE ARTISTS	CAROLEEN GREEN, CHRIS EVANS, FRANK ORDAZ
MATTE CAMERA SUPERVISOR	CRAIG BARRON
ASSISTANT MATTE CAMERAMAN	WADE CHILDRESS
MODELMAKERS	BARBARA AFFONSO, JEFF MANN, LARRY TAN, CHUCK WILEY
HEAD EFFECTS ANIMATOR	BRUCE WALTERS
ASSISTANT ANIMATOR	BARBARA BRENNAN
VISUAL EFFECTS EDITOR	BILL KIMBERLIN
ASSISTANT EDITOR	MICHAEL MOORE
STAGE TECHNICIANS	DICK DOVA SPAH, LANCE BRACKETT
MINIATURE PYROTECHNICS	TED MOEHNKE, PETER STOLZ, ROBERT FINLEY Jr.
STILL PHOTOGRAPHY	KERRY NORDQUIST
EQUIPMENT ENGINEERING SUPERVISOR	
	MICHAEL MACKENZIE

GOONIES

VISUAL EFFECTS PRODUCED AT

INDUSTRIAL LIGHT & MAGIC
MARIN COUNTY, CALIFORNIA

SUPERVISOR OF VISUAL EFFECTS	MICHEAL McALISTER
VISUAL EFFECTS ART DIRECTOR	DAVID CARSON
OPTICAL SUPERVISOR	JOHN ELLIS
MATTE PAINTING SUPERVISOR	CHRISTOPHER EVANS
SUPERVISING MODELMAKER	BARBARA GALLUCCI
ANIMATION SUPERVISOR	CHARLIE MULLEN
CHIEF VISUAL EFFECTS EDITOR	HOWARD STEIN
PRODUCTION COORDINATOR	PATRICIA BLAU
GENERAL MANAGER, ILM	WARREN FRANKLIN
VISUAL EFFECTS CAMERAMAN	KIM MARKS
ASSISTANT CAMERAMEN	MARTY ROSENBERG, BESS WILEY
OPTICAL CAMERA OPERATORS	KENNETH SMITH, DON CLARK
OPTICAL LINE-UP	ED JONES, RALPH GORDON, TOM ROSSETER
OPTICAL TECHNICIANS	TIM GEIDEMAN, JEFF DORAN
MATTE ARTISTS	FRANK ORDAZ, CAROLEEN GREEN
MATTE CAMERA SUPERVISOR	CRAIG BARRON
ASSISTANT MATTE CAMERAMAN	WADE CHILDRESS
CHIEF MODELMAKER	BILL GEORGE
MODELMAKERS	CHUCK WILEY, RANDY OTTENBERG, JOHN REED
ANIMATOR	WES TAKAHASHI
ROTOSCOPE ARTISTS	ELLEN LICHTWARDT, JACK MONGOVAN, BARBARA BRENNAN
INK & PAINT	SANDY HOUSTON, DONNA BAKER
ASSISTANT EDITORS	MICHAEL MOORE, TERRY PECK
STAGE TECHNICIANS	PETER STOLZ, JOHN LISTER, CARL ASSMUS, BOBBY FINLEY III, DAVE CHILDERS, DAVE HERON, BRAD JERRELL
STILL PHOTOGRAPHY	ROBERTO McGRATH
EQUIPMENT ENGINEERING	MICHAEL MACKENZIE, GREG BEAUMONT, LANNY CERMAK, DAVE HANKS
PRODUCTION BUYERS	PAULA KARSH, NED GORMAN, RON FODE

BACK TO THE FUTURE

VISUAL EFFECTS PRODUCED AT	INDUSTRIAL LIGHT & MAGIC MARIN COUNTY, CALIFORNIA
SUPERVISOR OF VISUAL EFFECTS	KEN RALSTON
VISUAL EFFECTS ART DIRECTOR	PHILLIP NORWOOD
OPTICAL SUPERVISOR	JOHN ELLIS
SUPERVISING MODELMAKER	STEVE GAWLEY
ANIMATION SUPERVISOR	CHARLIE MULLEN
SUPERVISING VISUAL EFFECTS EDITOR	HOWIE STEIN
PRODUCTION COORDINATOR	LAURIE VERMONT
GENERAL MANAGER, ILM	WARREN FRANKLIN
CAMERA OPERATORS	BOB HILL, SCOTT FARRAR, KIM MARKS
ASSISTANT CAMERA OPERATORS	BOB HILL, RAY GILBERTI, RANDY JOHNSON, MARTY ROSENBERG
OPTICAL CAMERA OPERATORS	KENNETH SMITH, DON CLARK, JAMES LIM, JIM HAGEDORN
OPTICAL LINE-UP	RALPH GORDON, ED JONES, PEG HUNTER
OPTICAL TECHNICIANS	JEFF DORAN, TIM GEIDEMAN, LOUIS RIVERA
MODELMAKERS	IRA KEELER, MIKE FULMER, MIKE COCHRANE, WESLEY SEEDS
ROTOSCOPE SUPERVISOR	ELLEN LICHTWARDT
ANIMATORS	WES TAKAHASHI, PEGGY REGAN, JACK MONGOVAN, A.J. RIDDLE III, BARBARA BRENNAN
ROTOSCOPE ARTISTS	DONNA BAKER, SANDY HOUSTON
INK & PAINT	PETER ALBRECHT, ELLEN FERGUSON, JOANNE HAFNER
EFFECTS EDITOR	BILL KIMBERLIN
ASSISTANT EDITORS	MIKE MOORE, TERRY PECK
STAGE TECHNICIAN	BOB FINLEY, JR.
PYROTECHNICIANS	TED MOEHNKE, PETER STOLZ

I N D U S T R I A L
L I G H T &
M A G I C

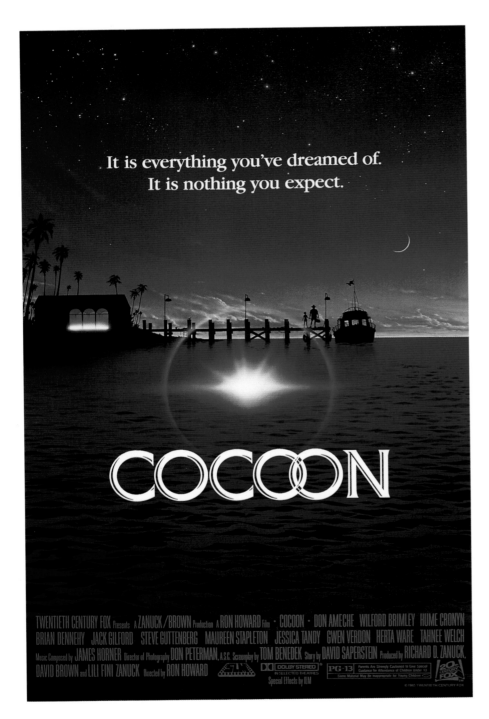

COCOON

VISUAL EFFECTS PRODUCED AT

INDUSTRIAL LIGHT & MAGIC
MARIN COUNTY, CALIFORNIA

SUPERVISOR OF VISUAL EFFECTS	KEN RALSTON
VISUAL EFFECTS ART DIRECTOR	PHILLIP NORWOOD
VISUAL EFFECTS CAMERAMAN	SCOTT FARRAR
OPTICAL SUPERVISOR	DAVID BERRY
SUPERVISING MODELMAKER	STEVE GAWLEY
ANIMATION SUPERVISOR	CHARLES MULLEN
VISUAL EFFECTS EDITOR	BILL KIMBERLIN
GENERAL MANAGER, ILM	WARREN FRANKLIN
PRODUCTION COORDINATOR	LAURIE VERMONT
MATTE PAINTING SUPERVISOR	CHRIS EVANS
ASSISTANT CAMERAMEN	ROBERT HILL, RAY GILBERTI, RANDY JOHNSON
STAGE MANAGER	ED HIRSH
STOP MOTION SUPERVISOR	DAVID SOSOLLA
ROTOSCOPE ARTISTS	ELLEN LICHTWARDT, JACK MONGOVAN, BARBARA BRENNAN
OPTICAL CAMERA OPERATORS	KENNETH SMITH, DONALD CLARK, JAMES LIM
OPTICAL LINE-UP	ED JONES, RALPH GORDON, PEG HUNTER
MATTE CAMERA OPERATOR	PAUL HUSTON
MODELMAKERS	IRA KEELER, MARTY BRENNEIS, BILL BECK, MIKE FULMER
MATTE ARTIST	CAROLEEN GREEN
SUPERVISING STAGE TECHNICIAN	PAT FITZSIMMONS
CLOUD TANK TECHNICIAN	BOB FINLEY JR.
STOP MOTION TECHNICIANS	TOM ST. AMAND, MARGOT PHILLIPS, ANTHONY LAUDATI, SEAN CASEY
STILL PHOTOGRAPHY	KERRY NORDQUIST
ASSISTANT EFFECTS EDITORS	MICHAEL MOORE, TERRY PECK
EQUIPMENT MAINTENANCE	MICHAEL MACKENZIE

1985

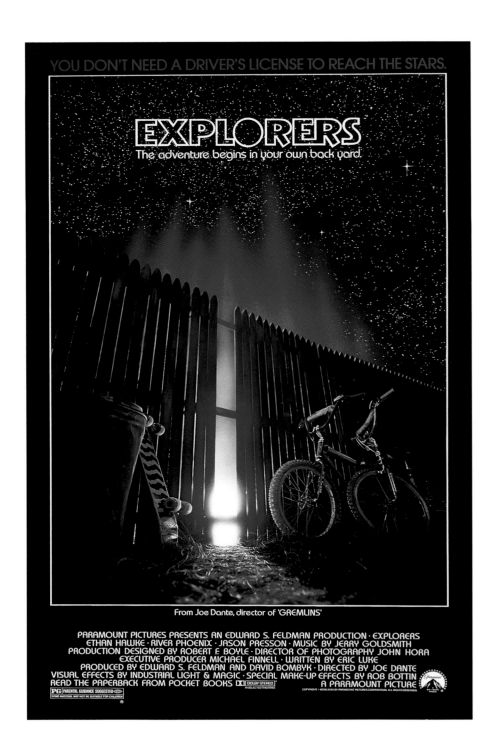

EXPLORERS

VISUAL EFFECTS PRODUCED AT	INDUSTRIAL LIGHT & MAGIC, MARIN COUNTY, CALIFORNIA
VISUAL EFFECTS SUPERVISOR	BRUCE NICHOLSON
DIRECTOR OF VISUAL EFFECTS PHOTOGRAPHY	DON DOW
VISUAL EFFECTS ART DIRECTOR	NILO RODIS-JAMERO
MATTE PAINTING SUPERVISOR	MICHAEL PANGRAZIO
MODEL SHOP SUPERVISOR	EASE OWYEUNG
ANIMATION SUPERVISOR	BRUCE WALTERS
SUPERVISING STAGE TECHNICIAN	PAT FITZSIMMONS
VISUAL EFFECTS EDITOR	MICHAEL GLEASON
PRODUCTION COORDINATOR	CHRISSIE ENGLAND
GENERAL MANAGER, ILM	WARREN FRANKLIN
VISUAL EFFECTS CAMERAMEN	SELWYN EDDY III, MIKE OWENS, PATRICK SWEENEY
ASSISTANT CAMERAMEN	PETER DAULTON, TOBY HEINDEL, PATRICK McARDLE, PATRICK TURNER
ASSISTANT ART DIRECTOR	PHILLIP NORWOOD
OPTICAL CAMERA OPERATORS	JAMES LIM, DON CLARK, KENNETH SMITH, JAMES HAGEDORN
OPTICAL LINE-UP	TOM ROSSETER, RALPH GORDON, ED JONES, PEG HUNTER, BRAD KUEHN
LAB TECHNICIANS	JEFF DORAN, TIM GEIDEMAN, LOUIS RIVERA
MODELMAKERS	BARBARA AFFONSO, BILL BECK, BILL GEORGE, JEFF MANN, CLAUDIA MULLALY, RANDY OTTENBERG, JOHN REED, WESLEY SEEDS, LARRY TAN, MARC THORPE
ASSISTANT MATTE ARTIST	SEAN JOYCE
MATTE CAMERA SUPERVISOR	CRAIG BARRON
MATTE PHOTOGRAPHY	WADE CHILDRESS, PAUL HUSTON
VISUAL EFFECTS ANIMATORS	ELLEN LICHTWARDT, BARBARA BRENNAN, JACK MONGOVAN, A.J. RIDDLE III, PEGGY REGAN, WES TAKAHASHI

ASSISTANT EDITORS	MICHAEL MOORE, TERENCE PECK	*PRODUCTION ASSISTANTS*	PAM MARCOTTE, JIM CAPANA
STAGE MANAGER	ED HIRSCH	*THE BETSY FLYER*	BETSY BURKE

STAGE TECHNICIANS   TED MOEHNKE, DICK DOVA SPAH, BOB FINLEY III, CARL ASSMUS, LANCE BRACKETT, DAVE CHILDERS, ROBERT FINLEY, JR., JOE FULMER, DAVID HERON, BRAD JERRELL, JOHN LISTER, JOHN McLEOD, MERLIN OHM, BILL PELKEY, MIKE SPEAKMAN, PETER STOLZ

ENGINEERING   MICHAEL MACKENZIE, MARTY BRENNEIS, GREG BEAUMONTE, LANNY CERMAK, DAVE HANKS, CRAIG HOSADA, KRIS BROWN

MACHINE SHOP   UDO PAMPEL, CHRISTOPHER RAND

CHARACTER MINIATURE SUPERVISOR   DAVE SOSALLA

CHARACTER MINIATURE CREW   CHARLIE BAILEY, SEAN CASEY, ROBERT COOPER, ANTHONY LAUDATI, MARGHE McMAHON, MARGO PHILLIPS

ADMINISTRATIVE STAFF   CHERYL DURHAM, PAULA KARSH, PAM KAYE, KAREN DUBE, NED GORMAN, JODI MUGGENTHALER, LORI NELSON, KIM NELSON

STILL PHOTOGRAPHERS   KERRY NORDQUIST, ROBERTO McGRATH

The Third Dream Sequence is Lovingly Dedicated To The Memory of Edward Peter Hirsh

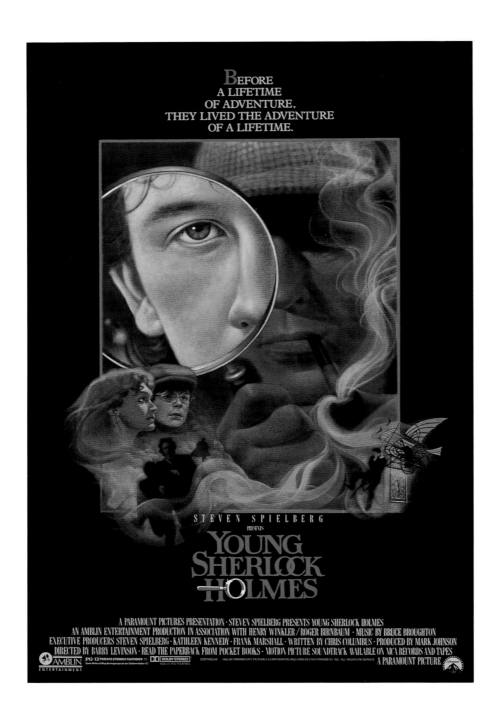

YOUNG SHERLOCK HOLMES

VISUAL EFFECTS PRODUCED AT	INDUSTRIAL LIGHT & MAGIC, MARIN COUNTY, CALIFORNIA
SUPERVISOR OF VISUAL EFFECTS	DENNIS MUREN

PASTRY SEQUENCE

MOTION SUPERVISOR	DAVID ALLEN
EFFECTS CAMERAMAN	SCOTT FARRAR

GLASS MAN SEQUENCE

PIXAR COMPUTER ANIMATION GROUP,
A DIVISION OF LUCASFILM LTD.

HARPY SEQUENCE

EFFECTS CAMERAMAN	MICHAEL OWENS
GO-MOTION ANIMATION	HARRY WALTON
OPTICAL SUPERVISOR	JOHN ELLIS
HEAD OPTICAL CAMERAMAN	KENNETH SMITH
EFFECTS ART DIRECTOR	DAVE CARSON
VISUAL EFFECTS EDITORS	MIKE GLEASON, HOWARD STEIN
GENERAL MANAGER, ILM	WARREN FRANKLIN
PRODUCTION COORDINATOR	ERIK JENSEN
CREATURE FABRICATION	DAVID SOSALLA
ANIMATION SUPERVISORS	BRUCE WALTERS, ELLEN LICHTWARDT
MATTE PAINTING SUPERVISOR	CHRIS EVANS
GLASS MAN COORDINATORS	DOUGLAS SCOTT KAY, GEORGE JOBLOVE
OPTICAL CAMERA OPERATOR	DON CLARK
OPTICAL LINE-UP	RALPH GORDON, ED JONES
PROCESSING	JEFF DORAN, TIM GEIDEMAN
ASSISTANT CAMERAMEN	PATRICK McARDLE, ROBERT HILL, DAVID HANKS
PUPPETEERS	JAY DAVIS, BOB COOPER, BLAIR CLARK, ANTHONY LAUDATI, MARGHE McMAHON, SEAN CASEY

MATTE PHOTOGRAPHY SUPERVISOR	CRAIG BARRON
EFFECTS ANIMATORS	JACK MONGOVAN, BARBARA BRENNAN, GORDON BAKER, KIM SINGHRS, CHUCK EYLER
ROTOSCOPE ARTISTS	DONNA BAKER, SANDY HOUSTON, TERRY SITTIG
INK/PAINT	JOANNE HAFNER, PETER ALBRECHT, ELLEN FERGUSON
ASSISTANT EDITOR	KIM COSTALUPES, TERRY PECK
GLASS CONSULTANT	ERIC CHRISTIANSEN
EQUIPMENT ENGINEERING	MICHAEL MACKENZIE, UDO PAMPEL

COMPUTER SOFTWARE	CRAIG HOSODA
STAGE TECHNICIANS	BOB FINLEY III, DAVID HERON, TIM MORGAN, DAVID CHILDERS, PETER STOLZ
COMPUTER ANIMATION GROUP	WILLIAM REEVES, JOHN LASSETER, DAVID DeFRANCESCO, EBEN OSTBY, DAVID H. SALESIN, ROBERT L. COOK, DON CONWAY, CRAIG GOOD, SAM LEFFLER, THOMAS L. NOGGLE
COMPUTERS BY	COMPUTER CONSOLES, INC.

EWOKS: THE BATTLE FOR ENDOR

VISUAL EFFECTS CREATED BY	INDUSTRIAL LIGHT& MAGIC
VISUAL EFFECTS SUPERVISOR	MICHEAL McALISTER
STOP MOTION SUPERVISOR	PHIL TIPPETT
MATTE PAINTING SUPERVISORS	CHRIS EVANS, CRAIG BARRON
OPTICAL PHOTOGRAPHY SUPERVISOR	DAVID BERRY
ANIMATION SUPERVISOR	BRUCE WALTERS
CREATURE DESIGNER	JON BERG
CREATURE SUPERVISOR	ELAINE BAKER
VISUAL EFFECTS EDITORS	MICHAEL MOORE, HOWARD STEIN
ROTOSCOPE SUPERVISOR	ELLEN LICHTWARDT
ILM PRODUCTION COORDINATORS	LAURIE VERMONT, SUSAN MONAHAN
GENERAL MANAGER, ILM	WARREN FRANKLIN
POST PRODUCTION SUPERVISOR	CHARLIE MULLEN
PRODUCTION MANAGER	ED HIRSH
STOP MOTION ANIMATORS	TOM ST. AMAND, RANDY DUTRA
STOP MOTION PHOTOGRAPHY	HARRY WALTON, TERRY CHOSTNER, MICHAEL OWENS, PATRICK McARDLE
STOP MOTION MINIATURES	TAMIA MARG, SHEILA DUIGNAN
VISUAL EFFECTS CAMERAMAN	SCOTT FARRAR
ASSISTANT CAMERAMAN	ROBERT HILL
OPTICAL CAMERA OPERATORS	KENNETH SMITH, JAMES HAGEDORN, DON CLARK, MIKE SHANNON
OPTICAL LINE-UP	ED JONES, RALPH GORDON
LAB TECHNICIANS	TIM GEIDEMAN, LOUIS RIVERA
MATTE ARTISTS	MICHAEL PANGRAZIO, LAZARUS, CAROLEEN GREEN, SEAN JOYCE
MATTE PHOTOGRAPHY	WADE CHILDRESS, PAUL HUSTON
ANIMATOR	BARBARA BRENNAN
ASSISTANT EFFECTS EDITORS	TERRY PECK, KIM COSTALUPES

EQUIPMENT ENGINEERING   MICHAEL MACKENZIE, GREG BEAUMONTE, LANNY CERMAK

CREATURE MAKERS   LAUREL LICHTEN, KEVIN BRENNAN, ESCOTT NORTON, EBEN STROMQUIST, JONATHON HORTON, BILL STONEHAM, GUNNER FERDINANDSEN, DAVE JOHNSON, JOHN REED III, ALAN PETERSON

STAGE TECHNICIANS   BOB FINLEY III, DAVID HERON, DICK DOVA SPAH, PETER STOLZ

PRODUCTION PROCUREMENT.   PAULA KARSH, NED GORMAN, KIT STEVENS

ADDITIONAL VISUAL EFFECTS BY   VCE, INC./PETER KURAN

VCE STAFF   BEVERLY BERNACKI, STEVEN BURG, BRUCE WOODSIDE, CHRIS CASADY, JACQUELINE ZIETLOW, MEGAN WILLIAMS, JAMIE FRIDAY, ED HARKER

ENEMY MINE

VISUAL EFFECTS PRODUCED AT
INDUSTRIAL LIGHT & MAGIC, MARIN COUNTY, CALIFORNIA

SUPERVISOR OF VISUAL EFFECTS — DON DOW

VISUAL EFFECTS ART DIRECTOR — DAVE CARSON

OPTICAL PHOTOGRAPHY SUPERVISOR
BRUCE NICHOLSON

MATTE PAINTING SUPERVISOR — CHRIS EVANS

SUPERVISING MODELMAKER — MIKE FULMER

ANIMATION SUPERVISORS — BRUCE WALTERS, ELLEN LICHTWARDT

VISUAL EFFECTS EDITOR — BILL KIMBERLIN

PRODUCTION COORDINATOR
SUSAN FRITZ MONAHAN

GENERAL MANAGER, ILM — WARREN FRANKLIN

PRODUCTION SUPERVISOR — CHARLIE MULLEN

PRODUCTION MANAGER — ED HIRSH

CAMERA OPERATORS — SELWYN EDDY III, PATRICK SWEENEY, KIM MARKS

CAMERA ASSISTANTS — RAY GILBERTI, PETER DAULTON, MARTY ROSENBERG, TOBY HEINDEL

OPTICAL CAMERA OPERATORS — JAMES LIM, DON CLARK, JIM HAGEDORN, MIKE SHANNON

OPTICAL LINE-UP — TOM ROSSETER, PEG HUNTER, ED JONES

OPTICAL TECHNICIANS — JEFF DORAN, TIM GEIDEMAN, LOUIS RIVERA

SUPERVISING MATTE PHOTOGRAPHER — CRAIG BARRON

MATTE ARTISTS — MICHAEL PANGRAZIO, FRANK ORDAZ, CAROLEEN GREEN, SEAN JOYCE

MATTE CAMERA ASSISTANTS — WADE CHILDRESS, PAUL HUSTON, RANDY JOHNSON

MODELMAKERS — SEAN CASEY, MIKE COCHRANE, STEVE GAWLEY, BILL GEORGE, IRA KEELER, WESLEY SEEDS

ANIMATION CAMERAMAN — A.J. RIDDLE III

EFFECTS ANIMATORS — CHUCK EYLER, GORDON BAKER

ROTOSCOPE ARTISTS   PETER ALBRECHT,
DONNA BAKER, BARBARA BRENNAN,
ELLEN FERGUSON,
JOANNE HAFNER,
SANDY HOUSTON, JACK MONGOVAN,
TERRY SITTIG

ASSISTANT EDITORS   KIM COSTALUPES,
TERRY PECK

CREATURE SHOP   CHARLIE BAILEY, BOB COOPER,
JAY DAVIS, ANTHONY LAUDATI

STAGE TECHNICIANS   PAT FITZSIMMONS,
DICK DOVA SPAH, BOB FINLEY III,
DAVE CHILDERS, BRAD JERRELL

MINIATURE PYROTECHNICS   PETER STOLZ,
BOB FINLEY, JR.

EQUIPMENT ENGINEERING SUPERVISOR
MIKE MACKENZIE

EQUIPMENT ENGINEERING   UDO PAMPEL,
GREG BEAUMONTE,
LANNY CERMACK, DAVE HANKS,
VINCE TILKER, MARTY BRENNEIS

STILL PHOTOGRAPHY   KERRY NORDQUIST,
ROBERTO McGRATH

ADMINISTRATIVE STAFF   CHERYL DURHAM,
PAM KAYE, KAREN DUBE,
LORI NELSON, KIM NELSON,
HEATHER MacKENZIE,
PAULA KARSH, NED GORMAN,
KITT STEVENS

GLOSSARY

AERIAL IMAGE PRINTER A camera that rephotographs two or more images onto one piece of film. The principle of an aerial image printer is a particularly intriguing one: if a picture is projected on a white card and then the card is removed, the "image" is still there in space, as long as the projector remains on—even though it's become invisible to the naked eye.

However, should someone peer through another lens at the exact spot where the white card was, they will see the image again, just as clear and well focused as if it were projected on a card. It is at this exact plane, where the image is aerially in focus, that a second film is placed; thus, the two images are combined. The optical printer's camera is pointed and focused on the combined images. The camera is now capable of rephotographing the two pieces of film as if they were one.

No other optical tool is as versatile as a fully equipped aerial image printer. Several filmed images can be combined at once, using multiple projectors and prismatic beam splitters; in successive passes of the camera, literally scores of images can be fitted together into matted spaces. Most of the optically combined shots at ILM are created on one or more of the three aerial image printers: the "Work Horse," the "Quad," and the "Anderson."

ANAMORPHIC PROCESS The method of fitting a wide-screen image onto a standard, almost-square film frame by optically "squeezing" it. This is accomplished by photographing through a cylindrically shaped lens in addition to a spherical one). When the image is shown it is "unsqueezed" by projecting it through the same kind of lens.

Anamorphic films were originally introduced to American audiences as Cinemascope, though now they are more commonly seen under the Panavision brand name. When an anamorphic lens is used on a camera, the developed film image appears squeezed in the horizontal axis, making it half as wide as it should be. A circle becomes an upright oval; a square becomes a rectangle with its top and bottom half the size of its height. These distorted images are particularly difficult to deal with in the creation of optical effects, so the ILM technicians usually use a nonanamorphic camera system (VistaVision) when they composite images. If a film is to be released anamorphically, the images are transferred to that medium at the very last stage.

ANDERSON PRINTER An aerial image printer with two projectors and one camera, designed thirty years ago for Paramount Pictures by the optical specialist Howard Anderson and now rebuilt and used in the ILM optical department. It is designed to handle only VistaVision format (see "eight-perf"). Much of the spectacle for De Mille's *The Ten Commandments* was created on the Anderson printer, for which it was originally built. In honor of the movie, an aging poster of the De Mille epic still hangs above the printer at ILM.

ANGLE, CAMERA The camera's point of view of the subject—low angle, high angle, Darth's point-of-view, etc. When filming a scene that will be combined with an ILM matte painting, the choice of camera angle is critical. Such basic elements of perspective as lines-of-convergence, left and right vanishing points, and so on, must be identical in the painting and the live-action material or the scene will appear askew.

ANIMATICS   A television or animation version of special effects shots, used to temporarily fill in scenes in the workprint until the final effects are completed.

ANIMATION CAMERA AND STAND   A camera mounted above or beside a table on which animation artwork is photographed. The table centers the artwork, moves it right or left, up or down, illuminates it from above or below (in the case of translucent animation cells), and with a built-in computing mechanism does many of these operations automatically. The camera is controlled by a mechanism that exposes one frame at a time, allowing the animation operator to position the next cel. The camera's movement between exposures, advancing the film, is engineered to provide an especially steady image.

Animation cameras are supported on vertical or horizontal stands. Vertical stands (sometimes called "downshooters" or rostrum cameras) mount the camera on an up-and-down, vertical axis aimed at the artwork table. On a horizontal stand, the camera runs on tracks along the floor and the artwork is mounted upright on an easel. Horizontal stands may be quite large, with tracks extending twenty feet or more from the artwork.

Modern animation stands closely resemble the motion control devices used in model photography for special effects. In the technique of aerial image animation, for instance, a filmed scene is projected onto a field where artwork (animated mattes, for instance, or painted titles) is placed. Usually the image is projected from below so that the artwork blocks it. The art is painted on clear sheets of plastic, so the filmed scene shows through where there is no paint.

ANSWER PRINT   The first print of a completed movie, usually combined with an optical sound track. The answer print is used to check that the original negative was cut and spliced correctly and to establish the quality of the images' color and density. Sometimes a laboratory must produce many answer prints before it delivers an acceptable one.

APERTURE   When referring to the camera lens, the aperture means the f/stop of the lens—an expression of the ratio of the focal length to the diameter of the iris of the lens. (For instance, if a lens has a focal length of 50 millimeters and the iris opening is 25 millimeters, the lowest possible f/stop is f/2.)

In a camera or projector, aperture refers to the rectangular opening behind the lens. The aperture provides a frame for the image on the film. The camera (or projection) aperture is also sometimes called the "gate."

ARMATURE   A skeleton of machined steel, with ball joints, encased inside a stop-motion puppet. The armature allows the manipulated figure to hold its form while being photographed.

ASA RATING   A measurement of the sensitivity of a film emulsion, rated by the American Standard Association. Films with higher ASA numbers are more sensitive to light. Lower ASA films require more light for proper exposure, though they are usually less grainy looking than the higher-rated, more sensitive films. Film ASA ratings have been gradually rising over the years, allowing movies to be shot with less light and opening up greater creative possibilities for cinematographers.

BACKLIGHTING   The illumination of a scene from behind the actors or set, with the light source facing the camera. Usually combined with front or side lighting. Backlighting creates a dramatic rim of light around the subject, and also serves to separate actors and furnishings from the background.

In animation, backlighting refers to the illumination of translucent cels from behind or below.

BASE   The actual plastic that constitutes movie or still film. Transparent, usually made of acetate or Estar material, onto which the film emulsion is fused. (Most film bases are made of acetate.) For many years ILM specified that special effects be shot on Estar base films, as they are less prone to shrinkage and almost indestructible. However, Estar is very difficult to splice and can damage a camera's mechanisms if it should jam. All intermediate film stocks used in the optical department must have an Estar base.

Prior to World War II, film base was made of a flammable and, in some cases, explosive nitrate material that gave off poisonous fumes when it burned. Frequent fires involving this material were responsible for the deaths of many film workers by fire and asphyxiation. After years of storage, nitrate stock is liable to become brittle, and even deteriorate into dust. Thus, many classic films have been irretrievably lost.

BEAM SPLITTER   A partially silvered mirror that reflects some of the light striking it and transmits the rest. Beam splitters can also be cube shaped, formed by joining two prisms. Both the silvered and cubic devices are used extensively in special effects, as they are means by which an image can be sent off in two directions or several images can be combined. The heart of the Quad printer in the ILM optical department is a cubic beam splitter that directs light from the projectors to two cameras. Front projection systems also use a beam splitter as a central element.

BI-PACK   Two films that run through a camera or projector at the same time, packed one on top of the other. In special effects work, one usually functions as a matte that will create an un-exposed area on the film to be filled in later by some other image, the other may be the fresh, unexposed film or print to be matted. Bi-pack cameras and projectors are commonly used in optical departments and sometimes in special effects or model photography. The matte paintings for the first Star Wars film were photographed with a bi-pack camera system.

Bi-pack cameras are equipped with twin sets of magazines, one for the unexposed film and the other for the matte. They run through the camera with their emulsions touching.

Early color cinematography relied on bi-packing the film. The Technicolor camera contained three rolls of black-and-white film, all running at the same time, filtered so that each saw only one color. Two films were bi-packed and a third received the image through a beam splitter.

At ILM bi-pack cameras and projectors are frequently used on optical printers and aerial image printers in the creation of elements for traveling mattes.

BLOW-UP   The rephotographing of a film in order to magnify some detail within the image. Also a term commonly used when 16mm film is rephotographed, or "blown up," to 35mm for theatrical release.

There are high-speed 16mm cameras that are capable of filming much faster than 35mm cameras, and they are sometimes useful for special effects shots—as in *Raiders of the Lost Ark,* for instance, where a high-speed 16mm camera was used to photograph an explosion. The footage was then blown up to the VistaVision format, sixteen times its original image size.

BLUE-SCREEN PROCESS   A photographic process that involves filming in front of a brightly illuminated blue screen. After optical rephotography, the process yields film of actors or objects placed against a black background, and also film of their silhouettes against a clear-white background. With these two elements—moving subjects and their identical, moving silhouettes—it is possible to place the subjects into any background scene. The silhouette is used to make a moving black space in the background environment, and the image of the actors is inserted into that hole.

At ILM the blue screens are self-lit with fluorescent tubes. The subject in front is lit with white or amber light, and care is taken that no blue from the screen reflects off the subject and none of the light on the subject spills onto the blue screen.

After the film is developed it is rephotographed twice: once with a filter that turns all the blue to black and leaves the subject unaltered, and then with a filter that turns the blue to white and blocks out all other colors, so that the subject becomes a silhouette.

BLUE SPILL   A common traveling matte process, Blue Screen, requires that an object or actor be photographed in front of a blue screen. When light from this blue screen illuminates the object and is seen by the camera, this is called "blue spill." If uncorrected during photogarphy, these contaminated areas may become transparent during the optical compositing process and create an undesirable matte line wherever the blue light fell on the object. This condition usually occurs when the subject is glossy or white or placed at an undesirable angle to reflect light, and certain lenses are more susceptible to blue spill than others. An experienced blue screen cinematographer is often able to eliminate or minimize "blue spill" through special lighting techniques.

CALLIGRAPHIC or LINE-DRAWING DISPLAY   This is the display that draws lines or "vectors" on a screen. The Picture System is a calligraphic display. The image can be changed very quickly, and since it responds immediately to input it is called a "real-time" device. The Death Star Simulation was filmed on this device.

CATHODE RAY TUBE (CRT)   The picture tube of a television set and the means for displaying computer-generated special effects. A TV screen is the front surface of a large picture tube, properly called a cathode ray tube. Streams of electrons from the cathode of the tube bombard the phosphorous screen in front, stimulating it to glow. The electrons are deflected one way and another by magnets, thus forming the lines and thousands of dots that make up a television picture. When computers are programmed to create special effect images, the images are usually drawn on a cathode ray tube and then photographed for the film. In the future, we expect that laser beams will replace cathode rays, giving images of higher resolution and greater color clarity.

CEL   Originally made of celluloid, now a thin sheet of plastic on which animation art is drawn or painted.

CLOSE-UP   A camera shot showing a detail of a subject, often the head and shoulders of an actor.

COLOR DYNAMICS   Refers to the range of color saturation that a medium is capable of reproducing. Television, for example, has a much smaller range than motion picture film.

COLOR TEMPERATURE   Refers to the temperature of a light source. Thus sunlight is said to be about 6000 degrees Kelvin, meaning that sunlight, as it strikes objects at sea level, acts like a "black body" that has been heated to 6000 degrees Kelvin and is illuminating the scene. Similarly, incandescent light, a normal electric lightbulb, is said to be about 3200-3400 degrees Kelvin—a lower temperature that makes colors drift toward the red end of the color scale (while sunlight sends colors toward the blue end of the color scale). A third kind of light, fluorescent, is missing a number of narrow bands of color from its spectrum; therefore fluorescent-illuminated scenes can never be as truly color-correct as a sunlit scene.

Motion picture film in America (but not in Eastern Europe) is generally balanced to record true color under incandescent light ("movie" lights). Thus, to shoot outside and avoid colors swinging toward the blue shades, an amber-colored filter must be placed over the camera lens to alter the color.

COMPOSITE   A special effects shot combining two or more separate elements. Used as a verb, "to composite" or the process of "compositing" describes the combining of images to create a new special effects shot.

COMPUTER ANIMATION   Animation usually displayed on a cathode ray tube under the control of a computer. The computer does not create the image—programmers and artists do that—but the computer can make it move, rotate it, distort it, color it, shade it, etc.

Some computer animation is complex and realistic looking. ILM first included such a shot in *Star Trek II* to illustrate the evolution of a planet. Computer animation was also used in *Return of the Jedi* to simulate a holographic representation of the Death Star during a Rebel battle briefing. The latest development involves laser scanned images. This technique was used in ILM's work for the film *Young Sherlock Holmes*. These sequences were programed and filmed at ILM's sister facility, the Lucasfilm Computer Division.

CONTACT PRINTER   A motion picture printing machine that places original processed film in emulsion-to-emulsion contact with unexposed duplicating film. Light passes through the original and exposes the undeveloped film: Contact printers are most commonly used for printing quantities of release prints, where microscopically precise registration of the images is not so important. Most special effects work requires prints in perfect registration (or else one part of an image will shift and ride against another), so "registered," rather than "contact," prints are made for effects elements.

CONTINUOUS STEP PRINTER   A printer that employs an aperture frame and registers the original with the unexposed duplicating print stock. The two films move through an intermittent mechanism, similar to one found in a projector or camera. As each frame is printed, the film momentarily comes to a complete stop and a light exposes the image.

DAILIES (also called rushes)   The unedited film from a day's shooting. An important part of each production day is screening the previous day's dailies.

DEPTH OF FIELD   The nearest and farthest point in front of a lens in which an image appears to be in focus. Small three-dimensional objects photographed up close tend to have a very limited depth of field—that is, either the front or back of them will be out of focus. Thus, when photographing miniatures for special effects, extraordinary measures must be taken.

Depth of field increases as the camera lens' f/stop increases; for a higher f/stop, more light is required. The f/stop can also be raised if the shutter speed is slowed down—for instance, from ¼8th of a second to one second per frame. Models filmed with motion control cameras are often given such relatively long exposures, so correspondingly the lens is set at a high f/stop, providing sharp focus from the front to the back of the model.

Conversely, when a miniature is filmed with a high-speed camera in order to slow down its action, great amounts of illumination must be used—100,000 to 200,000 watts of light are not uncommon—in order to achieve as high an f/stop as possible, and therefore a deep depth of field.

DIFFUSION   The decreasing of the sharpness of an image without altering its focus. Anything seen through a fine cloth or finely etched glass will seem softer, less clearly defined, and farther away. Such diffusing of images is a technique used frequently in special effects cinematography. Bridal veiling or glass diffusion filters in a wide range of grades can be placed in front of the lens. Optical camera operators will often use diffusion on their lenses to create a better blending of elements.

In studio filming, lights are often softened by placing them behind diffusion materials such as translucent shower curtains or spun glass, scattering the light and rendering a softer light source.

DISSOLVE   A way of going from one shot to the next by fading out the first scene at the same time that the second is fading in, one blending or merging into the next. Traditionally, dissolves have been used to indicate a short passage of time. In the early days these effects were actually done by controlled double exposure inside the production camera—either on location or in the studio. Now dissolves are created long after the film is shot, as an optical effect.

DIGITAL IMAGES   Images created with the use of a computer and projected on a cathode ray tube for filming or scanned directly on the film with a laser.

DIGITAL PRINTER   A device, still in development, that will "read," encode, and store a shot in digital form. Later it can be "printed" on film or videotape, and manipulated in innumerable ways. ILM's work on *Young Sherlock Holmes* was the first practical demonstration of the device.

DOUBLE EXPOSURE   The exposure of two separate shots on one film.

DYKSTRAFLEX   The first sophisticated, electronically controlled motion-control camera system, developed at ILM for the visual effects on *Star Wars*. Its improved descendants are still in use at ILM today. The original Dykstraflex was named after the first ILM visual effects supervisor, John Dykstra, who was primarily responsible for the development of the camera system.

EFFECTS ANIMATION   Visual effects, such as lightning, laser swords, and flying pixies, photographed from artwork one frame at a time with an animation camera. Most effects animation, however, has another function: blocking out unwanted images that are the by-products of other special effect processes.

EIGHT PERF   A much larger motion picture image size, used in special effects preparation. Film usually runs vertically through the camera with each frame having four sprocket holes along its edge. But in preparing special effects, more image area is needed to minimize the quality loss that results from rephotographing images, so the film is run through VistaVision-type cameras, going horizontally from right to left. Now the picture area is as wide as eight sprocket holes—twice as much area, half the film grain, and more resolution. In the final stage, the image is reduced back to four-sprocket size, or "four perf."

EMULSION   The film layer that is light sensitive. It is supported by the film base, usually made of acetate.

ESTABLISHING SHOT   Usually an introductory wide shot of a setting or environment that leads into a series of closer shots that define the scene. ILM often produces matte paintings to be used as establishing shots.

EXPOSURE   The act of light striking the film emulsion and imprinting a "latent" image—latent because it remains invisible until washed with a chemical bath. Photographic exposure must take four mutually dependent elements into account: the amount of light reflected by the scene; the lens f/stop setting; the camera shutter speed; and the ASA or sensitivity of the film.

f/STOP (f/NUMBER)   A number relating to the amount of light a lens allows to pass through it. Camera lenses have two settings on them: the focus setting, usually given in feet or meters, and the f/stop setting. Most movie lenses range from approximately f/2.2 up to f/22 (f/.9 to f/45 at the extremes). The numbers are a relationship of the focal length of the lens and the width of the opening. The higher the number, the less light is allowed to reach the film. The amount of light that actually passes through the lens to the film, however, is influenced by the translucency of the glass lens elements. Because of this, lenses with many glass elements in them often use a "t/stop," which is a more accurate measure of the amount of light actually transmitted to the film.

FADE   A shot that smoothly goes from normal exposure to black is called a fade-out; one that goes from black to full exposure is called a fade-in. In traditional film grammar, a fade-out followed by a fade-in signifies the passage of time.

FIBER OPTICS   The method of sending light through thin, pliable glass fibers. A negligible amount of light "leaks out" along the way; even if the glass fiber is bent around a corner or is tied into a knot, nearly all light sent in at one end appears at the other.

Fiberoptical media are used in communications and often found in optical devices. At ILM, glass fibers have been used in model spaceships to channel light from a single source to hundreds of tiny outlets representing windows or running lights.

FILTER A glass or a gelatin sheet placed in front of a camera lens to modify light, control image contrast, or correct color differences in light sources and film emulsions.

FLASHING A photographic technique in which a latent image or unexposed film emulsion is briefly exposed to a light source, thereby changing the characteristics of the primary image recorded on the same film. It is often used to reduce the contrast of the primary image, as it tends to turn blacks in the picture to grays. In the days when black-and-white motion picture film was relatively insensitive and required high light levels for proper exposure, the film was sometimes "flashed" in order to increase the ASA (film's sensitivity).

Flashing is also done in ILM's optical department in order to alter the character of an element in a composite shot.

"FLAT FOUR" A shorthand term used in special effects work to describe a normal 35mm motion picture format. It is "flat" in that it is not squeezed with an anamorphic (Cinemascope) lens, and "four" in that each frame is four perforations high from top to bottom—in contrast to VistaVision (large-format film), which is eight perforations wide.

FOCAL LENGTH The dimension of a lens measured from the optical center to the point just behind the lens where the image is in focus. These dimensions are measured when the lens is set for a subject positioned at infinity. Long focal length lenses ("long lenses") bring distant objects up close, as a telescope does. Short focal length lenses push distant objects farther away, but have a much wider field of vision.

FOCUS Adjusting a lens on a camera or projector to produce the sharpest possible image on the film. All lenses actually form images in the air behind them, out of focus but for one razor-thin plane. When this plane falls exactly on the film emulsion, a focused image is exposed.

FORCED PERSPECTIVE A technique of set design to give the illusion of great depth. Background elements that are supposed to look very distant are made unnaturally small—distant buildings, boats, even furniture—while foreground elements are full size.

FRACTAL This is a technique for creating computer images of objects that occur in nature; fractal refers to the fact that an object actually looks like a smaller version of itself. For instance, a branch of tree looks like an entire tree. The "shapeness" of the object is independent of its size—a section of a mountain looks a lot like a mountain. Rivers, coastlines, plants, and a surprising number of natural phenomena share this quality. Of course, nature has a lot of randomness too, but the computer is also capable of generating randomness. If we combine these two notions, then we have a simple method for generating very complex shapes such as mountains and plants with very little information.

FRAME   A single picture on a film strip. It also is used to describe the field seen by the camera for a given shot ("in frame").

FRAMEBUFFER   This is a computer memory that holds an image; the image is scanned out on a display screen. The paint program uses a framebuffer to hold the image, and the monitor is used to show the artist the contents of the framebuffer.

FRONT PROJECTION   Also known as the "Alekan-Gerand Process" and the "Scotchlite Process." A highly reflective screen is placed behind the subject being photographed. A projector is next to the camera with its optical axis at 90 degrees to the camera. A beam splitter reflects the projected image toward the screen while allowing the camera to see through; thus the camera sees the projected image on the highly reflective screen with the subject in front of it. The screen is so reflective, in fact, that only a very dim projection light is used; consequently, the foreground objects do not reflect the projected image.

At ILM, front projection is most commonly used in photographing matte paintings. The paintings are prepared with a hole in them; an area of Scotchlite screen is behind the hole and the action is projected on this screen.

GARBAGE MATTES   Animated mattes that serve to block out "garbage" in shots, such as unwanted lights, cables, C stands, and so on. Often there are large areas of the shots in special effects elements that not used and need to be "plugged up," as it were, with garbage mattes. Usually they are quickly made with pieces of black paper placed above a light box and photographed with an animation camera.

GAUGE   The width of film stock, measured from edge to edge and expressed in millimeters, i.e., 8mm, 16mm, 35mm, 65mm, and 70mm. There are other special formats that are still larger and produce a bright and sharp image, but because of the enormous expense involved they are not widely used.

GENERATION   The successive printings that separate from the original camera negative a copy. Each generation decreases the color range and increases the grain and contrast of the image; therefore, it is desirable to limit the number of generations required to produce a final image.

GLASS SHOT   One of the earliest visual effects techniques, first used in movies by Norman Dawn, a pioneer matte painter early in the century. A painting is made on a sheet of glass, then placed between the camera and whatever is to be filmed. Almost anything can be added to a scene by means of a glass shot—clouds in the sky, a castle on a mountain, a refurbished Parthenon.

GO-MOTION   A refinement of stop-motion developed at Industrial Light and Magic and first used in 1980 for *Dragonslayer*. Puppets are made to move by rods, which are controlled by motors that are commanded through a computer. This permits the puppets to move while the camera shutter is open, thereby causing a natural blurring of moving parts. The jerky, stroboscopic movement often associated with stop-motion animation is largely eliminated and an eerily lifelike effect results. Particularly unsettling when used with monsters.

GRAIN   The small particles suspended in

film emulsion that form the image. Generally, the finer the grain, the more desirable the image.

IMPLOSION   The reverse of explosion: the crushing inward of an object upon itself.

IN-THE-CAMERA   Any special effect—especially combining images—which is executed entirely inside the camera before the film is developed. Some in-the-camera effects involve multiple passes of the film, while others, such as "glass shots," are completed in one exposure. An in-the-camera effect is a first-generation image that does not suffer the deficiencies of multiple generations. In the early days of cinematography all tricks were done in the camera, as optical printers were not commonly available.

KEY LIGHT   The principal light source in a scene.

LASER   A powerful light source, consisting of a narrow wavelength of extraordinary purity. Laser light has been used for such effects as the shock waves in *Poltergeist*. The best hope for high-quality images from computers appears to be painting digitized images on film with deflected laser light.

LATENT IMAGE   The exposed but undeveloped image on a piece of film.

"LAZY EIGHT"   A term used in the early days of VistaVision to describe the new format. The VistaVision frame is eight perforations wide and is pulled horizontally through the camera or projector.

LONG SHOT   A distant view of a scene showing the entire setting. Sometimes called a wide shot or a full shot (though the latter may refer to a head-to-foot shot of an actor). Film terminology is nothing if not exact. . . .

L.S. PRINTER   An electronically controlled single projector printer built by machinist/cameraman John Ellis (hence L.S.) and used in the ILM optical department.

MATTE   A mask that partially covers film as it travels through a camera. The matte keeps some part of a shot black—the sky, or the view through a window, or a shape of a person. Usually, whatever part is blacked out is filled with another image. Some mattes are painted on glass and placed before the camera, others are made of black tape or opaque cardboard. More sophisticated versions of matting are accomplished by using one film to mask another, the principle involved in traveling matte processes.

MATTE BOX   Usually a bellowslike device that attaches to the camera and shades the lens. It is also used to hold filters and support objects used in special effects work for matting out parts of a scene.

MATTE PAINTINGS   Large, realistic paintings made to be shot as a separate component, then composited with live-action scenes. Many of the spectacular backgrounds in ILM films are matte paintings.

MECHANICAL EFFECTS   Physical or practical effects that take place on the set during filming, such as explosions, wire tricks, bullet hits, etc.

MEDIUM SHOT   A camera position between a long shot and a close-up.

MINIATURES   Small-sized objects that are photographed to appear larger. Models of spaceships, buildings, land vehicles, airplanes—are all employed extensively at ILM. When skillfully photographed they can be effective in shots where it is not prudent or possible to use the full-sized objects. Most miniatures at ILM are created by the Model Shop.

The art of photographing miniatures is highly specialized, involving a whole repertory of lighting and photographic techniques.

MODEL MOVER   A device for moving a model during photography. At ILM motion control is extensively used; therefore models are generally subject to electronic control as part of the entire motion control system. Most model movers are used in front of a blue screen and have their own built-in blue-light coverings in order to make them invisible when composited.

MONOFILAMENT   A thin plastic thread commonly used as fish line but employed in visual effects to move objects with invisible (it is fervently hoped) support.

MOTION CONTROL   The computerized system that moves camera and models together in prearranged patterns. Because they are computer controlled, the model and camera can repeat their movements over and over—making traveling mattes, creating multiple spaceships from only one model, adding lights to models, adding engine glows, and so on.

The computer can direct the camera shutter to remain open while the camera is moving, so that the image blurs slightly, just as actual movie frames of fast-moving objects are blurred—and so the final effect appears as real live action.

A motion control system was first used in a feature film for ILM's effects work on *Star Wars*; it has now become an essential tool in any well-equipped special effects house, and similar systems are also becoming common on animation stands.

NEGATIVE   The film as it comes from the camera and is developed, with all colors and density exactly the reverse of what was photographed. Printing the negative onto print film stock brings the colors and density back to normal; this is called the positive print, and is used for projection.

OPTICAL PRINTER   A camera that rephotographs and combines separate images of motion picture film. Optical printers consist of a projector and a camera facing each other, with a lens that focuses the projector image on the film of the camera. Modern printers are controlled electronically, allowing strings of complex commands to be carried out with great accuracy.

OPTICAL COMPOSITE   A finished special effects shot, made up of two or more images that have been combined on an optical printer. An optical composite can be as simple as a flash of lightning in the sky (as in *Dragonslayer*) or as complicated as fifty individual spaceships in a space battle (*Return of the Jedi*). The most common optical composites place actors, photographed on a stage, into imaginary environments that combine actual live shots with matte paintings.

OPTICALS   any effects that are made using an optical printer.

PAN (a contraction of "panorama")   A camera movement sweeping horizontally across a scene.

PANCHROMATIC FILM   A black-and-white film stock that is sensitive to all colors. Early camera film stocks were orthochromatic, that is, they were not sensitive to red; and even today most black-and-white laboratory film used for printing is blind to red. This permits the laboratory to be illuminated in red light, so technicians can see what they are doing.

The quality of black-and-white films is important in special effects work, as all shots are rephotographed into their three primary colors on three rolls of black-and-white film when any optical work begins. Because these elements must be recombined onto color film at the compositing stage, fine-grain panchromatic film must be used for the black-and-white elements.

PASS   A run of film through the camera, projector, or optical printer. In compositing shots it may be necessary to run the film through the optical camera many times—hence, "multiple pass" shots.

PERFORATIONS   The holes on the edges of motion picture film, sometimes called sprocket holes. By means of perforations the film is advanced through the camera and held immobile in the camera's gate.

PERSISTENCE OF VISION   A quality of our vision that causes an image to seem to persist for a moment after the stimulus is gone. This residual image blends the individual frames that make up a motion picture viewing experience, giving it the impression of a continuous, moving shot. Without persistence of vision, there would be no motion pictures.

PHYSICAL EFFECTS   See "mechanical effects."

PIXAR   Developed by the Lucasfilm Computer Division, it manipulates images that have been scanned into the computer.

PIXELS   Pixels are elements of a picture that make up the image on the faceplate of a cathode ray tube (the "dots" on a TV picture). The resolution in a computer-generated digital image is directly related to the density of the pixels that make up the image. For instance, American commercial television is broadcast with 150,000 pixels per screen image, while in most of Europe television is broadcast with 210,000 pixels per screen (except France, which enjoys 440,000 pixels per screen—a relatively detailed image). However, computer-generated images of much less than 12,000,000 pixels cannot pass for motion picture—originated shots.

PLATES   A strip of motion picture film that serves as the background image for a composite that is being assembled. Sometimes a still transparent photograph is used for the same purpose.

POSITIVE   A print produced from a film negative, containing light values similar to the original scene.

PRINT   When used as a noun, a positive film made from the original or duplicate negative. As a verb, it is the act of making a film duplicate.

PROCESS CAMERA   A special camera used for effects work, designed to yield a rock-steady image, usually by means of a pilot-pin movement. Shots made with a process camera are usually designed for rear or front screen projection, or as an element in an optical composite.

PROCESS SCREEN   A translucent screen used for rear projection of a scene, while the camera films live action in front of the screen. For instance, when an actor looks out an airplane window at the clouds rushing by, he may actually be staring at a process screen with a shot projected on it.

PYLON   An ILM term describing the support used for miniature models. Most working pylons are enclosed in neon tubing and covered with blue plastic material, so they match the blue-screen background and hide the model's structural support. They are also connected to the motion control system and possess motors that can move the model as directed.

PYROTECHNICS   Effects dealing with fireworks and explosives. Because of the great dangers involved in the handling of these materials, pyrotechnicians must be licensed by the government, and strict laws govern the storage and handling of pyro material. Pyrotechnical accidents are rare in professional filmmaking, though they take a toll among amateurs.

QUAD PRINTER   A printer built at ILM in 1979 for use on *The Empire Strikes Back*, it originally consisted of four projectors and one camera with an anamorphic lens. Two of the projectors were placed at right angles to the camera and used a cubic beam splitter to reflect the images they projected. In 1982, the two right-angle projectors were removed and a camera with a non-anamorphic lens was put in their place. By reversing the beam splitter, the printer has the capability of filming in anamorphic *or* non-anamorphic formats.

 The electronic and optical features of this printer have made it the standard for all subsequent printers.

QUANTEL   A sophisticated image-mixing device used in television.

RASTER DISPLAY   Your home television is a raster display—the electron beam traces out horizontal scan lines. This is in contrast to the calligraphics display, where the beam draws the lines in any orientation on the screen.

RAW STOCK   Unexposed motion picture film.

REAR SCREEN PROJECTION   A system in which background scenes are projected onto a screen from behind, while actors perform in front of the screen for the camera. Miniatures may also be shot in front of a rear screen, though the most common use has been to supply the moving images seen outside car windows.

 Front-screen projection has replaced many rear screen effects in today's films.

RELAY LENS   In an aerial image printer, the lens that focuses the image of one projector onto another projector's film, this combined image is then rephotographed onto yet a third piece of film. Technically, any intermediate lens in an aerial image system is a relay lens.

RENDERING AN IMAGE   This is the process of converting the 3-D environment and models into a framebuffer for display on a color raster monitor. This is the single most expensive step in the computer graphics process—high-quality images can require an immense amount of computer power. While the Pixar is being designed to address this need, it should be emphasized that the goal is cost effective computing.

REYES A computer program developed by Lucasfilm Computer Division's Rob Cook and used to create complex synthetic images. The word has a double meaning: Point Reyes, a Northern California landmark, was the subject of a sophisticated synthetic image created by the device. "REYES" also stands for "Renders . . . Everything . . . You've . . . Ever . . . Seen."

ROTOSCOPE A technique in which individual frames of a movie are blown up and traced, one at a time, onto animation cels. Thus live action can be turned into animation (when the cels are rephotographed), ghostly effects can be added to live action (the ghoulies in *Poltergeist*), technical marvels can be put into real people's hands (the laser swords in *Star Wars*) and so on—in scores of examples every year at ILM.

SCANNER A device used to "read" images, converting the data into a form that can be stored and manipulated by a computer.

SCOTCHLITE™ A trademark of the 3M Company for the material used on the reflective screens for front projection. Strips of Scotchlite™ are also used as a safety precaution by applying them to clothing to reflect auto headlights on the streets at night.

SHOOTING SCRIPT The final version of the script, used during the shooting of a film.

SHOT A continuously filmed segment; the basic element of a scene.

SLIT-SCAN PHOTOGRAPHY A technique for filming artwork to give the impression that the camera is rushing headlong into the scene—as in the famous "light corridor" sequence at the end of *2001: A Space Odyssey*.

The camera is mounted on a track, and with the shutter opened, exposing one frame, it is moved toward a slit with backlit artwork behind it. Simultaneously, the artwork is moved laterally past the slit. When the camera stops moving forward, the shutter is closed. The cycle is repeated for the next single-frame exposure. Thus the image is distorted exactly as though one were moving within it—including the blurring effect that comes with live-action photography.

SLOW MOTION The technique of running film through a camera faster than normal, so that when it is projected at the normal speed of twenty-four frames per second the image appears to move unnaturally slowly on screen. For instance, when a camera's speed is twice as fast as normal, it will film forty-eight frames every second—but a projector will take two seconds to show those forty-eight frames, and, hence, actions will move at half speed.

In special effects work, moving miniatures are often filmed in slow motion in order to give them the appearance of having more mass and size. Some effects, such as miniature explosions, are shot at speeds as high as 500 frames per second and more, giving what was actually a momentary blast the illusion of a vast, galaxy-shaking eruption.

SPECIAL EFFECT Any shot that uses optical or mechanical devices to create an illusion on film. In location filming, mechanical effects are sometimes called practical or physical effects. Optical effects are achieved using the optical printer during the post-production period.

SPLINE ALGORITHM A mathematical procedure that traces moving objects' paths or positions at key points in space and time from point to point for each frame. It is used in both animation and digital effects work.

SPLIT SCREEN EFFECT Two or more images going on at the same time on screen, usually (but not always) separated by a clearly visible line.

Thus, half the frame might be matted off and the remaining half shot, then the film rewound in the camera, the opposite side matted off, and a second scene filmed on the other half of the frame. The final effect might reveal a talk show host conversing with a raccoon.

On a more sophisticated level, multiple split screens are a common part of the effects technician's repertoire of techniques for seamlessly combining images.

SPFX An abbreviation for Special Effects. Other common abbreviations are FX, EFX, and SFX.

STEPPER MOTOR An electric motor that is run by a series of electrical pulses rather than a continuous current. Stepper motors can be precisely controlled by computer-commanded devices, and are essential components of computer motion-control camera systems and the Go-Motion system.

STOP MOTION The technique of filming an inanimate object, one frame at a time, gradually moving it between exposures. Thus puppets are brought to life, odd aircraft whiz through the ether or plunge into the deepest forests at ungodly speed, bicycles fly, kitchen paraphernalia are flung about by poltergeists, and ancient heroes are done in by dragons.

Stop motion is sometimes called stop action.

STORYBOARD A drawing or set of drawings of the shots in a film. All special effects shots at ILM are storyboarded before filming. The ILM storyboards also contain a list of technical specifications required to execute the shot.

STRAIGHT CUT Two scenes spliced together directly, not connected with a dissolve or a fade-out/fade-in.

STROBOSCOPIC In special effects, the jerky movement of an object moving across a screen without the benefit of a blurred edge. Traditional stop-motion is often criticized as being "too stroboscopic."

t/STOP A number assigned to a lens aperture setting that relates to the amount of light the lens can actually transmit. A t/stop is a more useful gauge of a lens setting than the familiar "f/stop," which relates to the relationship of the diameter of the aperture and the focal length of the lens. While in many cases f/ and t/stops are very similar, lenses with a large number of glass elements can actually block more light than a reading of the f/stop would indicate. In such lenses, the t/stop is the only accurate measurement of the light passing through.

TEXTURE MAPPING A technique used in the creation of digital images. Sometimes it is difficult to make a model of an object that is very complex; a solution to the problem is to take a photograph or painting and apply (or "map") it onto a surface. A good example is the addition of craters to the planet in the Genesis Demo. We didn't really model all those craters; instead, a computer program generated images of craters and they were applied to a sphere. Likewise, the final image of the planet was painted by an artist and then applied to the sphere—once it is applied, we can look at the sphere from any direction. This technique is called texture mapping and can be applied to any surface to increase the visual complexity.

TILT   A camera movement sweeping up or down on a vertical axis.

TRACKING SHOT   A shot in which the camera moves forward, backward, or sideways along the ground, following the movement of an object. Tracking shots are graphically effective as they offer pleasing and complex changes in perspective as the camera moves.

Most tracking shots are made with the camera on a dolly—a little wheeled cart—that may be on a kind of miniature railroad track, or roll along on rubber tires.

An effect of tracking shots is to show clearly how things are shaped and how they are situated in relation to one another. Consequently, special effects design often relies on simulating the look of tracking shots so that unfamiliar objects become comprehensible to an audience. A strange black spaceship in a void means nothing until we begin moving past it, seeing its perspective change, sensing its mass and weight, and understanding it as a three-dimensional object.

TRAVELING MATTE   A system used in optical printing in which *moving* photographic silhouettes either obscure or reveal images during rephotography. Into the black shapes left by these photographic silhouettes, other images are placed—people, vehicles, anything that needs to move.

There have been many systems used over the years for creating perfectly registered traveling mattes, but the one most commonly used throughout the effects community today is the blue-screen process. Other methods include rotoscoping and the front-back alternate lighting of a model.

VISUAL EFFECTS   Any visual manipulation of motion picture frames, whether accomplished in cameras, projectors, optical printers, aerial image printers, front and rear screen systems, etc.

WORK HORSE PRINTER   An aerial image optical printer built at ILM prior to the production of *The Return of the Jedi*, it has two VistaVision format projectors and one camera with an anamorphic lens. The projectors and relay lens were cannibalized from the original Quad Printer, while the system's camera, anamorphic lens, and electronics were built expressly for it.

ZOOM   The effect of going from a close shot to a wider shot—or the other way around—by means of a zoom lens. While the effect is similar in basic respects to a dolly shot, the effect of the zoom is very different, because there is no change of perspective in the objects as the camera goes by them. A zoom shot seems to flatten out the space through which it moves. Zooms are usually avoided in special effects design, since the intent of special effects is to increase the three-dimensional realism of a set-up, not reduce it to two dimensions.

ZOOM LENS   A lens equipped with an adjustable optical assembly allowing for a continuous change in focal length while filming.

BIBLIOGRAPHY

Abbott, L.B., ASC. SPECIAL EFFECTS, WIRE, TAPE AND RUBBER BAND STYLE. California: The ASC Press, 1984.

Arnheim, Rudolf. FILM AS ART. University of California Press, 1958.

Bazin, André. WHAT IS CINEMA? University of California Press, 1967.

Call, Deborah. THE ART OF THE EMPIRE STRIKES BACK. New York: Ballantine, 1980.

Clark, Frank P. SPECIAL EFFECTS IN MOTION PICTURES. Scarsdale, New York: Society of Motion Picture and Television Engineers, Inc., 1966.

Clason, W.E. ELSEVIER'S DICTIONARY OF CINEMA, SOUND AND MUSIC IN SIX LANGUAGES. Amsterdam, London, New York, Princeton: Elsevier Publishing, 1956.

Dunn, Linwood G., ASC. THE ASC TREASURY OF VISUAL EFFECTS. California: The ASC Press, 1983.

Fielding, Raymond. A TECHNOLOGICAL HISTORY OF MOTION PICTURES. University of California Press, 1983.

Fielding, Raymond. THE TECHNIQUE OF SPECIAL EFFECTS CINEMATOGRAPHY (Revised Edition). New York: Hastings House, 1968.

Finch, Christopher. SPECIAL EFFECTS: CREATING MOVIE MAGIC. New York: Abbeville Press, 1984.

Fischer, Robert. TRICK PHOTOGRAPHY. New York: M. Evans & Company, Inc. 1980.

Goldstein, Laurence and Kaufman, Jay. INTO FILM. New York: E.P. Dutton & Co., Inc. 1976.

Halas, John and Manuell, Roger. THE TECHNIQUE OF FILM ANIMATION (Revised Edition). New York: Focal Press, 1976.

Imes, Jack Jr. SPECIAL VISUAL EFFECTS. New York: Van Nostrand Reinhold Company, Inc., 1984.

Lucasfilm Ltd. THE ART OF RETURN OF THE JEDI. New York: Ballantine, 1983.

Marner, Terence St. John. FILM DESIGN. London: The Tantivy Press/New York: A.S. Barnes and Co., 1974.

Mehrdad, Azarmi. OPTICAL EFFECTS CINEMATOGRAPHY: ITS DEVELOPMENT, METHODS, AND TECHNIQUES. Ann Arbor, Michigan: University Microfilms International, 1973.

Miller, Arthur, ASC and Strenge, Walter, ASC. AMERICAN CINEMATOGRAPHERS MANUAL. California: The ASC Press, 1969.

Monaco, James, HOW TO READ A FILM (Revised Edition). New York: Oxford University Press, 1981.

Nizhny, Vladimir. LESSONS WITH EISENSTEIN. New York: Hill and Wang, 1962.

Pollack, Dale. SKYWALKING: THE LIFE AND FILMS OF GEORGE LUCAS. New York: Crown Publishers, 1983.

Solomon, Charles and Stark, Ron. THE COMPLETE KODAK ANIMATION BOOK. New York: Eastman Kodak Co., 1983.

Surgenor, A.J. BOLEX GUIDE (7th Edition). New York: The Focal Press, 1962.

Titelman, Carol. THE ART OF STAR WARS. New York: Ballantine, 1979.

Wilkie, Bernard, MBKS. THE TECHNIQUE OF SPECIAL EFFECTS IN TELEVISION. New York: Focal Press/Hastings House, 1971.

INDEX

ABOUT THE AUTHOR

Born in Canton, Illinois, Thomas G. Smith also was raised in Wisconsin, France, Belgium, and Stockton, California. While an undergraduate at Northwestern University, he worked for an industrial film production company and as a Chicago radio announcer. He pursued graduate film studies in France under a Fulbright scholarship at the prestigious Institute of Higher Studies of Cinematography (IDHEC). After serving with the U.S. Air Force as an Audio Visual Officer, Smith worked as a producer/director for Encyclopaedia Britannica, then formed his own company to direct and produce documentaries, principally for public television. In six years he made thirty films, on subjects running the gamut from child development to physics to American history.

Smith entered the field of special effects with a highly successful 1977 Encyclopedia Britannica educational documentary, "The Solar System." To execute the technical aspects of space photography, he manufactured "Stone-Aged versions of what ILM has now in high-tech computer form," in a studio converted

from the back of a dress factory. In 1979 Tom was hired by Lucasfilm to join Industrial Light and Magic. He started as production supervisor and later became general manager.

While at the helm of ILM, Smith oversaw visual effects production on *Return of the Jedi, Raiders of the Lost Ark, Indiana Jones and the Temple of Doom, Star Trek II: The Wrath of Khan, Star Trek III: The Search for Spock, Dragonslayer, Poltergeist, E.T.: The Extra-Terrestrial,* and *The Neverending Story.* After this concentrated focus on special effects, Smith was eager to produce his first dramatic motion picture. George Lucas greeted his impending resignation from ILM by offering Smith the challenge to produce the Lucasfilm production of an ABC Movie-of-the-Week: *The Ewok Adventure* (distributed theatrically in Europe and Japan as *Caravan of Courage: An Ewok Adventure*). In 1985 he produced another Lucasfilm movie for television, *Ewoks*: The Battle for Endor. As of this writing, Smith continues as a producer and resides in Northern California.

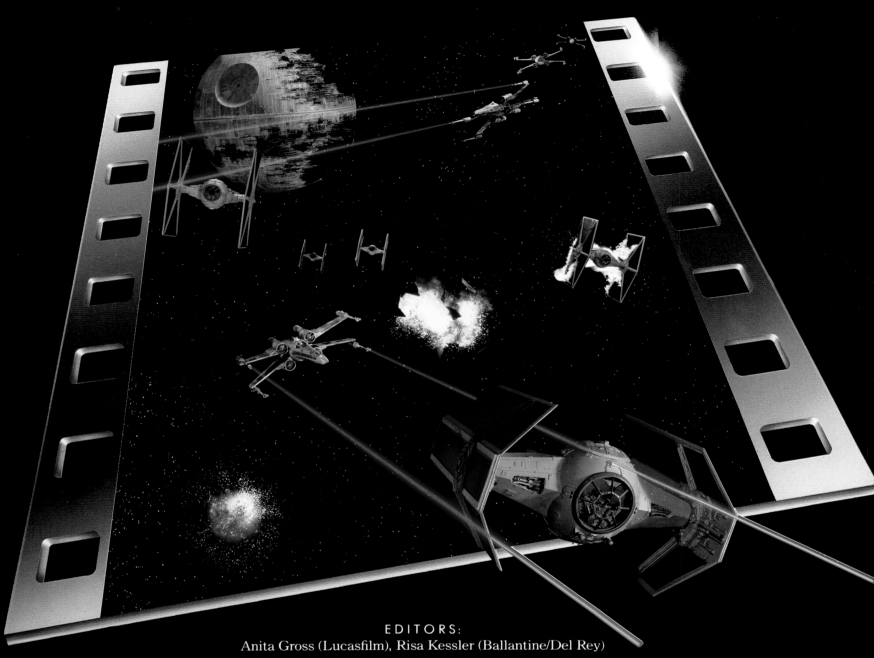

EDITORS:
Anita Gross (Lucasfilm), Risa Kessler (Ballantine/Del Rey)

PRODUCTION DIRECTOR:
Fred Dodnick

INTERIOR AND JACKET DESIGN:
Michaelis/Carpelis Design Associates Inc.

The text of this book was set in Binney Old Style by U.S. Lithograph, Inc.
The captions and incidental text were set in Futura by T.G.A.
Communications.
Color separations, printing, and binding by Dai Nippon, Japan.